Lonely planet

THE ISLANDS BOOK

A JOURNEY TO THE WORLD'S MOST AMAZING ISLANDS

Treasured Islands

Think of an island and your imagination will likely conjure up palm trees, silken sands and turquoise seas. And, yes, tropical islands are perfect for escapist fantasies.

But there are a lot more unusual and interesting islands to explore in the world's seas and oceans. This book introduces 150 of our most treasured islands

MYTHS & LEGENDS

Islands have long inspired myths and legends. The Greek god Zeus is said to have grown up on the island of Crete (which was also home to the half-man half-bull Minotaur). And the Phoenicians believed that the phoenix lived on Socotra in the Arabian Sea, as did the giant roc, another mythical bird. But reality can be just as extraordinary. We're still not sure why the giant stone *moai* (statues) of Easter Island/Rapa Nui were carved, although it's presumed that they honoured ancestors.

And are the dozens of unique plant and animal species that evolved in isolation on Madagascar any less remarkable than a bird that rises from flames?

STORIES TO TELL

In selecting the islands to explore in this book, we asked our Lonely Planet travel experts for their recommendations, earned through years of island-hopping. They came up with an extremely eclectic collection and each island has a distinct story to tell. Some, such as Malta and Sicily in the Mediterranean, were at historic crossroads, their architecture betraying influences from across the ages.

Hong Kong and Singapore are now global cities with international connections, while the remote Andaman and Nicobar Islands are inhabited only by indigenous peoples.

On Naoshima, in Japan's Seto Inland Sea, you'll encounter the trippy art of Yayoi Kusama – and on Cuba you couldn't mistake the sights or sounds for anywhere else.

NATURAL WONDERS

Natural wonders abound on many of the islands, from the unique wildlife of the Galapagos to the unspoiled coral reefs around the Raja Ampat islands. Sperm whales dive off Sri Lanka and orca patrol the shores of the San Juan Islands of the US.

Geological processes shaped many of the islands in extraordinary ways: Kaua`i and Iceland were formed by volcanoes yet couldn't be more different – one tropical and the other snowbound.

❶

1. Land snail from the Ogasawara Archipelago dubbed 'Japan's Galápagos' (p250)

2. Clifftop living in Corsica (p136)

3. Kaua`i's Wailua Falls, Hawai`i (p78)

SANCTUARY FROM DAILY LIFE

There's an endless variety of islands to visit. We seek out islands for all sorts of reasons, but often because they feel like a self-contained sanctuary, far from the routine of our daily lives. Who hasn't dreamed of an island to themselves? However, that's increasingly unlikely to happen. Too much of a good thing means that beautiful places like Ko Phi Phi in Thailand suffer from overtourism. To travel responsibly and take some pressure off these vulnerable destinations, consider visiting in the off-season and be sure to support businesses that give back to the local communities.

ISLAND EXPERIENCES

Each of the introductions in this book features five interesting island experiences, all plotted on a map. We hope that some inspire you to visit one of these islands for your next trip, which you can plan at lonelyplanet.com.

And if you really do want palm trees and warm seas, we can suggest those too: try Tobago in the Caribbean or the Mentawai Islands of Indonesia.

© Matt Munro | Lonely Planet, © Pete Seaward | Lonely Planet

AMERICAS

Kodiak Island

COUNTRY USA • **COORDINATES** 57.491° N, 153.495° W • **AREA** 9311 SQ KM (3595 SQ MILES)

Giants still roam the Earth on Kodiak Island. Some 50km (31 miles) off the coast of the Alaska Peninsula, the vast landmass known as Sun'aq to the native Alutiiq people is home to some 3500 Kodiak bears. Even bigger than grizzlies, these bears can weigh up to 680kg (1500lb) and can stand 3m (9.8ft) tall. Spying one of the world's largest carnivores – preferably while ensconced in a bear-proof force field – is one of the big draws to this wildly dramatic island. While there are pockets of development, including Alaska's largest fishing port, the indomitable wilderness stretches far and wide, encompassing chiselled peaks, dense spruce forests, wind-whipped grasslands and tundra where caribou graze to their hearts' content. Getting here is a big part of the Kodiak adventure, whether taking the slow scenic ferry from Homer or jetting in above the glacier-covered Kenai Mountains from Anchorage.

THE LOST MASKS OF THE ALUTIIQS

When anthropologist and Native Alutiiq Sven Haakanson heard the story, he was dumbfounded. A museum in a small French village contained dozens of rare Alutiiq ceremonial masks – and no one in Kodiak knew of their existence. The pieces had been cut off from their living culture for over 150 years.

In the early 1870s, French anthropologist Alphonse Pinart arrived in Kodiak to study Native Alaskan communities, gathering artefacts along the way. It was a time of great upheaval in Alutiiq society, with American missionaries presaging the end of many traditional Alutiiq customs. Pinart took extensive notes, recording ceremonies and stories associated with the 70 masks he took and later donated to the Boulogne-sur-Mer museum. In 2006, Haakanson and members of the Alutiiq community headed to France to see the collection; many of them had tears in their eyes upon seeing the masks. More than just beautiful objects, the masks were a vital record of cultural knowledge for the Alutiiq community. The museum shared Pinart's notes, which contained songs, many still untranslated, that were part of the creative process of making each mask. In 2008, 34 of the masks were reunited with the Alutiiq homeland in Kodiak, where they were displayed in a temporary exhibition at the Alutiiq Museum.

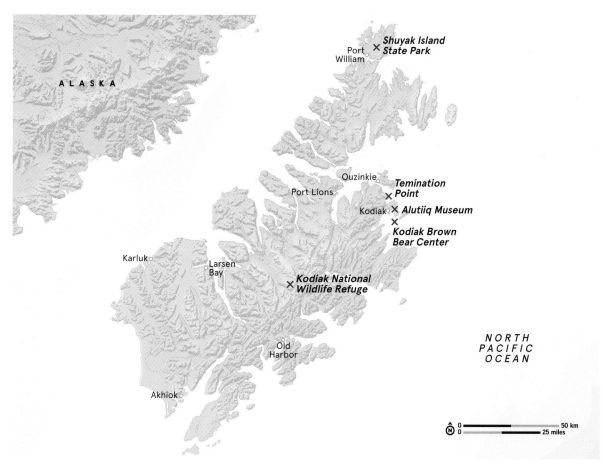

ALASKA

Shuyak Island State Park
Port William

Ouzinkie
Port Lions
Temination Point
Kodiak × Alutiiq Museum
Kodiak Brown Bear Center

Karluk
Larsen Bay
Kodiak National Wildlife Refuge

Old Harbor

Akhiok

NORTH PACIFIC OCEAN

0   50 km
0   25 miles

X MARKS THE SPOT

Kodiak Brown Bear Center Owned by the Alutiiq people, this remote lodge is one of Kodiak's top places to see brown bears in the wild.

Kodiak National Wildlife Refuge This massive preserve covers the southern two-thirds of Kodiak Island and has abundant wildlife – from oversized bears to some 200 bird species.

Alutiiq Museum Well-designed displays give insight into Kodiak's Native Alaskan heritage, from 1000-year-old petroglyphs to ceremonial dances.

Shuyak Island State Park Otters, sea lions and Dall's porpoises inhabit the waters off this spruce-covered island, which is best seen by kayak.

Termination Point An 8km (5-mile) out-and-back trail takes you along the edge of a spectacular peninsula jutting out into Narrow Strait.

1. Kodiak brown bear

2. Sunrise on Kodiak Island

3. Alutiiq mask

1. Kayaking off the Broken Group islands

2. Hiking near Tofino

3. Humpback whale off the coast of Vancouver Island

X MARKS THE SPOT

Vancouver Island Trail Ten years in the making, Canada's newest long-distance trail offers epic hiking on a 770km (478-mile) route connecting Victoria with Cape Scott.

Tofino The small west-coast town – and undisputed Canadian surf capital – lies near beaches with outstanding waves for pros and novices alike.

Craigdarroch Castle With its turrets, stained-glass windows and palatial interior, this Victoria mansion looks like it might have been teleported from the Scottish Highlands.

Pacific Rim National Park Reserve Dramatic beaches and misty forests make the perfect wilderness escape, whether you're kayaking, camping or trekking.

Ahtsik Gallery Near Port Alberni, you can see works by talented local First Nations artists at a gallery owned by a Tseshaht/Nuu-chah-nulth master carver.

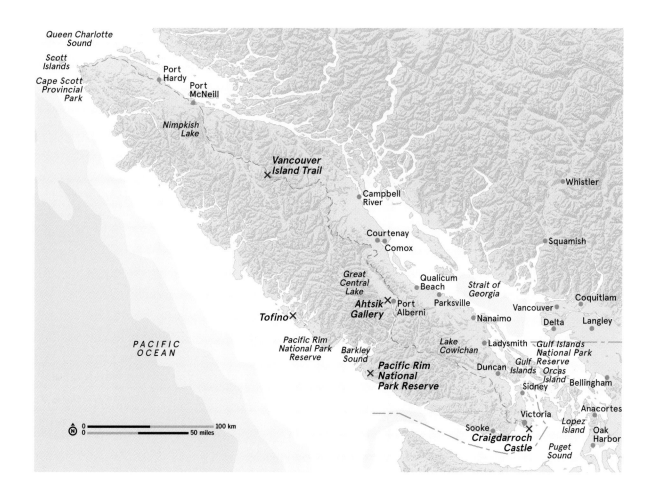

Vancouver Island

COUNTRY CANADA • **COORDINATES** 49.650° N, 125.449° W • **AREA** 31,245 SQ KM (12,064 SQ MILES)

Larger than the country of Belgium, Vancouver Island feels like a woodland nation unto its own. Vast tracts of wilderness are ever-present in this southwestern corner of British Columbia, with its towering old-growth forests, snow-covered peaks and thundering waterfalls. For hundreds of kilometres along the wave-kissed northern and western shores, there are no roads at all, and the only way in is by boat or floatplane. In the south, Vancouver Island's more genteel aspects shine through, from neo-Gothic castles and English-style gardens in the city of Victoria to small towns clinging to rocky coastline and verdant hinterlands dotted with farm fields and wineries.

COUGAR ANNIE

Vancouver Island has long attracted misfits, dreamers and other free spirits to the promise of untamed shores on Canada's far west coast. Among the first in a long line of iconoclastic pioneers was a young woman named Ada Anne Rae-Arthur, who took a steamer with her husband and three children to remote Mesquite Harbor in 1915. There, she unloaded her family and possessions into a dugout canoe, paddled ashore and set about making a home in the wilderness. She would remain for another 65 years, giving birth to eight more children, cycling through four husbands and

creating gardens and a small farm to provide vegetables and meat. She earned her nickname as a fierce markswoman after shooting dozens of cougars and bears – initially in order to protect her family and her livestock, and later for the bounty offered by the Province of British Columbia. Annie rarely left the property, and finally moved away in her 90s when she could no longer fend for herself. She died at age 96 in Port Alberni. Today, Annie's garden and the remnants of her homestead are managed by the non-profit Boat Basin Foundation, and are open to visitors who make the trip out by floatplane.

Haida Gwaii

COUNTRY CANADA

COORDINATES 53.001° N, 132.008° W • **AREA** 9596 SQ KM (3705 SQ MILES)

Centuries-old totem poles reach toward the skies on the edge of misty rainforests, while the roar of crashing waves echoes through the treetops. Around 80km (50 miles) off the coast of British Columbia, the islands of Haida Gwaii showcase a world where nature rules supreme. Sudden thunderstorms and icy winds can't blunt the power of seeing foraging black bears, nesting bald eagles and scurrying pine martens amid moss-laden forests that harbour some of the largest spruce and cedar on Earth. Haida Gwaii's cultural treasures are equally inspiring. The Haida people have lived on their ancestral land for over 10,000 years, with historic villages and ancient archaeological sites attesting to their age-old presence. About 2500 Haida live on the islands, and they continue to contribute to a thriving arts and crafts scene while also playing a critical role in helping to protect the natural environment of the islands.

THE POWER OF SYMBOLS

In the 1940s, once ubiquitous Haida artwork had virtually disappeared from the town of Masset where Robert Davidson grew up. Though Davidson was born to a notable family of artists, it wasn't until he moved to Vancouver to complete his education that he first saw some of his ancestors' stunning artworks on display in a city museum. The experience was an epiphany. He began working with other Haida Gwaii sculptors, including the well-known artist Bill Reid, and at the mere age of 22, he decided to carve a totem pole. Hoping to reconnect with the disappearing heritage of his ancestors, Davidson spent weeks transforming a massive cedar tree. On 22 August 1969, hundreds in the village of Masset gathered to witness the raising of the 12m (39ft) Mother Bear, its striking red-and-black figures silhouetted against the sky. The raising of the first totem pole in nearly a century helped spark rebirth: elders recalled songs, and the community danced and sang into the night. Numerous other artists would follow in Davidson's footsteps, helping to revitalise traditions that were nearly lost to the world.

❶

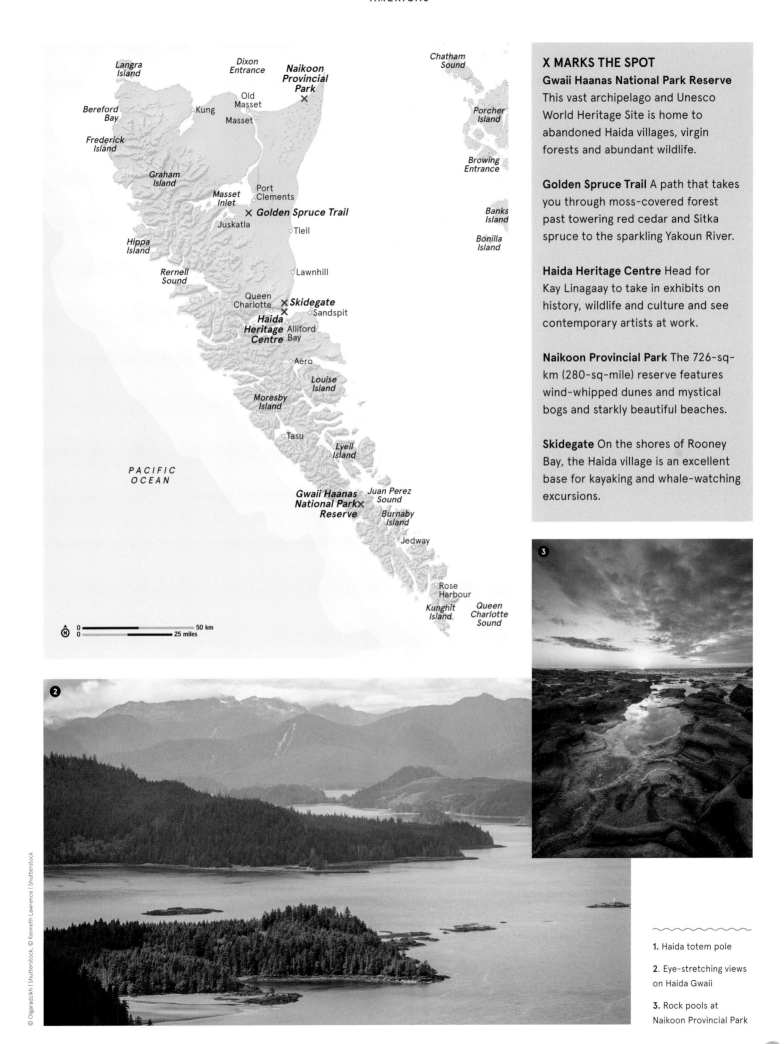

Langra Island
Dixon Entrance
Naikoon Provincial Park ✕
Old Masset
Kung
Masset
Bereford Bay
Frederick Island
Graham Island
Masset Inlet
Port Clements
✕ *Golden Spruce Trail*
Juskatla
Tlell
Hippa Island
Rernell Sound
Lawnhill
Queen Charlotte
✕ *Skidegate*
✕
Sandspit
Haida Heritage Centre
Alliford Bay
Aero
Louise Island
Moresby Island
Tasu
Lyell Island
PACIFIC OCEAN
Gwaii Haanas National Park ✕ *Reserve*
Juan Perez Sound
Burnaby Island
Jedway
Rose Harbour
Kunghit Island
Queen Charlotte Sound

Chatham Sound
Porcher Island
Browing Entrance
Banks Island
Bonilla Island

0 ————— 50 km
N 0 ————— 25 miles

X MARKS THE SPOT

Gwaii Haanas National Park Reserve
This vast archipelago and Unesco World Heritage Site is home to abandoned Haida villages, virgin forests and abundant wildlife.

Golden Spruce Trail A path that takes you through moss-covered forest past towering red cedar and Sitka spruce to the sparkling Yakoun River.

Haida Heritage Centre Head for Kay Linagaay to take in exhibits on history, wildlife and culture and see contemporary artists at work.

Naikoon Provincial Park The 726-sq-km (280-sq-mile) reserve features wind-whipped dunes and mystical bogs and starkly beautiful beaches.

Skidegate On the shores of Rooney Bay, the Haida village is an excellent base for kayaking and whale-watching excursions.

1. Haida totem pole

2. Eye-stretching views on Haida Gwaii

3. Rock pools at Naikoon Provincial Park

11

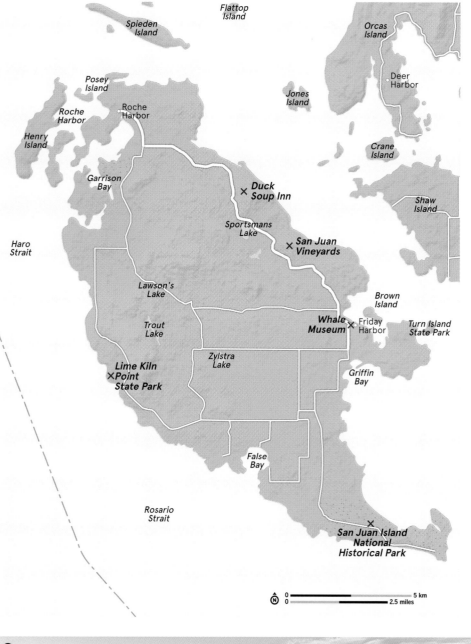

Spieden
Island

Flattop
Island

Orcas
Island

Posey
Island

Deer
Harbor

Roche
Harbor

Roche
Harbor

Jones
Island

Henry
Island

Crane
Island

Garrison
Bay

× Duck
Soup Inn

Shaw
Island

Haro
Strait

Sportsmans
Lake

× San Juan
Vineyards

Lawson's
Lake

Brown
Island

Trout
Lake

Whale
Museum × Friday
Harbor

Turn Island
State Park

Zylstra
Lake

Lime Kiln
× Point
State Park

Griffin
Bay

Rosario
Strait

False
Bay

×
San Juan Island
National
Historical Park

0   5 km
0   2.5 miles

X MARKS THE SPOT

Lime Kiln Point State Park The well-placed park on the western shore has trails, a photogenic lighthouse and viewpoints for spotting orcas and humpback whales.

San Juan Island National Historical Park British and American military forces left behind 19th-century fortifications and other buildings during the so-called Pig War.

San Juan Vineyards A locally owned winery that produces unusual estate-grown varieties like Siegerrebe and Madeleine Angevine.

Whale Museum Giants of the deep (especially orcas) play a starring role at this small interactive museum in Friday Harbor.

Duck Soup The rustic woodsy dining room sets the stage for feasting on fresh-off-the-boat seafood.

San Juan Island

COUNTRY USA • **COORDINATES** 48.551° N, 123.078° W • **AREA** 143 SQ KM (55 SQ MILES)

Forest-covered hills, fertile farmlands and shimmering waters teeming with marine life form the backdrop to San Juan Island, a near-perfect microcosm of the Pacific Northwest. Even before arriving, nature's finery unfurls its emerald cloak as ferries glide past craggy-shored islets, over aquamarine seas backed by thick strands of evergreens. Out on the island – one of several hundred off the coastline of Washington state – bald eagles soar overhead, while orcas glide and leap through waters off the aptly named Whale Watch Park. Home to a year-round population of around 6000 residents, San Juan Island boasts some surprising human-powered attractions to match its green credentials, including wineries, farm-to-table restaurants and a vibrant arts scene.

PIG WAR

Sometimes seemingly trivial local disputes can have international repercussions. Such was the case in 1859 when an American farmer named Lyman Cutlar spotted a pig in his garden, eating his potatoes. Cutlar, exasperated at the repeated incursions onto his property, shot and killed the swine. Not surprisingly, the owner of the animal was incensed. Charles Griffin, an Irishman who managed a sheep ranch on the island, rebuffed Cutlar's paltry offer of compensation and demanded more. Tempers flared across San Juan Island, which at the time was part of an unresolved border disagreement between the US and the UK. British authorities viewed Cutlar and other American settlers as little more than squatters and threatened to arrest and evict them from the island. The American military intervened, dispatching soldiers to set up a fortification. Meanwhile, the British sent naval ships and prepared for combat. War was only narrowly avoided when word of the bizarre incident reached Washington, and high-ranking officials raced to calm tensions. Both countries then took part in joint rule until 1872, when international arbitrators named the San Juan Islands as American possessions.

1. Roche Harbor on San Juan's northwest coast

2. Whale Museum, Friday Harbor

3. Lighthouse, Lime Kiln Point State Park

13

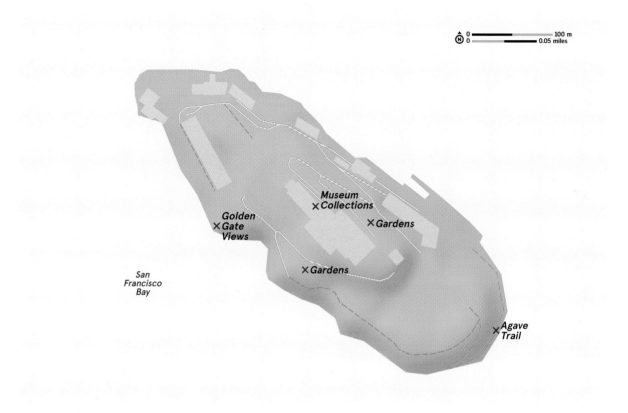

0 ———— 100 m
0 ———— 0.05 miles

Museum
✕ Collections

Golden
✕ Gate   ✕ Gardens
Views

San
Francisco
Bay

✕ Gardens

✕ Agave
Trail

Alcatraz

COUNTRY USA • **COORDINATES** 37.827° N, 122.423° W • **AREA** 0.1 SQ KM (0.03 SQ MILES)

Alcatraz: the name alone was enough to cause panic among hardened criminals facing
justice. For nearly 30 years, 'the Rock' in San Francisco Bay served as one of America's most
infamous federal penitentiaries. Bank robbers, murderers and notorious gangsters – including
Al Capone and George 'Machine Gun Kelly' Barnes – served time in the brutalist concrete cell
blocks, beyond which the cold fog enveloped the island like a shroud. Today, the remarkably
well-preserved prison gives an eye-opening perspective on life for the incarcerated, as well
as for the wardens, guards and their families who also lived on the island.

THE OCCUPATION OF ALCATRAZ

In November 1969, LaNada War Jack, a member of the Shoshone
Bannock tribe, boarded a boat along with a group of 88 other
Native Americans and headed to Alcatraz. At that time, the
island was abandoned – the prison had closed in 1963 – and she
along with the other activists sought to reclaim the land once
used by Ohlone peoples. So began a 19-month occupation of
Alcatraz that would focus attention on years of injustices by the
federal government against indigenous people. Made up largely
of students, the 'Indians of All Tribes' called for the creation of
a cultural centre and a Native American university on Alcatraz.

Their courage inspired hundreds of other Native American people
to join their cause, along with Jane Fonda and other celebrities;
the Isani Sioux artist and poet John Trudell made daily radio
broadcasts from the island. The occupation finally ended after
the government cut off power to the island and forcibly removed
the remaining occupiers in June 1971. The daring takeover,
however, wasn't in vain. President Richard Nixon promised to
restore Native American territory and strengthen self-rule, and
the US government later returned millions of acres of ancestral
land. Over 50 years later LaNada War Jack, now an author and
distinguished history professor, continues to fight for justice.

1. Alcatraz from San Fran's scarped streets

2. Proceed with caution at The Rock's Power House building

3. The prison's ruined Warden's House

X MARKS THE SPOT

Audio Tour The cell-house audio guide gives first-person accounts of daily life on the island, based on interviews with the incarcerated and with correctional officers.

Museum Collections See inmate artwork, historic photographs and other materials dating back to the 19th century, when Alcatraz was a military prison.

Golden Gate Views On clear days, the west side of the island offers striking views of the Golden Gate Bridge and the San Francisco skyline.

Agave Trail Nature flourishes in surprising places – head out beyond dense stands of agave to look for seabirds along this path around the south part of the island.

Gardens Reborn after decades of neglect, the flower-filled gardens showcase species planted by successive generations, from Civil War soldiers to the families of guards.

Channel Islands National Park

COUNTRY USA

COORDINATES 33.968° N, 119.991° W • **AREA** 9311 SQ KM (3595 SQ MILES)

Nicknamed the 'Galápagos of North America', the Channel Islands National Park is home to an extraordinary variety of plant and animal life, including some 150 species found nowhere else on Earth. Volcanic activity formed the mountainous archipelago, which lies just off the coast of Southern California and was never attached to the mainland. While vestiges of human presence remain, including that of Chumash communities who lived on the island for more than 13,000 years, today these uninhabited islands offer a remarkable opportunity to reconnect with primeval wilderness. You can hike, kayak, scuba dive or camp amid a raw, edge-of-the-world landscape – or simply enjoy the unrivalled wildlife-watching amid the islands' surprisingly diverse terrain.

ISLAND FOXES

Found nowhere else on Earth, the island fox has long been a symbol of the national park. These tiny, doe-eyed creatures descend from mainland gray foxes, which were likely brought to the islands over 6000 years ago by native people – the Chumash considered the fox to be a sacred animal. Once gray foxes reached the island they evolved into a separate species. Years of flourishing came to an end in the 1990s, when the fox population suddenly plummeted, going from over 2000 individuals to less than a hundred. The rare foxes teetered on the edge of extinction, and no one knew why.

Conservationists finally solved the mystery when golden eagles were spotted preying on the foxes. But why was this suddenly happening now? It turned out that nature was completely out of balance, owing (unsurprisingly) to the actions of humans. Feral pigs had been a presence on the islands during the ranching era (mid-1800s to the late 1970s), and wild piglets were a food source for the eagles. When the pigs were exterminated from the island in the early 1990s, foxes became the eagles' meal of choice. The solution: the eagles were relocated, and the canid population bounced back. In 2016, the island fox was removed from the endangered species list in the fastest mammal recovery ever accomplished.

X MARKS THE SPOT

Santa Rosa Campground One of the best of the island's campgrounds, tucked into a canyon and sheltered by eucalyptus trees.

Scorpion Beach The calm shoreline is ideal for launching a kayak onto crystal-clear waters backed by towering cliffs on Santa Cruz.

Point Bennett The 25km (15-mile) return hike on San Miguel leads to an astonishing overlook where you can spot thousands of seals and sea lions.

Inspiration Point At the end of a 2.4km (1.5-mile) trail on Anacapa Island, you'll have spectacular views of mountains emerging from the sea.

Santa Barbara The smallest of the islands draws nature lovers, with brilliant yellow coreopsis flowers, abundant birdlife and humongous northern elephant seals.

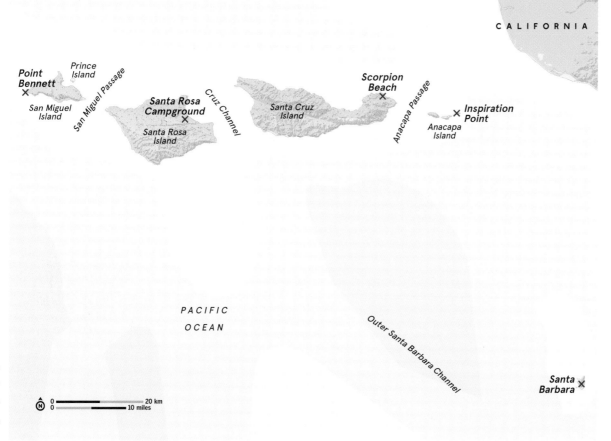

CALIFORNIA

Point
Bennett
✕

Prince
Island

San Miguel Passage

San Miguel
Island

Santa Rosa
Campground
✕

Cruz Channel

Santa Rosa
Island

Santa Cruz
Island

Scorpion
Beach
✕

Anacapa Passage

Anacapa
Island

✕ Inspiration
Point

PACIFIC

OCEAN

Outer Santa Barbara Channel

Santa
Barbara ✕

N
0 ——————— 20 km
0 ——————— 10 miles

1. Dive the Channel
Islands NP to spot
colourful species like
the Spanish shawl
nudibranch

2. California sea lions
near Anacapa Island

© Douglas Klug | Getty Images

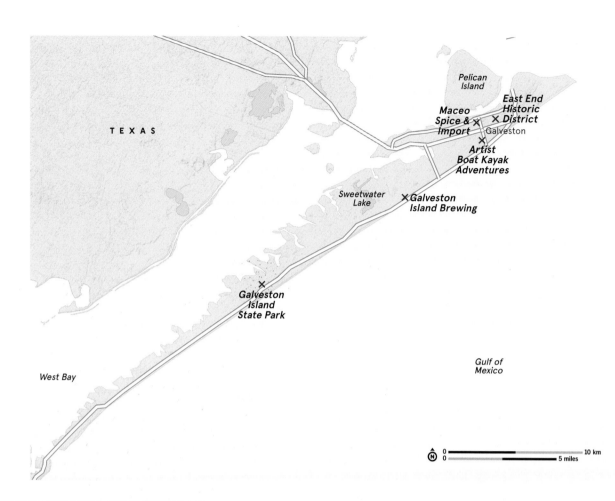

Pelican
Island

Maceo
Spice &
Import ✕

East End
Historic
District ✕

Galveston

✕
Artist
Boat Kayak
Adventures

TEXAS

Sweetwater
Lake

✕Galveston
Island Brewing

✕
Galveston
Island
State Park

West Bay

Gulf of
Mexico

0 _____ 10 km
Ⓝ
0 _____ 5 miles

~~~~~~~~~~

1. A day on the beach
at Galveston Island

2. Bishop's Palace, a
star of the East End
Historic District

Galveston Island

COUNTRY USA
COORDINATES 29.241° N, 94.909° W • AREA 170 SQ KM (66 SQ MILES)

During Mardi Gras, revellers line the streets watching brass-blaring marching bands and elaborate floats roll past. The crowd roars as masked riders shower the crowds with beads. If you imagine yourself standing on St Charles Ave in New Orleans, guess again. Galveston has been celebrating Fat Tuesday for over a hundred years and today hosts the third-largest Carnival celebration in the country. Not unlike the Big Easy, the Texas enclave has a deep-rooted independent streak, and residents sometimes jokingly call their hometown the 'free state of Galveston'. The appeal is undeniable: the 50km-long (31-mile) barrier island boasts wide beaches, an historic cobblestone-lined downtown, and wild, undeveloped spaces where coyotes still roam. The dining scene is in a class of its own, an eclectic mix of Cajun-style gumbo and crawfish étouffée as well as sizzling Texas barbecue and authentic Mexican street fare.

DWELLING OF THE UNDEAD

The worst hurricane in American history struck Galveston on 8 September 8 1900. With storm surges of nearly 4.8m (17.7ft), the hurricane killed over 6000 people and destroyed nearly every structure on the island. In the aftermath, Galveston built a massive seawall and raised the city by as much as 5.2m (17ft). In hopes of revitalising the economy, civic officials focused on tourism, and in 1911 they opened the Hotel Galvez, a grand resort described by *Hotel Monthly* as 'the most richly furnished seaside hotel in America'. There was just one snag: the Galvez had a ghost problem. Visitors reported seeing the ghoulish forms of children wandering the halls, or hearing phantom laughter in empty chambers. Others claimed to see the hazy outline of a nun in darkened corridors.

Some suspect that the Galvez was built over a mass grave. Ten Sisters of Charity and 90 children from the St Mary's Orphans Asylum died during the storm, and they were buried where they were found – perhaps directly beneath the future luxury hotel.

Still operating today, the Galvez is considered the most haunted hotel in the state of Texas.

X MARKS THE SPOT

East End Historic District Dotting the streets of Galveston's photogenic historic district are grand 19th-century mansions, including the jaw-dropping four-storey Bishop's Palace.

Artist Boat An eco-friendly non-profit that melds nature with art and science via kayak tours of Galveston's wetlands.

Maceo Spice & Import This 1940s grocery also serves the best Cajun food in town at tables crammed between the shelves.

Galveston Island State Park Near the island's centre, this 810-hectare (2000-acre) reserve has a white-sand beach and trails through coastal dunes, salt marshes and mudflats.

Galveston Island Brewing Local icon with a grassy yard and sunset views, brewing up some excellent quaffs, served out of 13 taps on-site.

❷

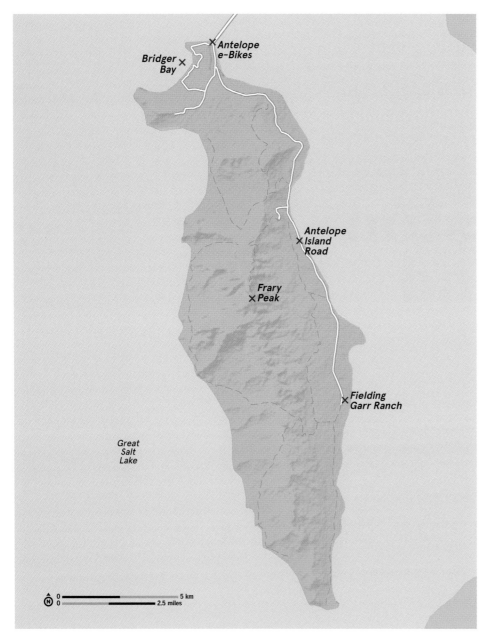

X MARKS THE SPOT

Fielding Garr Ranch Well-preserved structures tell the story of the ranchers who worked the land from 1848 to 1981.

Bridger Bay On the north of the island, a long beach provides access for a dip in the Great Salt Lake.

Frary Peak An 11km (7-mile) out-and-back trail takes you to the highest point on Antelope, with 360-degree views of the lake and other islands.

Antelope Island Road This paved 17.7km (11-mile) road follows the island's eastern shore and offers prime viewing of bison and other wildlife.

Antelope e-Bikes A reliable outfitter that hires out fat-tyre bikes with electric motors for help on the hills; they also run biking tours.

1. Loggerhead shrike

2. North American bison

3. The mirror-calm Great Salt Lake at Antelope Island

Antelope Island

COUNTRY USA · **COORDINATES** 40.958° N, 112.214° W · **AREA** 109 SQ KM (42 SQ MILES)

At first glance, the Great Salt Lake seems like an unlikely setting for wildlife. Fringed by arid desert, the lake boasts a salinity so high that it can support little life apart from brine shrimp and algae. And yet even here in northern Utah, life finds a way to flourish. Jutting out into the lake, Antelope Island harbours dozens of freshwater springs that support massive animals like bison, mule deer and bighorn sheep, as well as pronghorn antelope, the fastest land mammal in the western hemisphere. Entirely protected as a state park, the island draws outdoor lovers who visit in hopes of spotting wildlife while hiking, mountain-biking or horseback-riding some 70km (43 miles) of trails. You can also sleep out under the stars and see vestiges of the old Wild West.

BISON ROUNDUP

Clouds of dust swirl through the October air as hundreds of bison thunder across the island, flanked by wranglers on horseback. The riders whoop and holler as they near the corrals, the sense of relief palpable after a long day in the saddle. It's the Bison Roundup on Antelope Island, an annual event that draws horseback riders from across the country. They come to help out (or watch from a safe distance) as one of the nation's largest and oldest public bison herds is gathered and driven from the island's southern reaches up to holding pens in the north.

Following the roundup, the herd – which numbers about 700 most years – is sorted and separated to receive an individual check-up that includes vaccinations, screening for pregnancies and other health issues. Once they're checked, around 500 of the bison are released back into the wild, with the other 200 sold at auction. With no natural predators on the island and 200 or so calves born each year, it's essential to maintain a herd size that the habitat can support.

To learn more about volunteering, or just watching it all unfold, visit Utah State Parks (stateparks.utah.gov).

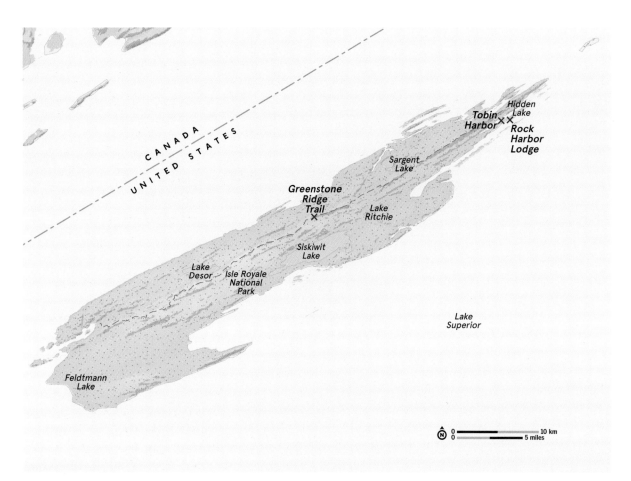

CANADA

UNITED STATES

Tobin
Harbor ✕✕

Hidden
Lake
✕

Rock
Harbor
Lodge

Sargent
Lake

**Greenstone
Ridge
Trail**
✕

Lake
Ritchie

Siskiwit
Lake

Lake
Desor

Isle Royale
National
Park

Lake
Superior

Feldtmann
Lake

N
0 ————— 10 km
0 ————— 5 miles

1. Kayaking around Isle
Royale

2. A new generation
of the island's wolf
population

❶

Isle Royale

COUNTRY USA

COORDINATES 47.976° N, 88.931° W • **AREA** 535 SQ KM (206 SQ MILES)

For centuries humans couldn't leave Isle Royale alone. Copper mining by Native Americans was followed by commercial fishing, logging and the building of summer resorts for wealthy Chicago families. Despite its troubled past, the remote island tucked into the northwest corner of Lake Superior retains its untamed beauty – thanks in large part to the preservationists who helped Isle Royale become a national park in 1940. Dense forests and the return of wildlife serve as powerful symbols of nature's rejuvenation. Lumberjacks and golfers have been replaced by moose, beavers and the elusive wolf, along with some 150 bird species. Today some 99% of the island is designated as wilderness, with over 270km (168 miles) of trails and seemingly endless shorelines drawing hikers and kayakers eager to experience Isle Royale's enduring allure.

WOLF VS MOOSE

The helicopter swooped low along the edge of the snow-covered forest. As a wolf darted out across the frozen lake, the pilot banked in close pursuit. The crew fired the netgun and ensnared the bounding animal. While lying entangled, the wolf was tranquilised, then loaded into the helicopter and carried off. After a health check at a veterinary station, the apex predator continued its journey to a new home: Isle Royale. She would be the first of over a dozen wolves brought to the island between 2018 and 2020.

Since 1958, researchers have been conducting the world's longest-running study of a predator-prey system: exploring the delicate connection between wolves and moose in Isle Royale, and learning about the surprising repercussions when nature was out of balance. As the wolf population plummeted and the moose population soared, the whole ecosystem was affected as overgrazing destroyed plant diversity and impacted other animals (like snowshoe hares) that rely on the same food source. With just two wolves left on the island, the park decided to reintroduce new members in hopes of bringing equilibrium to Isle Royale. So far, the results are promising. New wolf pups have been born on the island, and the moose population has stabilised.

X MARKS THE SPOT

Tobin Harbor Sunrise or sunset is a magical time to be at this scenic cove, where you might spy moose on a lucky day.

Diving Lake Superior The waters off Isle Royale are riddled with 10 major wrecks, all relatively easy to see in the lake's clear water.

Rock Harbor Lodge Isle Royale's only full-service accommodation makes a great base for exploring the nearby wilderness, offering kayak and canoe rentals and guided excursions.

Greenstone Ridge Trail The 64km (40-mile) trail barrels over the backbone of Isle Royale and tops out at 396m (1299ft), with glorious views to Lake Superior.

Boat Tours National Park Service rangers lead narrated cruises aboard the MV *Sandy*, including stops at remote islands on some trips.

❷

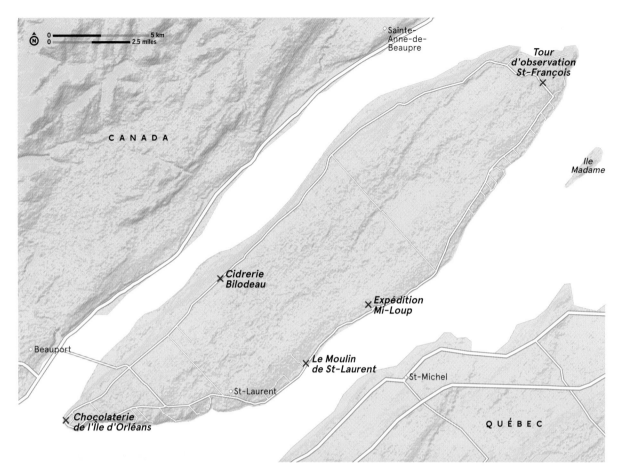

CANADA

Sainte-Anne-de-Beaupre

Tour d'observation St-François

Ile Madame

Cidrerie Bilodeau

Expédition Mi-Loup

Beauport

Le Moulin de St-Laurent

St-Laurent

St-Michel

Chocolaterie de l'Île d'Orléans

QUÉBEC

1. Pont de l'Île d'Orléans

2. A log cabin in the woods on l'Île d'Orléans

Île d'Orléans

COUNTRY CANADA
COORDINATES 46.965° N, 70.906° W • **AREA** 193 SQ KM (74 SQ MILES)

To the Huron First Nations people it was known as Minigo (meaning 'Enchantress'). When 16th-century explorer Jacques Cartier first visited, he called it Isle de Bacchus (Bacchus Island) owing to the wild grapes growing in abundance. Though its name changed many times over the centuries, this fertile island downriver from present-day Québec City never failed to captivate. Sparsely populated, Île d'Orléans is famed for its pastoral roots and today lies at the epicentre of Québec's artisanal food and craft movement. The island also has a rich historical heritage, with some village manors and churches dating back more than 300 years.

THE CHEESE OF ÎLE D'ORLÉANS

At the turn of the 21st century, Gérard Aubin was the only person alive who had the ancestral recipe for a raw-milk cheese that had been made on the island for over 300 years. In fact, production dated back to 1635, when colonists from France settled on the island and began making cheese according to a recipe from the Champagne region. Handed down from generation to generation, cheesemaking continued well into the 20th century. Just after the WWII, over three dozen families on the island still made cheese. But in 1965, production collapsed when the government passed a law requiring the mandatory use of pasteurized milk for all cheeses matured for less than 60 days. Farmhouse-style Île d'Orléans had a much shorter ageing process; after a month it turned to liquid. Unable to comply, Aubin ended commercial production. That would have been the end of the story – and the end of North America's oldest cheese – until several scientists in the 1990s managed to isolate and identify the microorganisms that matured the island cheese, which could then be reproduced and added directly during the production process. In 1999 Gérard Aubin, then in his late 80s, played a pivotal role in keeping the recipe alive by passing it along to island resident Jocelyn Labbé, who announced plans to bring back cheesemaking to Île d'Orléans. In 2004, Labbé's dream became a reality with the opening of the artisanal cheesemaking operation Les Fromages de l'Isle d'Orléans – where visitors can once again taste the continent's oldest variety of cheese.

X MARKS THE SPOT

Tour d'observation St-François Near the island's north end, a wooden observation tower provides views of the St Lawrence River and the mountains beyond.

Expédition Mi-Loup In winter, you can zip through the snow-covered forest on the back of a dogsled on adventures offered by this island-based venture.

Cidrerie Bilodeau An orchard and distillery that offers apple picking and cider tasting; there's also a small petting zoo.

Chocolaterie de l'Île d'Orléans Using cocoa beans from Belgium, chocolatiers churn out tasty concoctions including almond bark and flavoured truffles.

Le Moulin de St-Laurent In a converted 19th-century flour mill on the edge of a waterfall, chef Martin Pronovost prepares French-accented fare with locally sourced ingredients.

Governors Island

COUNTRY USA • **COORDINATES** 40.689° N, 74.016° W • **AREA** 0.7 SQ KM (0.2 SQ MILES)

Stretching out on the grass, while enjoying the view of the Statue of Liberty and looming skyscrapers: it's hard to think of a better spot for a picnic than a peaceful island on the edge of a great American metropolis. A mere 10 minutes after boarding the ferry from either Brooklyn or Lower Manhattan, you arrive on a vehicle-free space of open lawns, breezy seaside promenades and lush hills with sweeping harbour views. During the summer, a regular lineup of events feature site-specific art installations, concerts and dance performances, backed up by an array of food trucks and craft beer vendors. Until recently, the island was strictly off limits to the public owing to a military (and later coast guard) presence. Historic spots include several forts and the elegant 19th-century officers' quarters known as Colonels Row.

WILD GOOSE CHASE

Throughout the year, Canada geese pass through Governors Island, sometimes in 'super flocks' numbering up to 500 birds. While lovely to behold, the birds can wreak havoc, devouring the grass and leaving massive amounts of waste. Park authorities tried various strategies to humanely drive away the birds using lasers, remote-control cars and even strobe lights, though nothing worked as effectively as one particularly enthusiastic park 'volunteer' brought on board in 2014. That's when a Border collie named Max became the island's official goose herder.

Previously employed on a sheep farm in Maryland, Max learned to run around the flock without barking or biting, causing them to quickly fly off. Since Max's successful appointment, four other dogs have joined the Governors Island herding team: Quinn, Chip, Aspen and Leader. All are rescue dogs, taken from the Mid-Atlantic Border Collie Rescue Program in Maryland. When not out on goose patrols, they greet visitors and happily welcome a bit of human interaction. The furry canines even have a following on Instagram: @giworkingdogs.

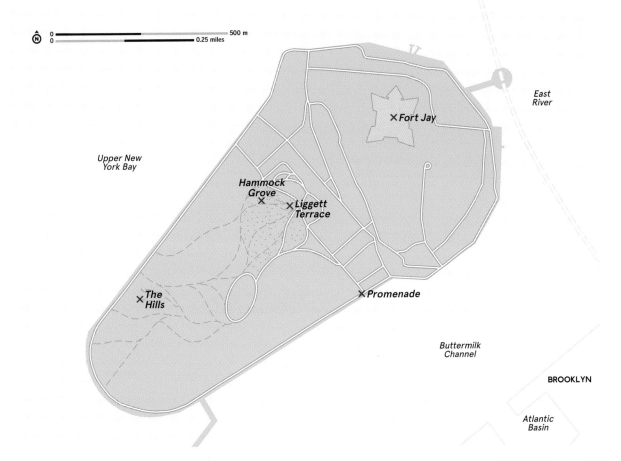

N
0 — 500 m
0 — 0.25 miles

East River

Upper New York Bay

× Fort Jay

Hammock Grove ×
×Liggett Terrace

×The Hills

×Promenade

Buttermilk Channel

BROOKLYN

Atlantic Basin

X MARKS THE SPOT

Promenade The 3.5km (2-mile) round-island loop is a scenic spot for a leisurely spin, with various bikes (including two-, four- and six-seaters) for hire.

Liggett Terrace Vendors sell kimchi tacos, fish and chips, souvlaki and other treats, best enjoyed on the grassy expanse of the Parade Ground.

Hammock Grove Oversized red hammocks big enough for two set the stage for cloud-gazing amid lush island greenery.

The Hills Four artificial mounds, partially made from recycled demolition debris, range in height from 8m (26ft) to 21m (69ft) and offer the island's best harbour views.

Fort Jay Free guided tours on weekends give insight into this star-shaped fort, built in 1794.

2

3

GOVERNORS

1. Ferries make the 10-minute journey from Lower Manhattan

2. Governors Island and Brooklyn from above

2. Governors Island ferry dock

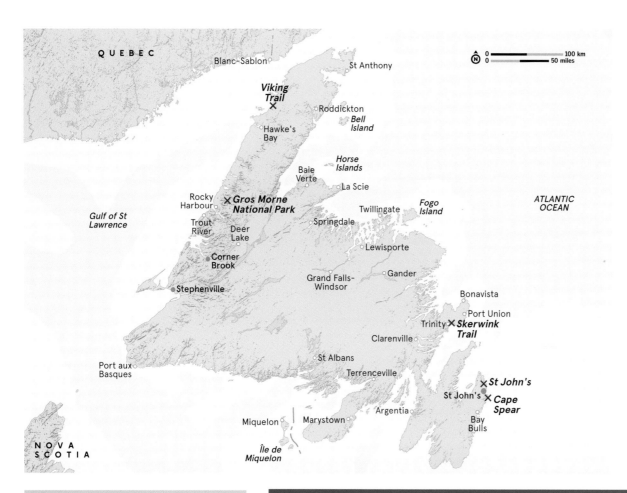

QUEBEC
Blanc-Sablon
St Anthony
Viking Trail
×
Roddickton
Hawke's Bay
Bell Island
Horse Islands
Baie Verte
La Scie
Rocky Harbour
× *Gros Morne National Park*
Twillingate
Fogo Island
ATLANTIC OCEAN
Gulf of St Lawrence
Springdale
Trout River
Deer Lake
Lewisporte
Corner Brook
Grand Falls-Windsor
Gander
Stephenville
Bonavista
Port Union
Trinity × *Skerwink Trail*
Clarenville
St Albans
Port aux Basques
Terrenceville
St John's
St John's ×
× *Cape Spear*
Argentia
Bay Bulls
Miquelon
Marystown
Île de Miquelon
NOVA SCOTIA

0 — 100 km
0 — 50 miles

X MARKS THE SPOT

St John's In North America's oldest city, you can wander past rainbow-hued houses, munch on fish and chips and hear live Newfoundland folk music.

Gros Morne National Park Remnants of a mountain chain formed 1.2 billion years ago, this Unesco World Heritage Site features craggy mountains, fjords, beaches, bogs and barren cliffs.

Skerwink Trail A 5km (3-mile) coastal loop leads out to astonishing views over sea stacks and icebergs – with the occasional moose and bald eagle sighting, too.

Cape Spear On a rocky headland, winds whip past an 1835 lighthouse and fragments of WWII bunkers in Canada's easternmost point.

Viking Trail The scenic drive along Newfoundland's west coast winds past foggy coves and sun-kissed fjords as well as the famous L'Anse aux Meadows National Historic Site.

1. Hike the Skerwink Trail to eyeball mighty icebergs

2. Newfie architecture at east-coast Trinity

3. Kayaking the Newfoundland coast

Newfoundland

COUNTRY CANADA • **COORDINATES** 53.135° N, 57.660° W • **AREA** 109,000 SQ KM (42,085 SQ MILES)

The wooden boards shake as couples twirl across the dancefloor, propelled by the frenetic rhythms of a fiddler, guitarists and a fife player crowding the small stage. Outside the wind howls, waves crash against the shore and unseen icebergs drift along the horizon. Canada's easternmost province is a mesmerising mash-up of ancestral traditions and awe-inspiring wilderness. Towering sea cliffs, fjord-like lakes and misty boreal forests form the backdrop to a vast subarctic island that's home to half a million residents. Newfoundlanders are proud of their idiosyncratic heritage as the first place in the Americas where Europeans came ashore, and the last province to join Canada in 1949.

IN SEARCH OF VINLAND

Nobody knows who wrote the Icelandic sagas, a set of historical works from the 13th and 14th centuries detailing the deeds of Vikings in centuries past. One of the most fascinating tales describes the travels of Leif Erikson, who was blown off course while sailing from Greenland and arrived in a mountainous land with fjords, tall grasses and wheat. In some places wild grapes grew, and the Vikings founded a settlement and dubbed the area Vinland. Although the sagas were full of ghost stories and sorcery, historians believed Erikson had made landfall somewhere in the New World roughly 500 years before Columbus. For decades Scandinavian archaeologists had fruitlessly searched the coast of

North America from Massachusetts to Labrador. Then in 1960, after months of following clues from the sagas, the Norwegian archaeologists Helge Ingstad and Anne Stine Ingstad sailed to L'Anse aux Meadows on Newfoundland's northernmost peninsula. There they found strange seaside mounds similar in outline to the ancient Viking longhouses of Iceland and Greenland. Later they unearthed hundreds of bronze, bone and stone artefacts that confirmed the site's Norse origins. Geochemical dating techniques placed the exact year of Viking presence at 1021. Declared a Unesco World Heritage Site in 1978, L'Anse aux Meadows today preserves one of Canada's most significant archaeological discoveries.

Chincoteague Island

COUNTRY USA • **COORDINATES** 37.933° N, 75.378° W • **AREA** 24 SQ KM (9.2 SQ MILES)

Hidden away just off Virginia's eastern coast, Chincoteague feels like a forgotten relic of decades past. Flower baskets dangle from lampposts on the tranquil main street, with a one-screen cinema, old-fashioned seafood restaurants and the whitewashed town library all just a few steps from the waterfront. Nearby, on a long fishing pier, locals cast for flounder as gulls wing past. Meanwhile, just across the Assateague Channel, whip-thin Assateague Island harbours a wilderness wonderland of beaches, marsh, dunes and maritime forest. The diverse habitats are home to waterfowl, wading birds, shorebirds and song birds – not to mention the wild horses for which the island is famed.

A FILLY NAMED MISTY

Wild ponies still gallop across sand dunes and over secluded beaches on Assateague, the 60km-long (37-mile) barrier island that lies a few minutes' drive from the heart of Chincoteague. According to legend, the freely roaming quadrupeds are descendants of survivors from a Spanish galleon that wrecked off the island of Assateague sometime in the 1700s. Since then, they have adapted to the harsh island environment and flourished. In fact, with approximately 60 new foals born each spring, the herd would soon overpopulate the island without intervention. And so each year on the last Wednesday in July, a handful of riders dubbed the 'saltwater

cowboys' climb into the saddle and drive a herd of wild ponies across a small channel in northeast Virginia. The pony-swim, famously described in Marguerite Henry's Newberry award–winning *Misty of Chincoteague*, is followed by a pony parade down Main St en route to the Carnival Grounds, where an auction is held the next day. Misty, incidentally, was a real-life pony who even appeared in the eponymous film made about her in 1961. Shot on location in Chincoteague, *Misty* premiered at the Island Theatre, where its equine namesake strutted down the aisles before the showing. Her hoofprints are still set in concrete in front of the cinema.

1. Wild horses of Assateague

2. Climb the Assateague Lighthouse for stellar island views

3. Marshland on the Chincoteague coast

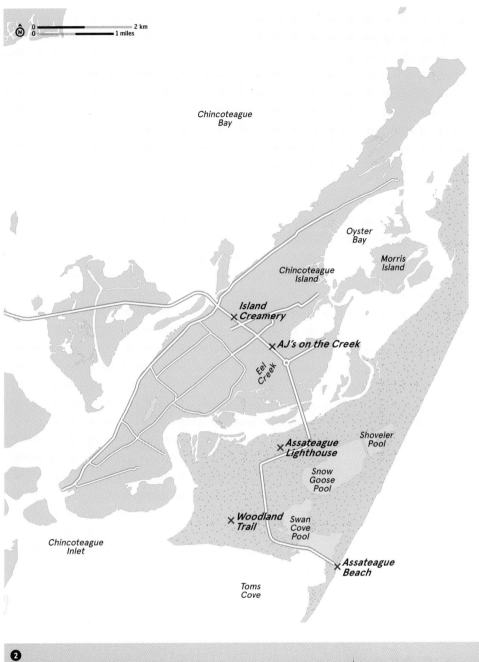

Chincoteague
Bay

Oyster
Bay

Morris
Island

Chincoteague
Island

× Island
Creamery

× AJ's on the Creek

Eel
Creek

Shoveler
Pool

× Assateague
Lighthouse

Snow
Goose
Pool

× Woodland
Trail

Swan
Cove
Pool

Chincoteague
Inlet

× Assateague
Beach

Toms
Cove

0   2 km
0   1 miles

X MARKS THE SPOT

Woodland Trail The best walk in the Chincoteague National Wildlife Refuge follows a 2.6km (1.6-mile) loop through pine forest, with the chance to see wild ponies.

Assateague Lighthouse Dating from 1867, the 43m (141ft) red-and-white-striped lighthouse, which opens on weekends, has memorable island views.

Island Creamery Going strong since 1975, this small-batch, family-owned ice-cream shop serves up dozens of tempting flavours.

Assateague Beach One of Virginia's loveliest shorelines offers seemingly endless kilometres of beachcombing over pristine sands.

AJ's on the Creek At one of Chincoteague's best seafood restaurants, you can dine overlooking Eel Creek while feasting on oysters, crab cakes or bouillabaisse.

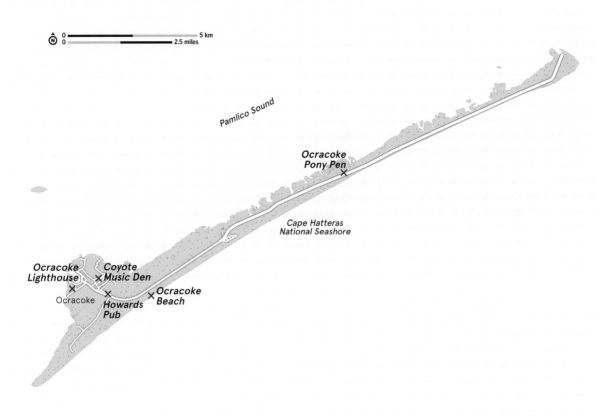

Pamlico Sound

Ocracoke
Pony Pen

Cape Hatteras
National Seashore

Ocracoke
Lighthouse

Coyote
Music Den

Ocracoke

Howards
Pub

Ocracoke
Beach

1. Looking down on
Silver Lake harbour and
Ocracoke village

2. Ocracoke Lighthouse

Ocracoke Island

COUNTRY USA
COORDINATES 35.114° N, 75.981° W • **AREA** 25 SQ KM (10 SQ MILES)

The history of Ocracoke sounds almost like a fairy tale. Blackbeard and other pirates used to hide in coves around this long, slender island off the coast of North Carolina, waiting to ambush unsuspecting ships. Wild ponies brought ashore by shipwrecked explorers in the 1600s shared space with the outlaws, and their descendants still graze amid some of the finest views on the island. Meanwhile, islanders on Ocracoke developed a unique brogue that stays true to its roots as a 17th-century British dialect. Today, it's not hard to reconnect with the island's unusual past. You can spot the descendants of the original ponies living out near the beach, see pirate artefacts in a museum, and hear the accent of older Hoi Toiders (so called because of the islanders' pronunciation of 'high tide') spoken on the street. Ocracoke also offers plenty of modern-day adventures, from frolicking in the waves off one of America's prettiest beaches to watching golden hues light up the sky on sunset kayaking tours.

X MARKS THE SPOT
Ocracoke Pony Pen The once free-roaming ponies are now cared for by the National Park Service, and you can catch views of them from the observation deck.

Ocracoke Lighthouse Built in 1823, this stolid brick lighthouse is the oldest in North Carolina, and is one of the island's most photogenic spots.

Coyote Music Den Inside a clapboard waterside house, this tiny musician-run venue hosts a regular lineup of folk, rock, blues and jazz.

Ocracoke Beach Dolphins are commonly spotted off Ocracoke's gorgeous, undeveloped 26km (16-mile) stretch of sandy beach.

Howard's Pub The best place on the island to indulge in freshly shucked oysters, peel-and-eat shrimp or grilled catch of the day.

HOWARD'S END

Few people can claim such a deep ancestral connection to their hometown as Philip Howard. He lives on a sandy lane named after his great-great-great-great-great-grandfather William Howard, who purchased 'Ye Island of Ocreecock' (for £105) in 1759; today, his family are the 10th generation of Howards who've called the island home. As the unofficial historian of Ocracoke, Philip Howard has collected a trove of stories, including a fair number related to Blackbeard – who met his bitter end on the island in 1718. One local villager named Roy Parsons told him about an encounter he had one late afternoon at Springer's Point. Parsons had docked his boat and was walking through the forest when he spotted a large bearded man sitting on a cistern. He got an eerie feeling from the man, so he turned back. The man followed him, and Roy began to run. Sensing him on his heels, Roy jumped into his boat, pulled up the anchor and oared off the shore. There the strange bearded man stood staring at him, thigh-deep in the water. As Roy watched, the frock-coated man just dissolved like smoke. Roy never saw him again – and he never set foot on Springer's Point again after dark. You can find Howard's latest Ocracoke writings on his website Village Craftsmen (villagecraftsmen.com).

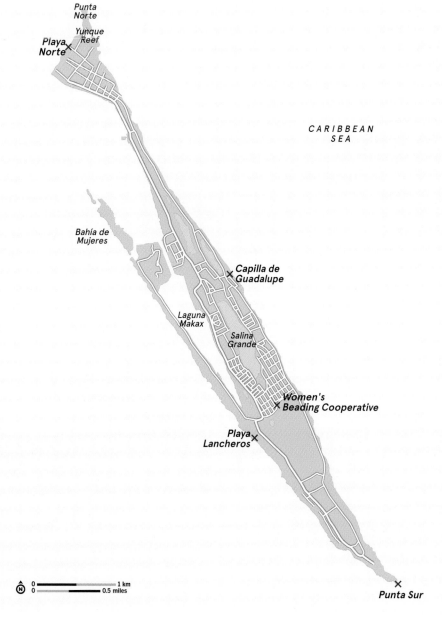

Punta
Norte

Yunque
Reef

Playa
Norte×

CARIBBEAN
SEA

Bahía de
Mujeres

× Capilla de
Guadalupe

Laguna
Makax

Salina
Grande

Women's
× Beading Cooperative

Playa ×
Lancheros

Punta Sur ×

0 ——————— 1 km
0 ——————— 0.5 miles

X MARKS THE SPOT

Playa Norte Greater Cancún's most alluring beach, with shallow gem-coloured waters, swaying palms and powdery white sands.

Punta Sur Crowds flock to this historic park on the island's southernmost tip to stroll alongside suntanning iguanas and explore the Maya ruins.

Women's Beading Cooperative This colourful co-op showcases the work of more than 50 women who make beaded jewellery, purses, earrings and more by hand.

Playa Lancheros This southern beach is a quieter alternative to Playa Norte, with rentals of kayaks, SUPs and other watersports gear.

Capilla de Guadalupe The views sure are heavenly at this revered oceanfront chapel dedicated to the Virgin of Guadalupe, a potent symbol of Catholic Mexican identity.

❶

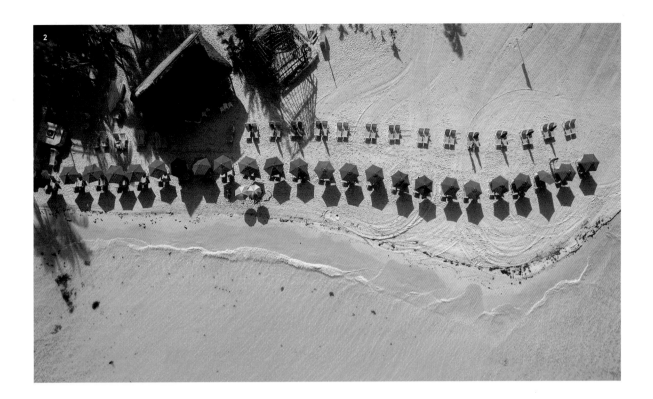

Isla Mujeres

COUNTRY MEXICO

COORDINATES 21.232° N, 86.734° W • **AREA** 4 SQ KM (1.5 SQ MILES)

Isla Mujeres may lie just off the coast of Cancún, but this tiny pencil-thin island feels a world away from the hubbub of Mexico's largest beach resort, with tranquil turquoise waters, white sands and prismatic corals along the Mesoamerican Barrier Reef. The island was revered by the Maya as a sanctuary for Ixchel, the jaguar goddess of midwifery and medicine, but today its devotees are drawn by sun and sand. The scuba diving is sublime, the mood is laid-back (golf carts are the only transportation here), and the margaritas go down like lemonade as the sun plunges into the Caribbean Sea.

CANCÚN UNDERWATER MUSEUM

Cancún boomed with energy and investment at the start of the 21st century, but as it did, the offshore reefs that lured so many of its visitors began to deteriorate rapidly. Marine Park Director Jaime Gonzalez Canto wanted to find a creative way to relieve pressure on the local reefs by diverting divers and snorkellers to new waters off Isla Mujeres. So, he enlisted the help of British sculptor Jason deCaires Taylor, who was keenly interested in the relationship between art and the environment. Together, they would submerge a series of statues in 2009 on a barren seabed about 8m (26ft) below the surface. Each would be cast from people who represented a cross-section of Mexican society. The sculptures would be made out of pH-neutral concrete, which would, over time, encourage coral growth and attract marine life, thus spawning a brand-new reef. The Cancún Underwater Museum was born.

This pioneering project now features over 500 sculptures by deCaires Taylor and five Mexican artists. Many are already blooming with corals as they become one with the aquatic environment. From headless torsos searching the seabed to an abandoned Volkswagen Beetle, one never knows what to expect on a dive through the world's largest submarine sculpture park.

1. The coral-encrusted sculptures of Cancún Underwater Museum

2. Tempting turquoise seas at Isla Mujeres

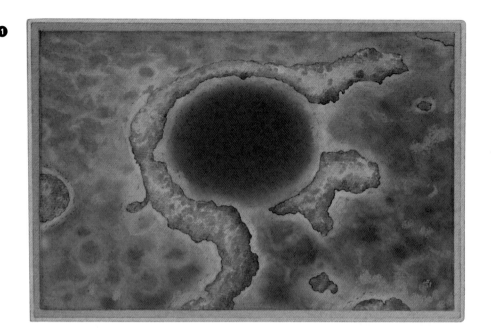

1

Turneffe Atoll

COUNTRY BELIZE
COORDINATES 17.438° N, 87.830° W • **AREA** 330 SQ KM (127 SQ MILES)

Turneffe Atoll, just 32km (20 miles) off the coast of Belize City, couldn't be more different to your run-of-the-mill Caribbean paradise. To understand what makes it so unique, you first need to understand what an atoll is. Typically associated with the South Pacific, atolls are ring-shaped coral islands that include a coral rim, which encircles a lagoon either partially or completely. Turneffe is one of just four atolls in the western hemisphere, and is the largest of the Mesoamerican Barrier Reef system. With 150 small cayes and mangrove islands, it has become a vital nursery for a wide variety of marine life. Anglers ply the offshore waters to achieve the prestigious 'Grand Slam' of bonefish, tarpon and permit – all caught in one day. Meanwhile, scuba types head to the dive resorts near the southernmost tip to search for eagle rays, hawksbill turtles, moray eels and harmless reef sharks.

GREAT BLUE HOLE

The year was 1971, and the famed French explorer Jacques Cousteau found himself descending from blue waters into black ones, diving to the unknown depths of a mysterious marine sinkhole off the coast of Belize. Deep down below, he was shocked to find 12m-long (39ft) stalactites, suggesting that this strange site was formed above ground. Indeed, further studies showed that it was once a limestone cave that collapsed, leaving in its wake a watery abyss that is, today, the largest underwater sinkhole in the world. Measuring 318m (1043ft) wide by 124m (407ft) deep, it is a a diving destination unlike any other (Cousteau himself declared it one of the top five in the world). A typical descent takes you to 40m (131ft) below the lip of the crater, where Caribbean reef sharks circle darkening waters. It's here that you begin to see the giant stalactites that make this submarine realm unlike anywhere else on Earth.

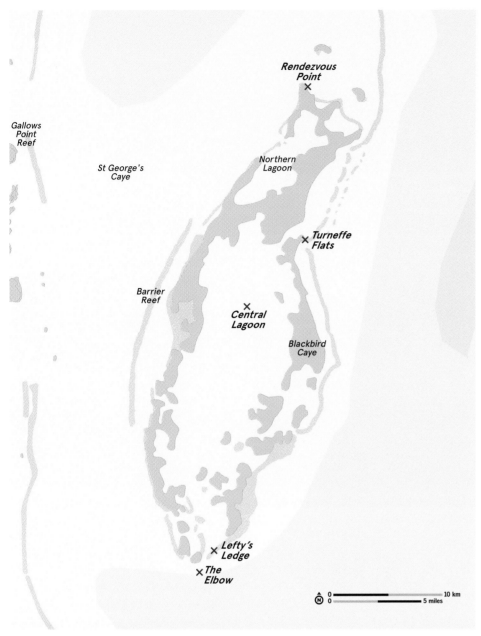

Gallows
Point
Reef

St George's
Caye

Rendezvous
Point
×

Northern
Lagoon

× Turneffe
Flats

Barrier
Reef

×
Central
Lagoon

Blackbird
Caye

Lefty's
× Ledge

×The
Elbow

0   10 km
N
0   5 miles

X MARKS THE SPOT

The Elbow Turneffe's most famous dive site offers a steep, sloping wall covered in tube sponges and frequented by eagle rays.

Central Lagoon The largest of Turneffe's three main lagoons is a natural playground dotted with mangrove islands, littoral forest and, yes, tons of American crocodiles!

Lefty's Ledge Coral growths jut out over a deep-water drop-off in this dive site frequented by pelagics, who enjoy its abundance of food and shelter.

Flats Fishing Anglers flock to the islands' resorts for catch-and-release flats fishing both on the edge of the atoll and in interior lagoons.

Rendezvous Point One of the few northerly dive sites, which is a popular first stop for daytrippers from nearby Ambergris Caye.

1. Turneffe Atoll

2. Kaleidoscopic corals at a Turneffe dive site

Little Corn Island

COUNTRY NICARAGUA
COORDINATES 12.293° N, 82.985° W • **AREA** 3 SQ KM (1.2 SQ MILES)

With its untouched gold-tinged beaches, whispering coconut and mango groves and refreshing absence of motorised vehicles, Little Corn Island feels like the kind of easy-breezy Caribbean hideaway you'll want to keep all to yourself. Reaching this tiny pocket of paradise, around 90km (56 miles) east of Nicaragua's Caribbean coast, is no simple task: usually a flight from capital Managua to Great Corn Island (13km/8 miles southwest of Little Corn), then a half-hour *panga* (boat) ride. But once you're swishing past the mangrove-lined cliffs in a kayak, tapping into the buzzy backpacker surf scene or digging into a fresh-fish spread overlooking a palm-sprinkled cove, the long journey instantly fades into the distance.

LITTLE CORN'S BACKSTORY

The origins of Little Corn's curious name (Isla Pequeña de Maíz in Spanish) are wrapped in mystery, and almost every islander has an original theory. Many believe that, with European sailors frequenting the archipelago from the 15th century onwards to stock up on meats, the Spanish word *carne* (meat) eventually trickled down as 'corn'. Along with its sister Great Corn, from the early 18th to the late 19th century Little Corn was controlled by the British, who brought enslaved African-Caribbean people to the island. Both Corn Islands were incorporated into Nicaragua in 1894, though between 1914 and the 1970s they were leased to the USA as a naval base.

Today, Little Corn's 1000-strong population, descended from African-Caribbean and indigenous Miskitu people, speak Creole, English and Spanish. Lobster fishing was the main occupation until tourism began to trickle through in the 1990s, and there was once also a flourishing coconut-growing industry, sadly destroyed by a hurricane in 1988.

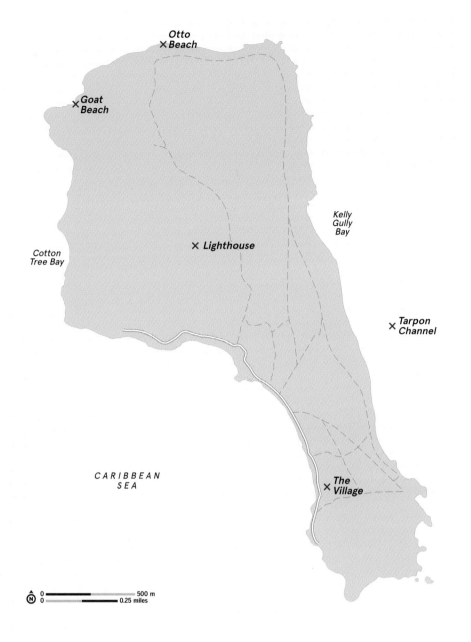

Otto
✕ Beach

✕ Goat
Beach

Kelly
Gully
Bay

✕ Lighthouse

Cotton
Tree Bay

✕ Tarpon
Channel

CARIBBEAN
SEA

✕ The
Village

N
0   500 m
0   0.25 miles

X MARKS THE SPOT

Otto Beach A blissful sweep of alabaster sand washed by aqua waves, the island's most beloved beach is tucked along the northern shoreline.

The Village Little Corn's main settlement hugs the southwest coast, with a few shops, hotels and restaurants.

Goat Beach Get away from it all on this remote cove in the island's north.

Lighthouse Built during the 20th-century US naval lease, Little Corn's metal lighthouse has been reincarnated as a terrific 360-degree viewpoint, especially popular as a place to take in the sunset.

Tarpon Channel Rays, rainbows of tropical fish and, in particular, hammerhead sharks patrol the depths of this standout dive spot.

1. Island life, Little Corn

2. Djembe drummer

3. Spotted eagle rays patrol the island's waters

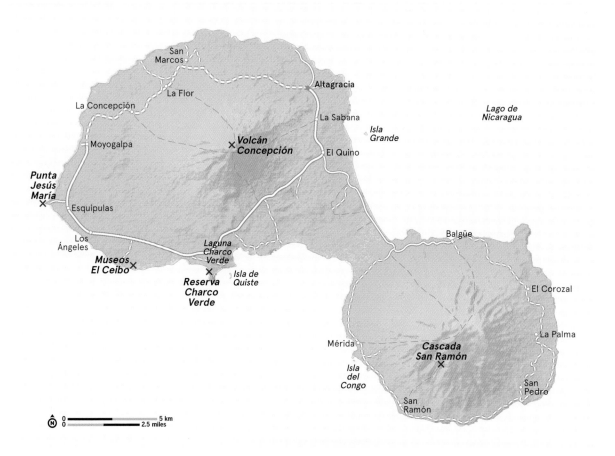

San
Marcos

La Flor

La Concepción

Altagracia

La Sabana

*Lago de
Nicaragua*

Moyogalpa

*Volcán
Concepción*

*Isla
Grande*

El Quino

*Punta
Jesús
María*

Esquipulas

Los
Ángeles

*Laguna
Charco
Verde*

Balgüe

*Museos
El Ceibo*

*Reserva
Charco
Verde*

*Isla de
Quiste*

El Corozal

La Palma

Mérida

*Cascada
San Ramón*

*Isla
del
Congo*

San
Pedro

San
Ramón

N   0 _____ 5 km
    0 _____ 2.5 miles

1. Thatched bungalow
at Totoco Eco-lodge
on the slopes of Volcán
Maderas

2. Diving in at Ometepe's
Ojo de Agua spring-fed
natural pool

Isla de Ometepe

COUNTRY NICARAGUA
COORDINATES 11.514° N, 85.581° W • AREA 276 SQ KM (106 SQ MILES)

Twin volcanic peaks connected by a low-lying isthmus poke above Lago de Nicaragua, forming this otherworldly hourglass-shaped island in Central America's largest lake. These two duelling cones are often referred to as 'fire' and 'water'. The former, Volcán Concepción, is a temperamental stratovolcano that erupts with great frequency. The latter, Volcán Maderas, is a smaller, dormant mound, blanketed in cloud forests that house playful white-faced capuchins and roaring howler monkeys – these noisy residents provide the morning wake-up call for the island's visitors, who travel here for low-impact ecotourism that benefits local communities. Ometepe is much more than just a natural paradise; it's been a sacred site for various indigenous peoples over thousands of years, including the Chorotega, Nahuatl and Maya. These ancient residents left their mark on the island, turning it into one of the world's greatest repositories of rock art. There are more than 1700 petroglyphs dating back to 1000 BCE, as well as large stone idols etched out of basalt.

THE NICARAGUA CANAL

Chinese businessman Wang Jing had a colossal dream for how Nicaragua could one-up its wealthier neighbour Panama: by creating a massive 278km (173-mile) shipping canal from the Rio Brito, on the Pacific side, to the Rio Punta Gorda, on the Caribbean.

In 2013, he made big promises and got a giant reward from Nicaraguan president Daniel Ortega, who offered him a 50-year concession to make the $40 billion plan a reality. The project faced strong opposition from the start as it would forever alter the freshwater ecosystem of Lago de Nicaragua, the large stretch of water at its heart, where giant cargo ships would sail right past the tranquil oasis of Ometepe.

Nevertheless, work began in December 2014, though it was halted indefinitely soon after when the Chinese stock market crashed, diminishing Wang's personal wealth. By 2018, Wang had closed all offices in Nicaragua.

X MARKS THE SPOT

Cascada San Ramón This 40m-high (131ft) waterfall tumbles down a mossy rock face into an emerald green pool, where you can cool off from the equatorial heat.

Punta Jesús María This narrow spit of sand juts out into the lake, forming a perfect backdrop for provoking Instagram envy.

Reserva Charco Verde Three hiking trails snake through this lush nature reserve, which holds a serene lake, a butterfly aviary and a black-sand beach.

Museos El Ceibo This small complex near the village of Esquipulas features two museums, including one dedicated to the pre-Hispanic archaeology of the region.

Volcán Concepción The challenging seven- to 10-hour round-trip trek to the fuming crater atop this 1610m (5282ft) volcano offers sweeping island views on a (rare) clear day.

Isla del Cocos

COUNTRY COSTA RICA
COORDINATES 5.528° N, 87.057° W • **AREA** 24 SQ KM (9.2 SQ MILES)

It took Costa Rica quite a while to figure out what it wanted to do with Isla del Cocos, a rectangular parcel of tropical forest marooned 480km (298 miles) away in the Pacific Ocean. After annexing it in 1832, it turned the uninhabited landmass into a prison colony. Then, spurred by rumours of loot and booty, it funded treasure-hunting expeditions following in the footsteps of the pirates who plied its waters in the early 1800s – all to no avail. Finally, in 1978, it landed on a more sensible idea: protect Isla del Cocos as a national park.

Blessed with a high level of endemic flora, Cocos is the only oceanic island of the eastern Pacific with a tropical rainforest environment. Encased by towering 90m (295ft) cliffs, it's accessible at just two natural harbours on its northern coast: Chatham Bay and Wafer Bay. Its 33 residents – park rangers – are split between the two. Divers flock to the deep waters just offshore to swim with giant shivers of hammerhead sharks, graceful manta rays and frenetic schools of pelagic fish. Yet, like all visitors, they must agree to stay on their boats in the evening; nobody (except the park rangers) is allowed to spend a night on this precious jewel of the Pacific.

TREASURE OF LIMA

Spain's prized New World possession of Lima was on the edge of revolt in 1820 when, according to legend, the Viceroy decided to ship its fabulous wealth to Mexico for safekeeping. Captain William Thompson was charged with the task, sailing away on the *Mary Dear*, but was soon overcome by the temptation to steal the loot he carried. The newly minted pirate headed for Isla del Cocos where, as the story goes, he buried precious jewels, silver and gold that could be valued now at more than $200 million. Countless hunters have searched for the Treasure of Lima, but its location remains a mystery to this day.

X MARKS THE SPOT

Chatham Bay The rare beach here is the island's easiest point of entry (and its best spot for lazing away an oceanside afternoon).

Wafer Bay A ribbon of water spills over a verdant cliff into the valley below before drip-dropping into the Pacific Ocean.

Hammerheads A chance to dive with the world's largest reported schools of hammerhead sharks is the island's biggest draw.

Genius River Bridge This local landmark was made with debris confiscated from shark-fin poachers, including nets, lines and buoys.

Cerro Yglesias Hidden in the cloud forests at 634m (2080ft), Cerro Yglesias is the island's highest point and most strenuous summit.

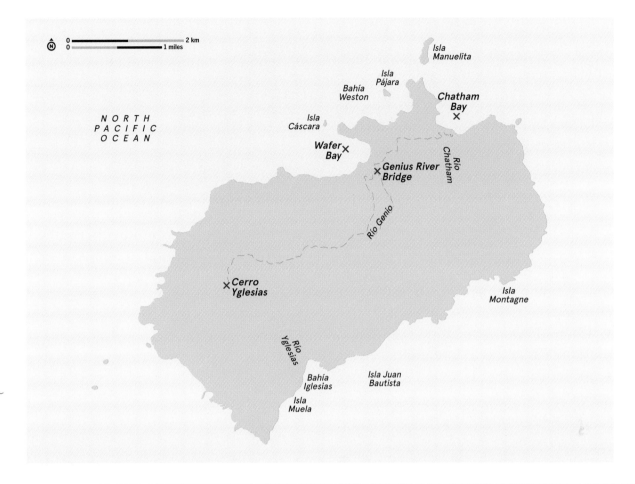

NORTH
PACIFIC
OCEAN

Isla
Manuelita

Isla
Pájara

Bahía
Weston

Chatham
Bay
×

Isla
Cáscara

Wafer
Bay ×

Genius River
Bridge ×

Río
Chatham

Río Genio

× Cerro
Yglesias

Isla
Montagne

Río
Yglesias

Bahía
Iglesias

Isla Juan
Bautista

Isla
Muela

1. Wafer Bay Waterfall

2. Bluestripe snapper
add a neon pop to the
Isla del Cocos reefs

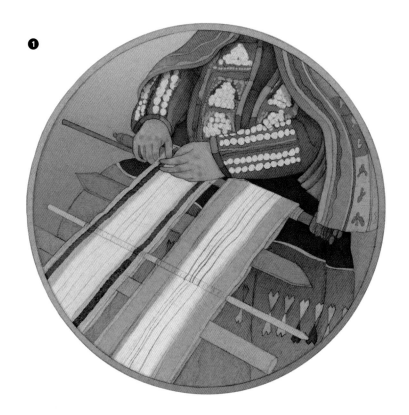

Islas San Blas

COUNTRY PANAMA • **COORDINATES** 9.570°N, 78.820° W • **AREA** 2.3 SQ KM (0.8 SQ MILES)

Studded with coconut palms and fringed by swirls of turquoise, the islands of the Archipiélago de San Blas are a vision of paradise. Stretching along the southern end of Panama's Caribbean coast, this remote string of around 365 islands (49 of which are inhabited) are autonomously controlled by the indigenous Guna Yala people, who maintain traditional ways of life despite modern pressures – including climate change – that threaten to erode them. Along with living out your wildest castaway fantasies, a San Blas highlight is the chance to spend time with Guna Yala people. The vibrant handmade textiles known as *molas,* sold by women artisans, don't just make fantastic travel mementoes; your purchases also help to preserve Guna culture.

Many travellers visit the San Blas as part of a multi-day yacht journey between Panama and Cartagena (Colombia) as an adventurous alternative to flying, as there is no road through the notorious Darien Gap that links the nations by land.

THE GUNA'S 'THIRD GENDER'

The Guna are Latin America's first indigenous group to gain autonomy, but perhaps the Guna peoples' most progressive tradition is their complete acceptance of gender fluidity.

Women enjoy an elevated status in Guna society, so much so that some boys choose to become Omeggid, literally 'like a woman'. This 'third gender' is a normal phenomenon in the San Blas. If a boy begins showing a tendency towards acting 'female', the family naturally accepts it. Often, Omeggid will learn a skill typically associated with women; for example, many Omeggid living on the islands become masters at crafting intricate *molas*.

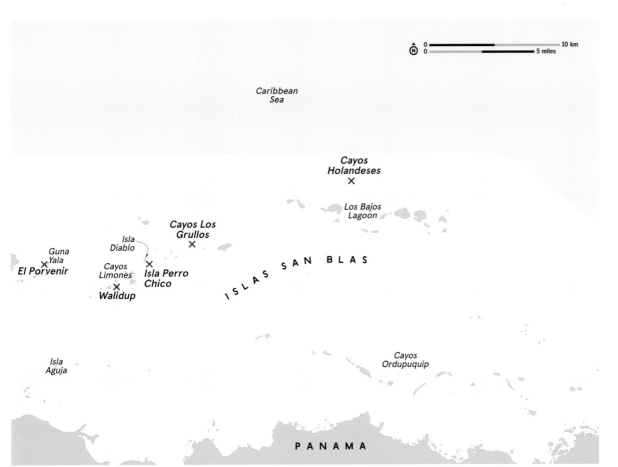

Caribbean
Sea

Cayos
Holandeses
✕

Los Bajos
Lagoon

Cayos Los
Grullos
✕

Isla
Diablo

Guna
Yala
✕
El Porvenir

Cayos
Limones
✕
Walidup

Isla Perro
Chico
✕

I S L A S   S A N   B L A S

Isla
Aguja

Cayos
Ordupuquip

P A N A M A

0 ────────── 10 km
0 ────────── 5 miles
N

1. Textiles are handmade
by Guna artisans

2. Just one of San Blas'
360 islets – perfect for
living out your tropical
castaway dreams

X MARKS THE SPOT

Cayos Los Grullos, Holandeses & Ordupuquip Popular with yachties, this triangle of three virtually uninhabited island chains are the gems of the archipelago.

Digir Dubu (Isla Tigre) This more traditional island is home to one of the San Blas' biggest festivals, October's Feria de Isla Tigre.

Yandup This small island, just five minutes by boat from Uggubseni, is home to one of the region's most atmospheric accommodation options, Yandup Island Lodge.

Assudubu Bibbi (Isla Perro Chico) With a small shipwreck just offshore that's perfect for snorkelling, 'Small Dog Island' is a popular day-trip destination.

Walidup This picturesque isle in the Cayos Limones has a sprawling beach and overwater bungalows.

❷

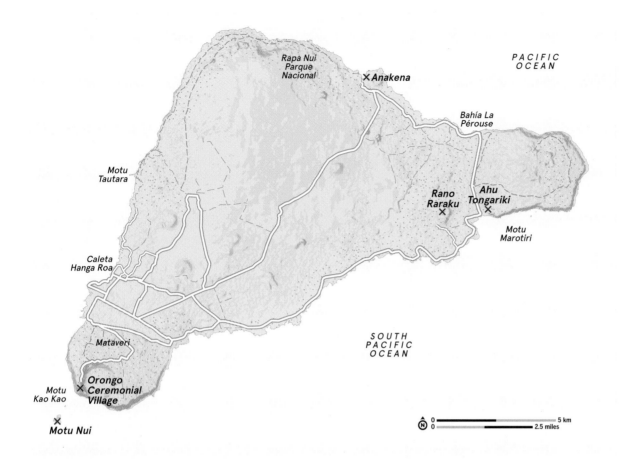

PACIFIC OCEAN

Rapa Nui
Parque
Nacional

✗ *Anakena*

*Bahía La
Pérouse*

*Motu
Tautara*

*Rano
Raraku*
✗

*Ahu
Tongariki*
✗

*Motu
Marotiri*

*Caleta
Hanga Roa*

*SOUTH
PACIFIC
OCEAN*

Mataveri

**Orongo
Ceremonial
Village**
✗

*Motu
Kao Kao*
✗

Motu Nui
✗

0 ———— 5 km
Ⓝ
0 ———— 2.5 miles

1. Looking down into the
Rano Kau crater

2. Stone *moai* gaze over
Ahu Akivi

© Walter Weinberg | 500px. © Eric Lafforgue | Lonely Planet

Easter Island/ Rapa Nui

COUNTRY CHILE

COORDINATES 27.112°S, 109.349°W • **AREA** 164 SQ KM (63 SQ MILES)

Few places on the planet possess a more mystical pull than this remote speck of land, some 3700km (2300 miles) northwest of Santiago. Endowed with the most logic-defying statues on the planet – the strikingly familiar *moai* – Easter Island (Rapa Nui to its native Polynesian inhabitants) emanates a magnetic, mysterious vibe.

But Easter Island is much more than an open-air museum. Diving, snorkelling and surfing are fabulous. On land, there's no better way to experience the volcanic island's savage beauty than on foot, from a bike saddle or on horseback. And while much of the island is surrounded by dramatic cliffs, there are a couple of superb white-sand beaches to enjoy.

Grasslands dominate the interior of Easter Island, roughly triangular in shape, and replating efforts are ongoing to help mitigate erosion, the island's most serious problem. Although visitor numbers are on the increase, everything remains small and personable in this spellbinding corner of South America.

MARCH OF THE MOAI

Easter Island's most pervasive image, the enigmatic *moai* are massive carved figures that probably represent clan ancestors. From 1m to 10m tall (3ft to 33ft), these stony-faced statues stood with their backs to the Pacific Ocean. Of the 887 known *moai*, just 288 made it to their *ahu* (ceremonial stone platforms), while 92 got derailed in transit.

For several centuries, controversy has raged over the techniques employed to move and raise the *moai*, which weigh an average of 12.5 tonnes. For many decades, most experts believed they were dragged on a kind of wooden sledge, or pushed on top of rollers, but in the early 2000s archaeologists came to the conclusion that the *moai* were not dragged horizontally but moved in a vertical position using ropes. This theory would tally with oral history, which says that the *moai* 'walked' to their *ahu*. It's a never-ending debate, which only adds to the island's sense of mystery.

X MARKS THE SPOT

Rano Raraku Take a lesson in archaeology at this 'nursery' of the *moai*, a volcano crater that served as an ancient quarry.

Ahu Tongariki Watching the sun rise above the island's largest row of *moai* is guaranteed to leave you spellbound.

Anakena Have a snooze under the swaying palms of this alluring north-coast beach, or spot unusual marine life on a snorkel excursion.

Orongo Ceremonial Village Ponder the island's mysterious past at this village perched on the edge of Rano Kau.

Moto Nui Excellent visibility makes for great diving around Easter Island, particularly around this tiny islet off its southwestern tip.

Isla Barú

COUNTRY COLOMBIA · **COORDINATES** 10.169° N, 75.657° W · **AREA** 25 SQ KM (10 SQ MILES)

Isla Barú is the kind of idyllic beach destination most travellers envision – but fail to find – when they land in the bustling city of Cartagena, just an hour to the north. This long and thin island, cut off from the mainland by a constructed waterway, Canal del Dique, is a place where turquoise water laps against white sands, shots of aguardiente flow and masseurs ply the beach in search of their next customer. Playa Blanca is the destination of the masses, with its ample beach bars and hordes of food vendors. More secluded beaches include Playa Manglares and Playa Puntilla nearby.

Just offshore from Isla Barú are the even more secluded Islas del Rosario, home to a national park that protects one of the most important coral reef systems on Colombia's Caribbean coast. These 27 small coral islands and islets lure divers and snorkellers alike, with the two most developed islands, Isla Grande and Isla del Rosario, boasting hotels, restaurants and serene interior lagoons. Many of Rosario's smaller islands are owned by a single hotel, though visitors can purchase day-passes to enjoy a private island experience with luxurious amenities.

THE BATTLE FOR SAN JOSÉ

It was 8 June 1708, and the Spanish galleon *San José* had been at battle with the British all day when it exploded and sank off the coast of Cartagena, taking with it 600 people and up to $20 billion in gold, silver and jewels. Gabriel García Márquez wrote about the buried treasure in *Love in the Time of Cholera*. Generations of explorers searched for it. Then, in 2015, the Colombian government announced that this holy grail had finally been discovered 600m (1968ft) deep off the coast of Isla Barú, where it remains to this day awaiting extraction. Will the legend of riches match the reality? It may be years before we find out due a complex legal battle over who should reap the rewards.

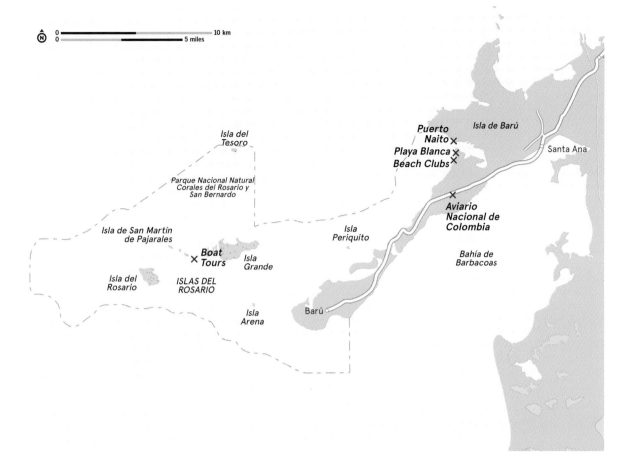

0   10 km
0   5 miles

Isla del Tesoro

Parque Nacional Natural Corales del Rosario y San Bernardo

Isla de San Martín de Pajarales

✕ Boat Tours

Isla del Rosario

ISLAS DEL ROSARIO

Isla Grande

Isla Arena

Barú

Isla Periquito

Bahía de Barbacoas

Puerto Naito ✕

Playa Blanca Beach Clubs ✕

✕ *Aviario Nacional de Colombia*

Isla de Barú

Santa Ana

X MARKS THE SPOT

Aviario Nacional de Colombia
This aviary includes 21 exhibits across three ecosystems that shelter some 190 species of native birds.

Beach Clubs Day-drinking is the chief activity on Playa Blanca, and you'll want a swanky four-poster beach bed to keep cool.

Puerto Naito Nighttime tours depart for the bay of Puerto Naito, where rare bioluminescent microorganisms dance in the water like fairly lights.

Lobster Lunches Caribbean lobster, coconut rice and *patacones* (twice-fried plantains) served at a table by the sea? Yes, please!

Boat Tours From Isla Barú, it's easy to schedule a boat tour to the nearby Islas del Rosario; some trips are pitched to snorkellers, others to partiers.

1. Boats of Isla Barú

2. Islas del Rosario

3. Palm-thatched beach hut on Isla Barú

Isla
Pallalla

Isla
Chullo

Isla
Kenata

*Lake
Titicaca*

Bahía
Machamachani   Isla
Lavasani
Bahía
Sabacera
× Chincana
Isla   Ruins
Jochihuata   **Cha'llapampa
Museum**
×
Bahía
Cha'lla

Bahía
Kona del   Bahía
Norte   Kea

Bahía
Pukhara

× Escalera
del Inca

Bahía
Kona

Pilko ×
Kaina   Isla
Chelleca

BOLIVIA

X MARKS THE SPOT

Museo del Oro Gold and silver figurines of both Tiwanaku and Inca origin are the highlights of this small museum in Cha'llapampa.

Chincana Ruins The labyrinthine Palacio del Inca here is the island's most spectacular sight, while the remaining ruins speak to the legendary origins of Inca gods.

Escalera del Inca This preserved stone stairway rises 200m (656ft) into the terraced gardens uphill from the ferry dock at Yumani.

Pilko Kaina The most prominent ruins on the island's south side, much of it is thought to have been built for Inca emperor Túpac Inca Yupanqui.

Hiking The journey from Yumani to Cha'llapampa passes terraced hills and lookouts with sweeping views all the way to the Cordillera Real's snow-capped peaks.

❸

Isla del Sol

COUNTRY BOLIVIA • **COORDINATES** 16.017° S, 69.178° W • **AREA** 14 SQ KM (5.4 SQ MILES)

Isla del Sol (Sun Island) is a veritable island in the sky, situated at a breathtaking 3812m (12,506ft) above sea level within the world's highest navigable body of water, Lake Titicaca. Continually occupied since at least 2200 BCE, it came to prominence in the 15th century during the Inca period, when most of the 80 ruins here were built. To this day, the island has no roads and most of its arid slopes are blanketed in terraced agricultural fields filled with quinoa. The southernmost village of Yumani holds most of the island's 800 families and is a hub for tourism, with traditional guesthouses overlooking Titicaca's azure waters. Dirt paths lead north from here through sun-dappled interior hills to the settlements of Cha'lla and Cha'llapampa, passing numerous Inca ruins along the way. Sun Island's smaller counterpart, Isla de la Luna (Moon Island), lies to the east – with more ruins but a fraction of the visitors.

THE BIRTH OF CIVILISATION

As the creator deity in pre-Inca and Inca mythology, Viracocha had his work cut out for him when he rose out of Lake Titicaca during the time of darkness and set about bringing forth light. First, he made the sun; then the moon, stars and civilisation itself. Later, he brought forth Manco Cápac and Mama Ocllo, founders of the Inca dynasty, who appeared on Isla del Sol and went on to establish the future Inca capital of Cusco near Machu Picchu in modern-day Peru. Both Isla del Sol and Isla de la Luna play key roles in Inca mythology as the birthplace of many of its gods, including Inti (the sun god) and Mama Killa (mother moon).

Meanwhile, the creation story of Viracocha is still shared by modern-day Aymara and Quechua peoples of Peru and Bolivia, who make pilgrimages to these holy sites every year.

1. Contemplating Titicaca from a reed-built Uros fishing boat

2. Chincana Ruins

3. Cha'llapampa village

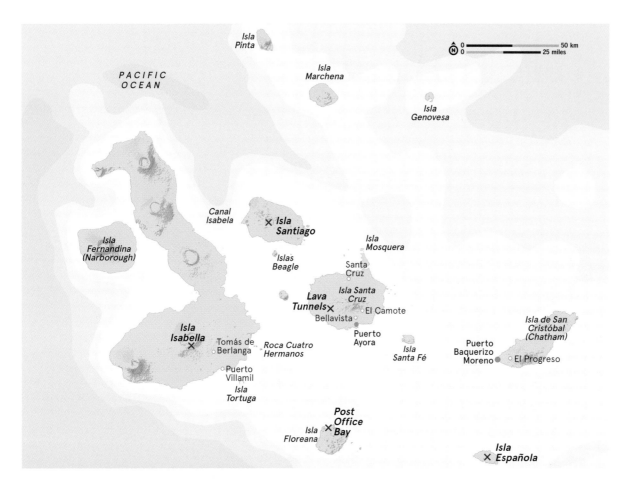

PACIFIC OCEAN

0 — 50 km
0 — 25 miles

Isla Pinta

Isla Marchena

Isla Genovesa

Isla Fernandina (Narborough)

Canal Isabela

× Isla Santiago

Isla Mosquera

Islas Beagle

Santa Cruz

Lava Tunnels×

Isla Santa Cruz

El Camote

Bellavista

Puerto Ayora

Isla Isabella ×

Tomás de Berlanga

Roca Cuatro Hermanos

Isla Santa Fé

Isla de San Cristóbal (Chatham)

Puerto Baquerizo Moreno ●

El Progreso

Puerto Villamil

Isla Tortuga

Post Office Bay

× Isla Floreana

Isla × Española

1. Puerto Ayora, Isla Santa Cruz

2. Galápagos land iguana

Galápagos Islands

COUNTRY ECUADOR
COORDINATES 0.953° S, 90.965° W • **AREA** 8010 SQ KM (3093 SQ MILES)

English naturalist Charles Darwin once described the Galápagos Islands as 'a little world within itself'. Nearly two centuries later, the remote Ecuadorian archipelago remains a place of wonder, where visitors can still get up close to some of the world's most unusual wildlife, from prehistoric-looking marine iguanas to blue-footed boobies. Of the 13 islands in the Galápagos, the four inhabited isles you can stay on offer a fascinating glimpse into how humans coexist with this wild place, a three-hour flight from mainland Quito. But arguably the best way to experience this otherworldly destination is on a small-ship cruise with an authorised operator. While choosing an itinerary can feel overwhelming, every island has its unique draws, from opportunities to snorkel with fur seals to unusual colonial-era heritage. And while the Galápagos' famed giant tortoises can be seen in the wild on several islands, a visit to the Charles Darwin Research Station on the main island of Santa Cruz, which runs breeding programmes for giant tortoises and land iguanas, is a travel highlight. Plus, visits support vital conservation work to protect the Galápagos into the future.

X MARKS THE SPOT

Lava Tunnels, Isla Santa Cruz
Walk through giant tunnels formed by molten lava near the modern-day village of Santa Rosa.

Isla Española Enormous waved albatrosses can be viewed nesting on this island.

Isla Isabella Stay a while to hike volcanoes, watch giant tortoises get jiggy at the local breeding centre, and enjoy sunset drinks as marine iguanas wander up the beach.

Post Office Bay, Isla Floreana
Leave a postcard for a future visitor to take home and send on in the tradition of early whalers.

Isla Santiago Marvel at surreal lava formations and prepare to fill your memory card with snaps of Sally lightfoot crabs.

BACK FROM THE DEAD

The 2012 death of Lonesome George, the last known individual of the Galápagos' *Chelonoidis abingdonii* giant tortoise species, was mourned across the world.

But in a boon for biodiversity, a giant tortoise found on Isla Fernandina in 2019 was identified in 2021 as the *Chelonoidis phantasticus* species, which had been considered extinct for more than a century.

The 'new' giant tortoise (which triggered an ongoing search for more members of her kin) is just one of many species that continue to be discovered in the Galápagos – including 30 new species of marine invertebrates announced in 2020 – which adds to the magic of visiting.

❷

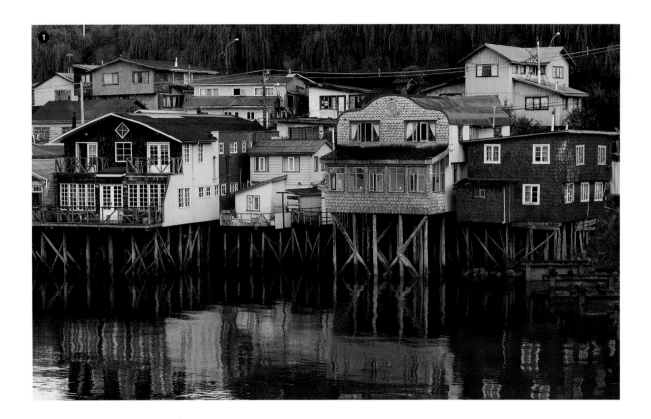

Chiloé Island

COUNTRY CHILE • **COORDINATES** 42.624° S, 73.926° W • **AREA** 8394 SQ KM (3241 SQ MILES)

This peanut-shaped island off the coast of Patagonia, 1100km (683 miles) south of Santiago, lures foreigners with its moss-covered rainforests, historic churches and untrammeled beaches. Yet, if you ask a Chilean why they're visiting, they'll likely wax poetic over the culture, dialect and aesthetic, which are distinct from the mainland following centuries of historic isolation. The wooden stilt homes of Chiloé's capital, Castro, are as colourful as the cast of characters in its local mythology, which includes fish-herding mermaids, sex-crazed forest goblins and lizards who predict the weather. Island meals, meanwhile, pair a rainbow of native potatoes with the fabulous fruits of the sea.

POTATO ISLAND

It's hard to imagine that the potato – so integral to diets everywhere from Ireland to Idaho to Irkutsk – is a relatively recent addition to global cuisine. While it journeyed around the world in the 16th century, indigenous communities in Chile have been cultivating the tuber for more than 8000 years. In fact, recent DNA studies show that more than 90% of modern spuds can trace their origins to Chiloé, where islanders historically cultivated more than 800 varieties (though only 286 survived into the 21st century).

These prismatic *papas chilotas* form a key part of the local diet and include *clavela lisa* (a creamy pink-skinned variety), *michuñe negra* (a fingery purple

potato) and *cabra* (which is both sweet and spicy). 'If you go to the home of a Chilote, there is not a single plate that is conceived without potatoes,' says Lorna Muñoz, a cookbook author and chef at Travesía in Castro. Muñoz uses distinct potatoes for bread (*chochoca*), dumplings (*chapalele*), stew (*cazuela chilota*), porridge (*mazamorra*) and even desserts: *mella de papa* is a cake-like dish made with potatoes that have remained in the soil from one harvest to the next, concentrating their sugars. Meanwhile, potatoes are also intrinsically linked to the island's unique mythology, with many islanders carrying them around in their pockets like amulets to ward off evil spirits.

1. Chiloé's sleepy capital, Castro

2. Chiloé Island wood-built church

3. Marine otter

0   50 km
0   25 miles

Calbuco

Ancud

*SOUTH
PACIFIC
OCEAN*

Isla
Quinchao ×

*Playa
Cole* × *Parque
Cole   Nacional
         Chiloé*

× *Castro*

Chonchi

*Muelle
De Las Almas* ×

*Parque
Tepuhueico*

Quellon

× *Parque
Tantauco*

*Parque
Nacional
Corcovado*

Patagonia

X MARKS THE SPOT

Castro Colourful *palafito* homes sit on stilts above the sea along the perimeter of Chiloé's sleepy capital, an emerging culinary hotspot.

Playa Cole The island's most spectacular crescent of golden sand (and best campground) lies at the end of a 16km (10-mile) hike through Parque Nacional Chiloé.

Muelle de las Almas Ripped out of a fairytale, Chiloé's 'Dock of Souls' curves over a cliff offering cinematic views of the Bay of Cucao.

Isla Quinchao Sample the simple life on one of the archipelago's smaller islands, photographing its Unesco-listed wooden churches.

Parque Tantauco Hike hut-to-hut through this remote reserve, searching for the world's smallest deer (pudu) amid the fuzzy ferns of its temperate rainforests.

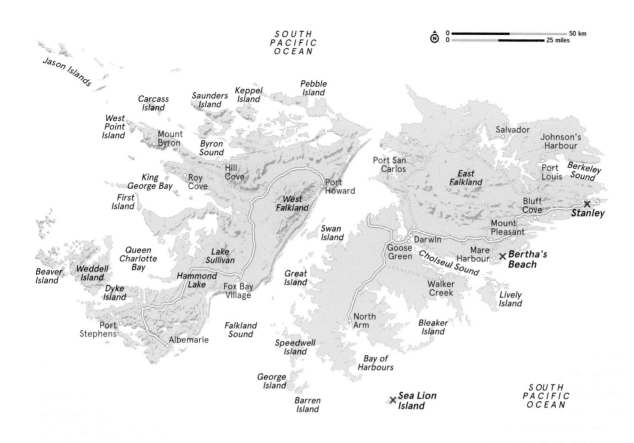

SOUTH
PACIFIC
OCEAN

0 ————————————— 50 km
0 ————————————— 25 miles

Jason Islands

West
Point
Island

Carcass
Island

Saunders
Island

Keppel
Island

Pebble
Island

Mount
Byron

Byron
Sound

King
George Bay

Roy
Cove

Hill
Cove

Port
Howard

West
Falkland

First
Island

Salvador

Johnson's
Harbour

Port San
Carlos

East
Falkland

Port
Louis

Berkeley
Sound

Bluff
Cove

Stanley

Beaver
Island

Weddell
Island

Queen
Charlotte
Bay

Lake
Sullivan

Swan
Island

Darwin

Goose
Green

Mount
Pleasant

Mare
Harbour

×**Bertha's
Beach**

Dyke
Island

Hammond
Lake

Fox Bay
Village

Great
Island

Cholseul Sound

Walker
Creek

Lively
Island

Port
Stephens

Albemarle

Falkland
Sound

Speedwell
Island

North
Arm

Bleaker
Island

George
Island

Bay of
Harbours

SOUTH
PACIFIC
OCEAN

Barren
Island

×**Sea Lion
Island**

1. Gentoo penguins on
Carcass Island

2. Wildflowers abloom
in Stanley

Falkland Islands

COUNTRY UNITED KINGDOM
COORDINATES 51.796°S, 59.523°W • **AREA** 12,173 SQ KM (4700 SQ MILES)

The wild and windswept Falkland Islands are a popular addition to many Antarctic voyages, but the remote British outpost is well worth seeing on its own, particularly for its spectacular penguin, seal and albatross populations.

Surrounded by the South Atlantic, the islands lie 490km (304 miles) east of Patagonia. Alternately settled and claimed by France, Spain, Britain and Argentina, the Falklands (known as the Islas Malvinas in Argentina) have been an overseas territory of the UK since 1833, a status the Argentines have fought and continue to contest.

There are two main islands, East Falkland and West Falkland, and more than 700 smaller ones. About 60% of Falklanders are native-born, some tracing their ancestry back six or more generations. Today more than 80% of the 2900 Falklanders (sometimes called 'Kelpers') live in Stanley, and about 1200 British military bunk at the Mt Pleasant base. The rest of the islanders live in 'Camp', the name given to all of the Falklands outside Stanley.

LAST OF THE LANDMINES

Until late 2020, there were still some beaches in the Falklands that locals wouldn't dare wander along. That changed when the territory was declared free of landmines – after almost 40 years of living in their midst.

The Falklands were peppered with an estimated 13,000 mines by Argentine forces during the 11-week conflict in 1982, which followed an invasion by Argentina to assert territorial claims over the islands. The then British prime minister Margaret Thatcher ordered a counter-invasion which claimed the lives of 649 Argentinian military personnel and 255 British troops, along with three Falkland Island women killed by a stray British mortar round.

With mine-warning signposts serving as a constant reminder of the grisly war, the removal of the last mines as part of a decade-long, UK-funded programme was described by locals as a form of closure. Britain now believes there are no anti-personnel mines on any of its territories around the world.

X MARKS THE SPOT

Bertha's Beach This remote stretch of sand in East Falkland is a penguin lovers' paradise.

Falklands Flora Among the Falklands' 13 endemic plants, several unusual species include Felton's flower (*Calandrinia feltonii*), a caramel-scented, magenta-blossomed annual that, until recently, was thought to be extinct in the wild.

Sea Lion Island Peace out with penguins, elephant seals and more while staying at Britain's most southerly lodge.'

Outlying Islands Away from the main island, wildlife is the biggest attraction on outlying landspits such as Carcass Island.

Stanley Get a taste of life in the 'big smoke', Falklands-style, where you'll find an interesting museum.

Ilha de Marajó

COUNTRY BRAZIL

COORDINATES 0.940° S, 49.639° W • **AREA** 40,100 SQ KM (15,483 SQ MILES)

This languid island where bicycles outnumber cars and water buffalo block traffic lies at the eastern end of the Amazon River, at the point where it prepares for its final push out into the Atlantic Ocean. Roughly the size of Switzerland, Marajó is the second-largest island in South America (after Isla Grande de Tierra del Fuego) and the largest fluvial island in the world. It's also the historic home of the Marajoaras, a pre-Columbian civilisation that left behind elaborate burial urns within large earthen mounds. The island's biggest village, Soure, maintains a strong artistic culture to this day, which is inspired by these ancient artefacts.

Marajó's eastern half, where Soure lies, is called the 'fields region'. It's characterised by low-lying fields and savannah, with palm-fronted beaches and mangrove swamps along the coast. Only the towns here – which lie within reach of the city of Belém – are accessible to tourists. The interior is a vast (and largely impenetrable) wetland home to thousands of birds, including the brilliantly red scarlet ibis. The island's little-visited western half – which edges up against the main flow of the Amazon River – is known as the forest region. It's blanketed in monkey-filled rainforests that flood during the rainy season (January to June).

POROROCA

The indigenous Tupi people, who first settled in the Amazon rainforest about 2900 years ago, noticed that, during new and full moons, when the ocean tide was at its highest, water from the Atlantic would mysteriously travel inland upstream the Amazon River (and its adjacent rivers) forming waves of up to 4m (13ft) high. They called this ephemeral phenomenon *pororoca* (the great roar), a name that has stuck to this day. Modern visitors flock to the waters off Marajó to surf this massive tidal bore, which reaches its visceral peak in the equinoxes of September and March during spring tides.

Map labels

Enlargement

Ateliê Arte Mangue Marajó
✕
✕ Soure
Salvaterra ✕
Ilha de Marajó
Baía de Marajó
✕ Joanes
○ Condeixa

0   40 km
0   20 miles

See Enlargement

● Soure
Camará do Marajó

Ilha de Marajó

Baía de Marajó

Ponta de Pedras
Belém ✕
Ilha da Trambioca
Ilha Grande
● Muaná
B R A Z I L
○ Breves
Ilha Sirituba
Abaetetuba
○ Curralinho

1. Mangoes of Marajó

2. Traditional riverbank stilt houses on the forest-fringed Amazon

X MARKS THE SPOT

Belém This gateway city to the eastern Amazon provides a comfortable launchpad for trips to Marajó, with once-opulent mansions bleaching in the equatorial sun.

Joanes This sleepy beach town lies just across the river from Belém, with laid-back hotels and the ruins of a 17th-century Jesuit mission.

Salvaterra Marajó's best beach lies in this eastern town near Joanes, which has low-key *pousadas* (inns) shaded in mango trees.

Soure The island's largest city (home to some 25,000 people) sits on the banks of the Rio Paracauari and is a top spot for fishing the notoriously toothy piranha.

Ateliê Arte Mangue Marajó This art studio in Soure carries on the artistic traditions of the Marajoaras with museum-grade ceramics and intricately carved sculptures.

❷

Ilha Grande

COUNTRY BRAZIL • COORDINATES 23.152° S, 44.228° W • AREA 193 SQ KM (74 SQ MILES)

As the largest island off the coast of Rio de Janeiro, it's incredible just how undeveloped Ilha Grande has remained. After all, it's got just one small town, Vila do Abraão, and zero cars. Covered by a dense canopy of brazilwood, cedar and ironwood, the island is a vital reserve within the Atlantic Forest, one of the most diverse woodlands in the world. Trails – instead of roads – lead through the forest to more than a hundred beaches that curve around its coast. Meanwhile, the twisted tale of how it avoided development is the stuff of Brazilian legend.

LOCKED UP IN PARADISE

The year was 1863, and Emperor Pedro II was opening the new Empire of Brazil to emigrants from Germany, Japan and Italy just as a cholera pandemic swept around the world. In order to quarantine new arrivals, and protect the empire, he set up the Lazareto Hospital on Ilha Grande where sick passengers were forced to disembark before journeying onward to a new life on the mainland in São Paulo or Rio de Janeiro. That hospital later morphed into a leper colony and, in the early 1900s, an Alcatraz-style maximum security prison known as Cândido Mendes, which housed some of Brazil's most violent criminals.

In 1979, during Brazil's repressive military dictatorship, conditions in the prison were so poor and its criminals so incensed that it gave rise to the Comando Vermelho (Red Command), a powerful criminal organisation in operation to this day. Human rights defenders launched a heated campaign to close the prison after the return of democracy in 1985. With tourism booming along the Brazilian coast, fears also grew that a prison escape could wreak havoc on nearby resort towns. So, authorities finally relocated all prisoners and detonated most of the prison in 1994, paving the way for the island to emerge from its dark past and begin a fresh chapter.

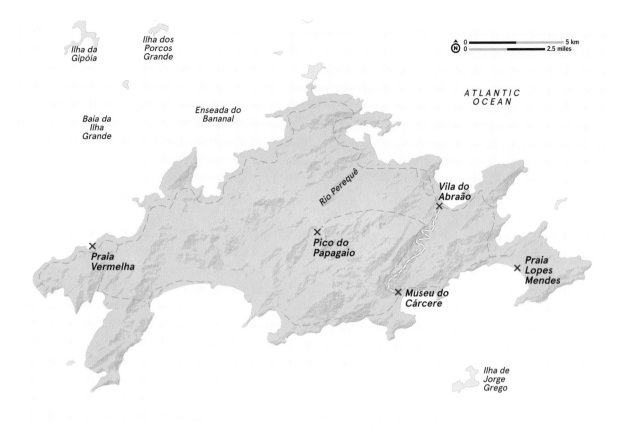

Ilha da
Gipóia

Ilha dos
Porcos
Grande

Baía da
Ilha
Grande

Enseada do
Bananal

ATLANTIC
OCEAN

0   5 km
0   2.5 miles
N

Rio Perequê

Vila do
Abraão

Pico do
Papagaio

Praia
Vermelha

Praia
Lopes
Mendes

Museu do
Cárcere

Ilha de
Jorge
Grego

X MARKS THE SPOT

Praia Vermelha A favourite for divers, this so-called Red Beach is the starting point for underwater adventures to the shipwrecks around Ilha Grande Bay.

Vila do Abraão The island's one true town (with 3000 residents) is mostly a jumble of *pousadas* (inns), seafood restaurants and boats bobbing in the harbour.

Museu do Carcere This museum in reconstructed ruins is the best place to learn about Ilha Grande's dark history as a penal colony.

Praia Lopes Mendes The island's most popular beach, with endless sand and gentle waves, is accessible by a 6km (3.7-mile) trek from Abraão.

Pico do Papagaio A parrot-shaped rock formation offering sweeping views is the highlight (and high point) of this 12km (7.4-mile) hike in the lush interior.

1. Ilha Grande beach

2. Forested coastline near Vila do Abraão

3. Boulder star coral

1. Laid-back Castara Bay on Tobago's Caribbean coast

2. Pigeon Point beach

3. Blue-chinned sapphire hummingbird

X MARKS THE SPOT

Pirate's Bay A steep flight of steps leads down to this sheltered cove where the crescent beach is as wowing as the offshore corals.

Hummingbird Gallery Sightings of at least six species of hummingbird are guaranteed at this Speyside nature centre.

Limbo Scenes of limbo dancing on Tobago in the 1957 film *Fire Down Below* are credited with spreading this local custom around the world.

Pigeon Point Manicured grounds, low-key bars, barbecue restaurants and a perfect palm fringe line the island's most famous beach.

Little Tobago An important seabird sanctuary, this hilly, arid island off the northeast coast lures birders in search of brown boobies, sooty terns and red-billed tropicbirds.

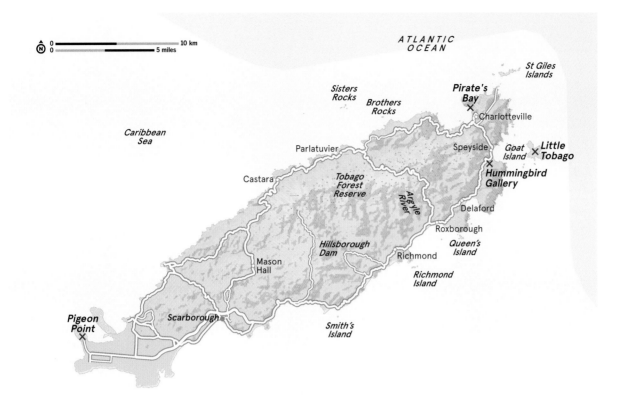

Tobago

COUNTRY TRINIDAD & TOBAGO · **COORDINATES** 11.23° N, 60.69° W · **AREA** 300 SQ KM (116 SQ MILES)

It's tough being the smaller half of a dual-island nation, but Tobago takes its second-tier status in stride. After all, while Trinidad bustles with 1.3 million people, Tobago holds just 60,000, leaving plenty of space for nature to thrive. Much of the coast here is lined in shallow corals, including the popular Buccoo Reef, while leatherback turtles return each year to nest on island beaches. In the hilly interior, you'll find a virgin rainforest left to prosper out of sight from any roads. It's no wonder, then, that Walt Disney Pictures chose Tobago as the backdrop for its iconic 1960s adventure film *Swiss Family Robinson*.

OLDEST PROTECTED FOREST

When the Treaty of Paris (1763) left Tobago in the hands of the British, they planned to do what they'd done on every other Caribbean territory: cut down trees and convert land into sugar plantations. Yet, around that same time, an enlightened commissioner of the Board of Trade, Soame Jenyns, was studying the work of British scientist Stephen Hales, who hypothesised a clear relationship between trees and rainfall. Fearing future droughts on Tobago, Jenyns spent the next decade lobbying Parliament to protect 40 sq km (15.4 sq miles) of the Main Ridge, a 29km-long (18-mile) chain of hills that slices through the

middle of the island. Finally, in 1776, Jenyns' convinced enough lawmakers to join his progressive cause. As a result, the Main Ridge Forest Reserve became the first protected forest in the western hemisphere. Now expanded to 56 sq km (21.6 sq miles), it holds 1500 kinds of flowering plants, 210 types of birds, 16 mammal species and 23 varieties of butterfly. Ecotourism – once a fledgling concept in the region – thrives here as birders, hikers and wildlife-watchers flock to the park, batting away mist-shrouded greenery on serpentine trails. This, of course, is what much of the Caribbean could have looked like if it, too, was protected sooner.

Barbados

COUNTRY BARBADOS • **COORDINATES** 13.193° N, 59.543° W • **AREA** 431 SQ KM (166 SQ MILES)

British, African-Caribbean and North American cultures collide in Barbados, a low-lying island nation known for its dazzling turquoise bays and rum-fuelled nightlife. But there's more to see – and learn about – in this corner of the Lesser Antilles, from quirky natural attractions to Barbados' turbulent past. Housed in a former military prison dating from the early 19th century, Bridgetown's excellent Barbados Museum provides a thought-provoking primer on the island's history – particularly its darkest chapter, when English colonists shipped in thousands of enslaved Africans to work its sugar plantations.

The history of enslavement in Barbados, and the cultivation of sugar cane here, are entwined with the nation's claim to fame as the birthplace of rum. Sanskrit texts suggest India may have beaten the Bajans to producing 'liquid gold' by several centuries, but Barbados' Mount Gay, established in 1703, holds the title of the world's oldest commercial rum distillery. Along with meticulously restored plantation house St Nicholas Abbey (also the product of forced labour by enslaved people), it's one of two historic distilleries visitors can tour. The 1700s saw rum shops pop up across the island, and today these atmospheric bars remain great places to 'fire one' (have a drink) with an eclectic Bajan crowd.

FEEL THE BEAT

Bajan contributions to Caribbean music are renowned in the region, having produced such greats as the Mighty Gabby, a calypso artist whose songs on cultural identity and political protest speak for emerging black pride throughout the region.

These days Bajan music leans toward the faster beats of soca (an energetic offspring of calypso), rapso (a fusion of soca and hip-hop) and dancehall (a contemporary offshoot of reggae with faster, digital beats and an MC). Hugely popular Bajan soca artist Rupee brings the sound of the island to audiences worldwide. And Bajan pop princess Rihanna – who often makes an appearance at the nation's mid-year Crop Over Festival – requires no introduction.

1. Barbados beach

2. Soup Bowl surf break, Bathsheba

3. Bartender lining up cocktails at Mullins Beach bar

The
Cabben

Spring
Hall

Fustic

Shermans

Boscobelle

Mile & a
Quarter

Speightstown

Belleplaine

Haggatts

Bathsheba
×

Holetown

× *Welchman
Hall Gully*

Four
Cross
Roads

ATLANTIC
OCEAN

Prospect

Brighton

Six Cross
Roads

Bridgetown ×

Rockley
× *Beach*

Charnocks

Cobblers
Reef

Rockley

Dover
Beach

Oistins
×

Silver
Sands

Caribbean
Sea

0 ———— 5 km
0 ———— 2.5 miles

X MARKS THE SPOT

Bridgetown The bustling capital, with its Unesco-listed downtown area and Garrison, buzzes with the rhythms of local culture.

Oistins At the heart of this south-coast fishing town is a lively seaside fish market, which on Friday hosts the island's most popular party, Oistins Fish Fry.

Rockley Beach On the south coast, unwind on one of the island's most blissful beaches.

Welchman Hall Gully Enjoy the lush beauty of this nature reserve in a collapsed cave system in central Barbados.

Bathsheba Take a road trip to the wild side, exploring the rugged shores around this fishing village on the northeast coast.

1

Dominica

COUNTRY DOMINICA

COORDINATES 15.415° N, 61.371° W • **AREA** 751 SQ KM (290 SQ MILES)

Forget everything you think you know about what a Caribbean island should look like: Dominica is the exception to the rule in so many ways. For starters, it's home to a whopping nine active volcanoes (all other volcanic islands of the Lesser Antilles have just one), which tower above the island at nearly 1500m (4921ft). Hidden in their midst are dense forests home to two parrots that live nowhere else on Earth. Then, there are the island's beaches, which are mostly black, and its waterfalls, which tumble over cliffs into steaming-hot pools. The nation's most famous attraction, meanwhile, is a remote lake that bubbles like a pasta pot with boiling water. On the Caribbean's so-called Nature Island, nothing is quite what it seems. Even the rum tastes different, infused as the bottles are with various botanicals meant to cure any ailment. Drink up, strap on a backpack and get lost – this is the Caribbean at its finest.

LAST LAND OF THE CARIBS

The year was 1492 and the Caribs (also known as the Kalinago) were living on islands across a region that would one day bear their name. What happened next is well known: Columbus 'discovered' the Americas, Europeans planted flags on Caribbean islands, and the Caribs lost their territory across the Lesser Antilles to warfare and disease. What most don't realise, however, is that the Caribs didn't disappear; a small population of around 3000 remain in northeastern Dominica, in a settlement established in the 1760s as a reserve for those forced to evacuate surrounding islands.

The Kalinago Territory, which lies in a remote and mountainous area, remained largely isolated from the rest of Dominica throughout much of the 20th century, receiving its first road in the 1970s and electricity in the 1980s. It contains eight villages, the largest of which, Salybia, serves as an administrative centre and hub for cultural tourism, which began in the early 2000s to provide the community with a source of revenue.

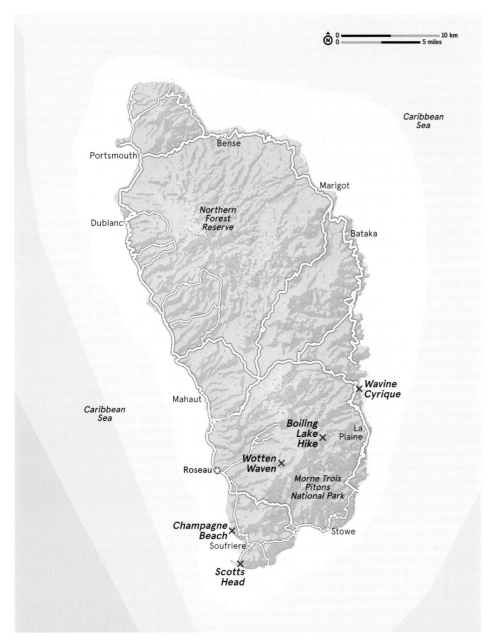

Portsmouth

Bense

Dublanc

Northern Forest Reserve

Marigot

Bataka

Mahaut

Wavine Cyrique ✕

Caribbean Sea

Boiling Lake Hike ✕

La Plaine

Wotten Waven ✕

Roseau ⊙

Morne Trois Pitons National Park

Champagne Beach ✕

Soufriere

Stowe

Scotts Head ✕

Caribbean Sea

X MARKS THE SPOT

Boiling Lake Hike This 9.5km (6-mile) hike, which starts near the turquoise Titou Gorge swimming hole, crosses the steam vents of the Valley of Desolation en route to a flooded, bubbling fumarole.

Wotten Waven The hot springs and thick mudpools of this tiny village provide an atmospheric end to forest hikes as you soothe weary bones in natural spas.

Champagne Beach Sure, maybe you've had champagne on a beach. But have you ever been on a beach with water that bubbles like champagne?

Scotts Head This tiny fishing village lies on the edge of a marine reserve that's one of the most pristine dive environments in the Caribbean.

Wavine Cyrique On an island full of waterfalls and beaches, Wavine Cyrique offers both at once with its namesake cascade hurtling over a cliff onto black sands.

1. Diving off the coast of Dominica

2. Titou Gorge, near the Boiling Lake trailhead

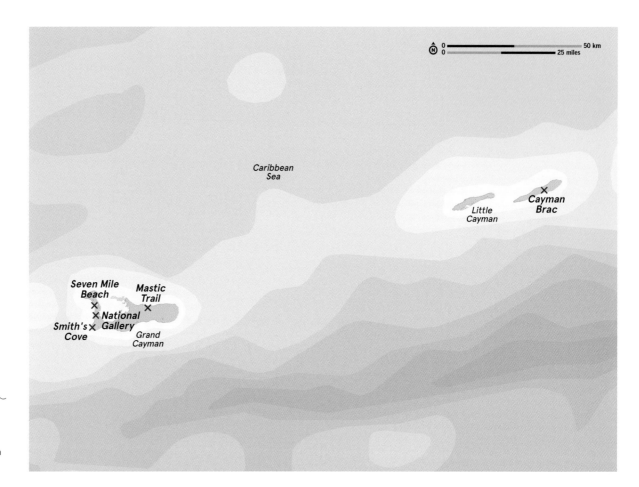

0   50 km
0   25 miles

Caribbean
Sea

Little
Cayman

Cayman
Brac

Seven Mile
Beach   *Mastic*
Trail

National
Gallery

Smith's
Cove

Grand
Cayman

1. Snorkeller and a
cushion sea star

2. Endangered Cayman
Brac parrot

Cayman Islands

COUNTRY BRITISH OVERSEAS TERRITORY
COORDINATES 19.313° N, 81.254° W • **AREA** 264 SQ KM (102 SQ MILES)

The Cayman Islands is one of the Caribbean's most multicultural and cosmopolitan corners, with residents hailing from more than 130 different nations. Most live on the main island, Grand Cayman, which looks as if it were fashioned after a curved pirate hook. Little Cayman and Cayman Brac are like tiny scribbles of green in the blue sea 130km (81 miles) to the east. Little Cayman holds just 175 permanent residents (most from abroad), while the more populous Cayman Brac is covered almost entirely by a bluff, which reaches up to 43m (141ft) above the sea. Both are primarily visited by divers. For the rest of the world, Grand Cayman may as well be the Cayman Island; it holds nearly all of the territory's bone-white beaches, lavish resorts and ritzy yacht clubs. This is also the global financial centre you read about in the news, with the wealth and prosperity to prove it.

TAX HAVEN

In 1966, the Cayman Islands followed the lead of several other British Overseas Territories and enacted a set of laws giving it no income tax, property tax, capital gains tax, payroll tax or corporate taxes, paving the way for it to become a tax haven. The move proved astonishingly successful. The Caymans quickly emerged as a preferred tax refuge for the wealthy, a favoured base of operations for hedge funds and a prime locale for multinational corporations to establish shell companies where they could channel their profits to shield corporate income from taxation.

Some 600 financial institutions and trust companies now operate on Grand Cayman, including 43 of the world's 50 largest banks. Their presence has made the Cayman Islands fabulously wealthy, giving it the 10th-highest GDP per capita in the world – though the islands' tax refuge staus means that, in real terms, this figure is skewed toward the wealthy.

X MARKS THE SPOT

Seven Mile Beach It's only 8.8km (5.4 miles) long, but this flawless stretch of white sand is undeniably alluring (and perennially packed).

Mastic Trail Swap sandals for shoes on this rocky 7.4km (4.5-mile) trail through the centre of Grand Cayman, which traverses mangrove wetlands and old-growth forest.

Smith's Cove This beloved snorkelling spot just off the South Sound in Grand Cayman is also the perfect west-facing beach for technicolour sunsets.

National Gallery This ambitious two-floor gallery is a surprising find that pairs rotating exhibitions with the national art collection.

Cayman Brac this bluff-lined island is the most peculiar of the Caymans, with climbing routes, caves and offshore dives that lure unhurried thrill-seekers.

Puerto Rico

COUNTRY US TERRITORY • **COORDINATES** 18.220° N, 66.590° W • **AREA** 9104 SQ KM (3515 SQ MILES)

With verdant rainforests, endless beaches and the second-oldest European-founded settlement in the Americas (San Juan), Puerto Rico is the ultimate amalgam of history, culture and nature. You can walk down empty sands in the morning, peruse modern art in the afternoon, dine on slow-roasted pork for dinner and then wash it all down with mojitos in the clubs of La Placita de Santurce, while chatting with *boricuas* about their strange political limbo. As an unincorporated US territory, Puerto Rico's residents have been US citizens for more than a century, though they get no voice in federal politics. They have, however, found plenty of ways to make their voices heard. This small Island (with less than three million residents) has an outsized reputation around the world thanks to the success of the Puerto Rican diaspora in sports, arts and culture, with figures like Jennifer Lopez, Rita Moreno, Ricky Martin and Carmelo Anthony all household names the world over.

ORIGINS OF REGGAETON

It was the early 1990s and the clubs of San Juan were throbbing with a new underground music style that threaded the *dembow* rhythms of reggae and dancehall with the grit of American hip-hop. Revving up the crowds at ad hoc venues were figures like Daddy Yankee, a young rapper who was making cassette tapes with the experimental DJ Playero. In 1994, the rising star gave the new genre a name: reggaeton. Soon, reggaeton cassettes were flying off the shelves. Meanwhile, Puerto Rican authorities did everything possible to confiscate them and stamp out the budding counterculture movement. Of course, that only made reggaeton music more desirable, and the genre soon spread across Latin America to become the most popular style of the region. Now, early Puerto Rican stars like Daddy Yankee and Ivy Queen have joined newcomers like Bad Bunny to put reggaeton atop music charts around the world.

X MARKS THE SPOT

Old San Juan San Juan's historic centre oozes colour and character at every turn of its cobblestoned streets, lined with 400-plus historically listed buildings.

El Yunque The only tropical rainforest in the US National Forest Service, with lush trails, cascading waterfalls and critically endangered wildlife like the Puerto Rican parrot.

Vieques Sure, the bioluminescent lights of Mosquito Bay get all the headlines, but this sleepy Spanish Virgin Island's lack of development is its real charm.

Gozalandia These off-the-beaten-path waterfalls and swimming holes in the forests of western Puerto Rico are a frolicker's dream.

Castillo San Cristóbal A visit to the largest fortification built by the Spanish in the New World pairs history with sweeping city views.

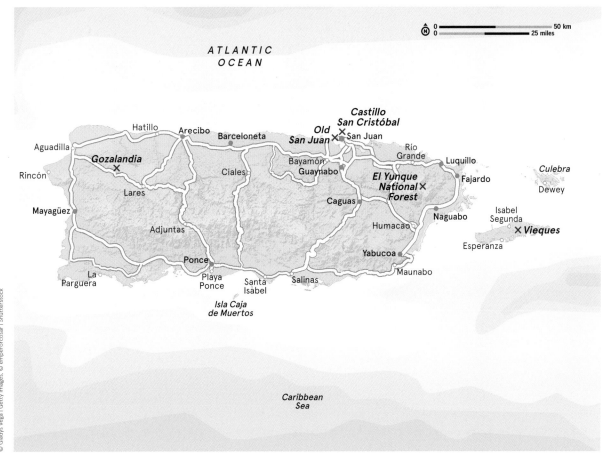

ATLANTIC
OCEAN

0 —————————— 50 km
0 —————————— 25 miles

Hatillo   Arecibo   Barceloneta

Aguadilla

Gozalandia

Rincón

Lares

Ciales

Castillo
San Cristóbal

*Old
San Juan*   San Juan

Río
Grande   Luquillo   *Culebra*

Dewey

Bayamón
Guaynabo

*El Yunque
National
Forest*   Fajardo

Mayagüez

Adjuntas

Caguas

Isabel
Segunda   ✕ *Vieques*

Naguabo

Humacao

Esperanza

Ponce

Yabucoa

La
Parguera   Playa
Ponce   Santa
Isabel   Salinas   Maunabo

*Isla Caja
de Muertos*

*Caribbean
Sea*

1. Queen of reggaeton, Natti Natasha, at the Reggaeton White Concert

2. Street in old San Juan

Eleuthera

COUNTRY THE BAHAMAS • **COORDINATES** 24.931° N, 76.190° W
• **AREA** 457 SQ KM (176 SQ MILES)

Eleuthera is kind of like the pretty little princess of Bahamian islands who believes everything is better in bright pink. The hibiscus and bougainvillea that crawl up buildings? Pink. The preferred paint in Governor's Harbour (the island chain's largest settlement)? Pink. Even many of its beaches have princess-approved pink sands. And, like most Disney princesses of yore, Eleuthera is also abnormally thin. In fact, the island is so thin that, at times, there is just a 1km (0.6-mile) strip of land separating the cobalt-blue Atlantic Ocean to the east from the turquoise-green Great Bahama Bank to the west. Viewed on a map, Eleuthera looks a bit like a doodle someone drew by accident. But it is, of course, no accident: it's a 180km-long (112-mile) coral formation that houses some of the most serene and secluded beach resorts in the nation.

PINK SANDS

When the sun rises over your New England–style cottage on Harbour Island and you step out onto its wooden porch, the long beach that unfurls in front of you can feel like some blurry early morning mirage. Surely, you must be dreaming. After all, the sand in front of you couldn't possibly be glowing pink on the edge of that gem-coloured bay?

And yet, that's exactly what happens here and all across the greater Eleuthera islands. So, what gives the sand its ethereal pink hue? Well, it actually comes from foraminifera, a tiny marine animal that lives on the underside of the offshore reefs. Foraminifera has a reddish shell which, when crushed and mixed with the sand, turns the beaches a fetching pink.

Viewed at midday, Eleuthera's shores don't look quite as radiantly rosy as the internet would have you believe (you can thank filters and editing software for that!). But at dusk or dawn, they are every bit as amazing as the Instagrammers make them out to be.

1. Cathedral Cave, near Rock Sound

2. Foraminifera shells, source of Eleuthera's rosy-pink sands

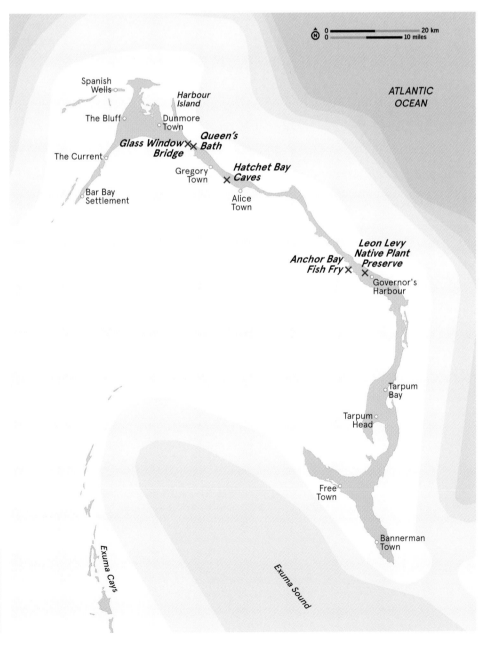

X MARKS THE SPOT

Leon Levy Native Plant Preserve Learn about endemic plants – including those used for traditional bush medicine – at this educational botanical garden with boardwalks and wetlands.

Queen's Bath Centuries of crashing waves have formed this rocky collection of natural pools and secluded grottoes, which glow turquoise at high noon.

Anchor Bay Fish Fry Locals converge in Governor's Harbour each Friday night for fried fish, *goombay* music and gallons of golden rum.

Glass Window Bridge This window-like geological formation on a thin isthmus lets you appreciate the vast differences in colour between bay and ocean.

Hatchet Bay Caves The walls of this former pirate hangout dazzle with cathedral-like stalagmites and stalactites, as well as 19th-century charcoal graffiti.

Cuba

COUNTRY CUBA

COORDINATES 21.521° N, 77.781° W • **AREA** 109,884 SQ KM (42,426 SQ MILES)

Tropical paradise? Crumbling mid-century time capsule? Political flashpoint? Cuba is many things to many people. Viewed as forbidden fruit by American tourists for nearly six decades, its sinewy strips of pearly-white sands were saved from the kind of rampant overdevelopment found elsewhere in the Caribbean. So, too, were its colonial-era cities like Trinidad and Cienfuegos, which appear frozen in time like outdoor museums of baroque and neoclassical architecture. Add in a hundred types of perky palms (90 of which are native), sultry salsa dancing in the streets and plenty of minty-fresh mojitos at sunset, and you have the recipe for an island escape like no other.

THE CUBAN CIGAR

Smouldering cigars hand moodily from the mouths of Cuba's famed revolutionaries in the black-and-white newspaper clippings of the 1950s. In one, Fidel Castro has his lips curled around a Cohiba. In another, Che Guevara hides behind the smoke of a Montecristo No 4. These images propelled Cuban cigars – which were first introduced to Europe's upper class by Christopher Columbus – to a new height of global popularity. When US president John F Kennedy made it illegal to import Cuban cigars to America in the early 1960s, their status as a hot commodity soared even

further. Even without the (legal) US market, Cuban cigar sales now top $500 million dollars annually, making them one of the nation's most important exports. So, what makes a cigar from Cuba so special? Some say it comes down to the soil in the southwest, which gives the tobacco those earthy coffee, chocolate and leather flavours that become gentler the longer you puff. Rolling stogies is also an art form here, and one that's been passed down from generation to generation, ensuring each cigar is a well-built vessel and prized piece of cultural cachet.

Map labels

FLORIDA (USA)
Florida Keys
Gulf of Mexico
New Providence
Eleuthera
ATLANTIC OCEAN
Andros Island
Cat Island
San Salvador
THE BAHAMAS
Great Exuma
Long Island
Crooked Island
Acklins Island

La Habana Vieja
HAVANA
Matanzas
Cárdenas
Valle de Viñales
Pinar del Río
Nueva Gerona
Isla de la Juventud
Santa Clara
Playa Pilar
Cienfuegos
Trinidad
Sancti Spíritus
Morón
Ciego de Ávila
Camagüey
Las Tunas
Holguín
Baracoa
Jardines de la Reina
Manzanillo
Bayamo
Guantánamo
Santiago de Cuba
CAYMAN ISLANDS (UK)
Cayman Brac
Little Cayman
Grand Cayman
Caribbean Sea
HAITI
JAMAICA

0   200 km
0   100 miles

X MARKS THE SPOT

La Habana Vieja A dazzling repository of monuments, Havana's historic quarter is arranged around four main plazas.

Playa Pilar Vying for the title of Cuba's prettiest beach is this blindingly white strip on Cayo Guillermo, which feels far removed from the bustle of neighbouring Cayo Coco.

Valle de Viñales Bulbous limestone outcrops soar above pancake-flat tobacco plantations, providing an epic backdrop for hiking and rock climbing expeditions.

Cienfuegos Known as the 'Pearl of the South', this port city claims an alluring jumble of eclectic 1920s-era palaces and serene seafront promenades.

Jardines de la Reina This uninhabited archipelago 80km (50 miles) off Cuba's southern coast is a diver's nirvana.

~~~~~~~

1. Vintage wheels in Camagüey

2. Valle de Viñales

3. Rolling a Cuban cigar the traditional way

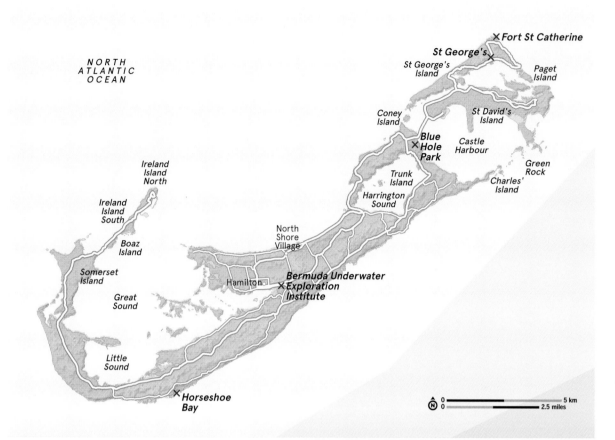

NORTH ATLANTIC OCEAN

✕ *Fort St Catherine*

St George's✕

St George's Island

Paget Island

Coney Island

St David's Island

✕ *Blue Hole Park*

Castle Harbour

Green Rock

Trunk Island

Charles' Island

Harrington Sound

Ireland Island North

Ireland Island South

North Shore Village

Boaz Island

Somerset Island

Bermuda Underwater ✕ *Exploration Institute*

Hamilton

Great Sound

Little Sound

✕ *Horseshoe Bay*

0   5 km
0   2.5 miles

1. Sea-kayaking Bermuda's coast

2. Horseshoe Bay

X MARKS THE SPOT

Horseshoe Bay Fringed by limestone cliffs, the pink sand beach faces cerulean seas and colourful reefs, ideal for snorkelling.

St George's Bermuda's oldest town and a Unesco World Heritage Site, has picturesque lanes packed with 400 years of history.

Bermuda Underwater Exploration Institute Interactive exhibits on marine life, underwater geology and shipwrecks, including mysterious disappearances in the so-called Bermuda Triangle.

Fort St Catherine Bermuda's most impressive fort has stood on a rocky promontory since 1614 and has well-preserved tunnels, ramparts and towers.

Blue Hole Park Trails through this verdant oasis lead past caves and grottoes as well as to the famous Blue Hole, an enticing lagoon backed by mangroves.

Bermuda

COUNTRY BRITISH OVERSEAS TERRITORY
COORDINATES 32.307° N, 64.750° W • **AREA** 54 SQ KM (21 SQ MILES)

'You can go to heaven if you want to – I'd rather stay in Bermuda,' wrote Mark Twain in 1910. Given the island's pink-sand beaches, turquoise seas and colourful, bougainvillea-draped streets, it's not surprising the illustrious American writer fell hard for the tiny archipelago located 1000-odd kilometres due east of North Carolina. Bermuda is one of England's oldest overseas territories, with cricket matches, wig-wearing judges and whitewashed Anglican churches all part of the landscape. And yet, the 181-island chain feels quite different from Britain, with its melding of African, European and North American influences.

THE GOMBEYS

Two dancers face off. Covered from head to foot in bright costumes, with layers of tassels in red, blue, yellow and green, they spin and twirl around one another. Narrow headdresses topped with ostrich feathers stretch high above their painted masks, while on their long velvet capes shimmering mirrors (said to ward off evil spirits) sparkle in the sun. Off to the side, a line of drummers pound out rapid-fire rhythms on bass and snare drums that match the dancers fast-moving footwork. The frenetic tempo culminates with high kicks, shimmying steps and acrobatic leaps, and the crowd roars its approval.

These are the Gombeys, an iconic, and much-cherished element of Bermudian culture that has been around since at least the 1800s. Although their exact origins are shrouded in mystery, the tradition has roots in West Africa (*gombey* is a Bantu word for 'rhythm') and also incorporates Native American, African-Caribbean and British elements. Each troupe (or 'crowd') is run by a different family and features its own unique style, which is handed down through the generations. One of the best times to see these high-energy street performances is during the Gombey Festival, held in September or October.

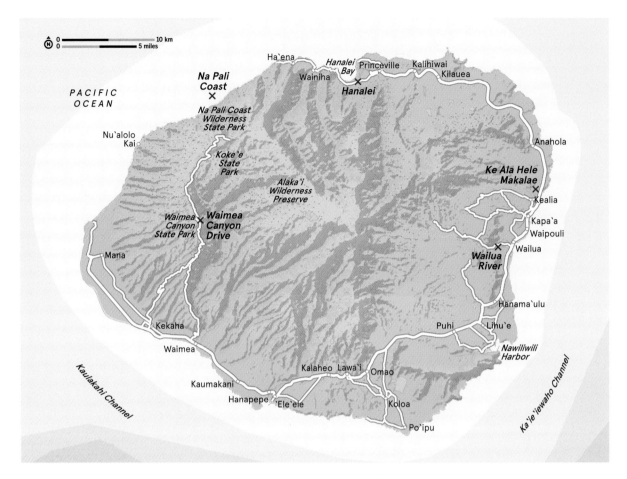

Kaua'i

COUNTRY UNITED STATES • **COORDINATES** 22.096° N, 159.526° W • **AREA** 1430 SQ KM (552 SQ MILES)

Near the far western edges of the Hawai'ian archipelago, the 'Garden Island' of Kaua'i is both an adventure seeker's playground and a destination for travellers keen on exploring a diverse and multicultural food scene. After a day of active exploring, oceanside restaurants and food trucks – many focused on blending Hawai'ian, Japanese, Korean and Filipino flavours and harnessing local and sustainable produce – are the relaxed focus for planning another day of kayaking, cycling and exploring. Away from the cosmopolitan influence of Honolulu, Kaua'i is also one of the island state's most traditional destinations, with regular events and festivals showcasing both hula and Hawai'ian slack-key guitar.

HIKING IN PARADISE

One of Hawai'i's smaller islands, Kaua'i offers some of the state's best opportunities for hiking. Versatile trails, often with views of a shimmering Pacific Ocean, meander through diverse tropical landscapes including forested mountains, lush waterfalls and valleys, and a world-famous red-rock canyon. Shorter routes offer the opportunity to return for an evening snack at a food truck or a mai tai at a sunset tiki bar, while travellers looking for the extended overnight adventure of a two-day hike are also catered to.

The island's most famous hiking route is the challenging Kalalau Trail, tracing a clifftop journey along the stunning Nā Pali Coast,

and taking in remote beaches, soaring cliffs of lava rock, and the spectacular Hanakapi'ai Falls. Most hikers begin the Kalalau's 36km (22-mile) two-day return adventure at Ke'e Beach on Kaua'i's North Shore.

Located on Kaua'i's more-sheltered South Shore, near the popular restaurants and resorts of Po'ipu, the Maha'ulepu Heritage Trail is an enjoyable 12km (7.4-mile) return coastal hike travelling from the popular beaches of Po'ipu through a wild and more rugged coastal landscape of secluded coves, jagged sea cliffs and surging blowholes.

1. The island has countless waterfalls

2. Kaua`i's serrated coastline

3. Frangipani flowers

X MARKS THE SPOT

Nā Pali Coast Scored by serrated and verdant valleys, Kaua`i's remote and spectacular northwest coastline is best observed from a gently-sailing catamaran.

Wailuā River Kayak up Kaua`i's most sacred river, before continuing the adventure on a forest hike to the 30m-high (98ft) Uluwehi Falls.

Waimea Canyon Drive Rent an open-top Jeep or Ford Mustang to negotiate the serpentine road leading to lookouts showcasing Waimea Canyon's unique red-dirt landscape.

Hanalei Ease into a blissful routine of bodysurfing and swimming followed by coffee and cocktails at Kaua`i's most relaxing North Shore destination.

Ke Ala Hele Makalae Meandering along Kaua`i's east coast, this shared-use path for walkers and cyclists is a perfect way to start the day at sunrise.

EUROPE

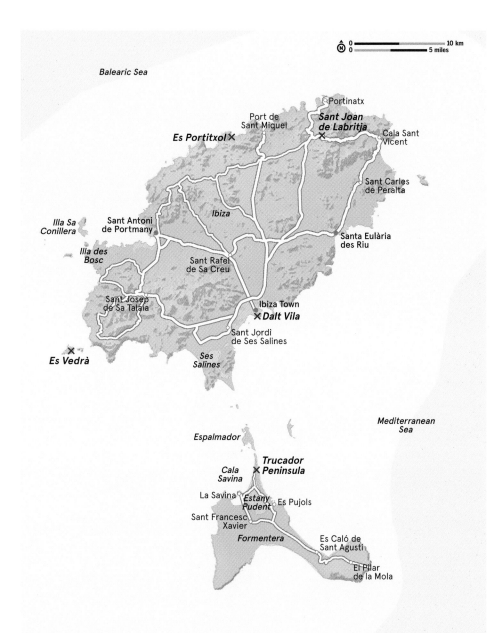

Balearic Sea

Portinatx

Port de
Sant Miquel

**Sant Joan
de Labritja** ✕

Es Portitxol ✕

Cala Sant
Vicent

Sant Carles
de Peralta

Ibiza

Illa Sa
Conillera

Sant Antoni
de Portmany

Santa Eulària
des Riu

Illa des
Bosc

Sant Rafel
de Sa Creu

Sant Josep
de Sa Talaia

Ibiza Town
✕ **Dalt Vila**

Sant Jordi
de Ses Salines

Es Vedrà ✕

*Ses
Salines*

0 —— 10 km
0 —— 5 miles

Mediterranean
Sea

Espalmador

Trucador
✕ *Peninsula*

Cala
Savina

La Savina

*Estany
Pudent* Es Pujols

Sant Francesc
Xavier

Formentera

Es Caló de
Sant Agustí

El Pilar
de la Mola

X MARKS THE SPOT

Dalt Vila Founded by the Phoenicians, Ibiza Town's historic core conceals medieval mansions, an ancient castle, formidable walls, a view-splayed cathedral and more.

Trucador Peninsula Silky white sands, gentle turquoise waves, a few barefoot-chic beach bars – this is Formentera's dreamiest corner.

Es Vedrà Swirling in mystery, the rocky islet off southern Ibiza is one of the Balearics' most mesmerising spots.

Es Portitxol A serene star among Ibiza's north-coast swimming spots, this rocky cove is accessible only on foot.

Sant Joan de Labritja Head north and inland for a taste of traditional Ibiza amid white-walled villages, somnolent churches and low-key farmers markets.

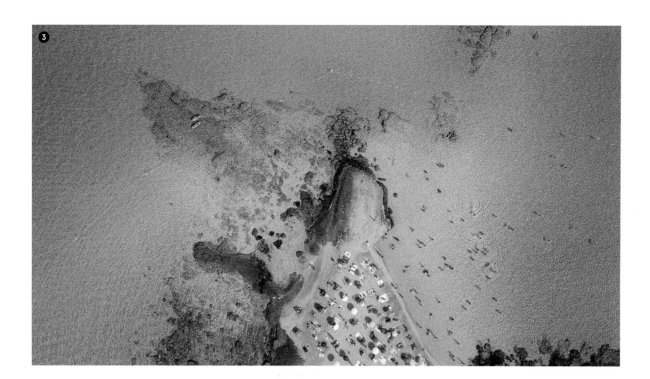

Ibiza & Formentera

COUNTRY SPAIN • **COORDINATES** 39.020° N, 1.482° E • **AREA** 572 SQ KM (221 SQ MILES)

No other Mediterranean island fires up the imagination quite like Ibiza, the beach-loving, party-all-night queen of Spain's Balearics. Away from the pounding beats and packed-out megaclubs, the White Isle reveals its quieter side: remote beaches and bays, curious ancient caves, awe-inspiring open-air galleries, coastal defence towers and delightful rural villages that revolve around a single tiny plaza with a church – not to mention the historical marvels of Ibiza Town's Unesco-protected Dalt Vila. Just wander off along Ibiza's northern coast, perhaps to one of its blissfully isolated horseshoe bays or a cash-only sand-side *chiringuito* (beach bar), and you'll see. Off Ibiza's south tip lies the delicious little island of Formentera, a barefoot back-to-nature beauty where tourism has been developed slowly and responsibly, and days revolve around dips in the azure sea, zipping about on two wheels, feasting on locally loved recipes and seeking out the next fiery sunset.

IBIZA'S HISTORY

On a stroll around the rocky, crisp-dry Puig des Molins necropolis, on the edge of Ibiza Town's magnificent Dalt Vila, time spins all the way back to the very beginnings of the island's inhabited history. Around 3000 burial tombs lie carved into the hillside here – a lineup, the story goes, of wealthy Carthaginians from all over modern-day Europe, laid to rest among terracotta vases, ancient jewels and countless other riches.

In the 7th century BCE, the Phoenicians founded a major trading port on the seaside spot now occupied by Dalt Vila, which eventually fell under Carthaginian control and later became a Roman settlement. The Moors seized power in 902 CE, bringing with them groundbreaking irrigation systems and transforming the island's capital into a booming port called Yabisa. Then, in 1235 CE, Catalan forces swept in, led by King Jaume I 'the Conqueror', and Ibiza fell into Christian hands. Having weathered countless tragedies during the Spanish Civil War in the 20th century, Ibiza and Formentera became part of the autonomous community of the Balearic Islands in the 1980s.

1. Dalt Vila, the historic hilltop core of Ibiza Town

2. Can Musón farm shop

3. Cala Conta on Ibiza's southwest coast

❶

Menorca

COUNTRY SPAIN

COORDINATES 39.949° N, 4.110° E • **AREA** 696 SQ KM (269 SQ MILES)

Welcome to the easternmost tip of Spain – a soulful, sun-soaked, beach-wrapped jewel of an island washed by the sparkling Balearic Sea, where sustainability was the cornerstone of local tourism long before it became a buzzword. Declared a Unesco Biosphere Reserve back in 1993, beautiful Menorca unveils inspiringly designed *agroturismes* (rural hotels), mystifying Bronze Age ruins, rippling wetlands, pine-scented coastal trails and a string of the country's most exquisite beaches. Its two elegant cities tell stories of its embattled past: harbourside capital Maó (Mahón) bursts with British-influenced architecture, while colourful Ciutadella brings a more Spanish feel. From its blissful protected beaches to its strong gastronomic heritage, this go-slow island is making waves as a responsible-travel destination.

MENORCAN GASTRONOMY

If you've ever wondered where the original recipe for mayonnaise came from, it was created right here in Menorca's capital Maó – just ask any *menorquin* and they'll proudly tell you, all while effortlessly whisking together golden olive oil, zesty lemon juice and bright-orange egg yolks. And this is only the beginning of the island's love affair with food. Menorcan gastronomy is an irresistible blend of classic Balearic flavours, rustic island recipes and deliciously fresh local produce, from homegrown vegetables sourced in the rippling hills to seafood plucked straight from the surrounding waters. And with creative chefs now throwing in international flair, the island's food scene is unstoppable. The fruits of the sea pop up in savoury stews such as the beloved *caldereta de llagosta* (lobster stew), best enjoyed with hunks of toasted garlic bread; or in oven-baked garlic-laced fish platters served with melt-away-soft potatoes. Another unmissable favourite is Mahón-Menorca cheese, a rich cow's cheese produced nowhere else in the world, which often appears alongside locally made charcuterie. Then there are sugar-dusted *ensaïmades* (a divine pastry inherited from neighbouring Mallorca), liquid-gold honeys infused with aromatic herbs and up-and-coming wines rooted in the island's Moorish history. Hungry yet? Wake up your taste buds with a locall a locally made Xoriguer gin and tonic and settle in – Menorca's food story is endless.

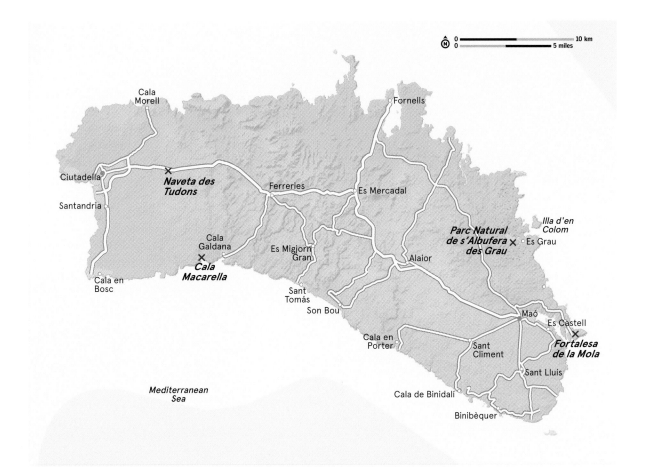

X MARKS THE SPOT

Camí de Cavalls This ancient 185km-long (115-mile) path travels all the way around Menorca's coastline, linking remote beaches, lonely lighthouses and shimmering wetlands.

Fortalesa de La Mola An imposing 19th-century military fortress keeps watch over the entrance to Maó's spectacular harbour.

Naveta des Tudons Among Menorca's most intriguing Talayotic archaeological sites is this stone burial chamber dating from around 1000 BCE.

Cala Macarella A duo of dreamy twinkling-turquoise bays on the south coast, reached by hiking along the pine-dusted cliffs.

Parc Natural de S'Albufera des Grau These protected 50-sq-km (19-sq-mile) east-coast wetlands are a delight for birdwatchers, kayakers and walkers.

1. *Ensaïmades* pastries

2. Cala Macarella

3. Naveta des Tudons

Mallorca

COUNTRY SPAIN
COORDINATES 39.695° N, 3.017° E • AREA 3640 SQ KM (1405 SQ MILES)

Few islands promise such an extreme cocktail of experiences. On the one hand there is the all-too-familiar, summer-holiday razzmatazz of hot and busy beaches, built-up coastal resorts and party-fuelled seaside buzz. Then there is its alter ego: Mallorca's serene interior, where ancestral vineyards, ancient hilltop monasteries and meadows stippled with olive, almond and carob trees promise peace and serenity in spades. For decades Mallorca's culture and conservation took a back seat to its beaches, but the tides are changing. Up and down the island, locals are embracing their roots, be it through a renewed appetite for zero-kilometre cuisine, revival of traditional arts and crafts like glass-blowing and leatherwork, or greener commitment to conserving nature and the island's extraordinary biodiversity.

SAVING EUROPE'S LARGEST RAPTOR

Mallorca is the only island in the world with a population of cinereous vultures. Europe's largest vulture species, also known as the Eurasian black or monk vulture, has a mesmerising wingspan of 2.5m (8.2ft) to 3m (9.8ft) and weighs in at 6kg to 11kg (13lb to 24lb). A scavenger at heart, this dark-brown raptor of Herculean proportion feeds on the carrion of wild rabbits, sheep, marmots and other medium- to large-sized mammals. Squirrelled away each winter atop towering pine and oak trees in Mallorca's Serra de Tramuntana mountains, their humongous nests, up to 2.5m (8.2ft) wide and more than 1m (3.2ft) tall, are testament to the island's unflagging conservation commitment.

By the late 1980s, a dwindling food supply and illegal hunting meant Mallorca's cinereous vulture population risked being wiped out completely. No more than 20 birds and one laying couple remained on the island, prompting an urgent restocking of the vulture population with 35 raptors. The Fundació Vida Silvestre Mediterrània (Mediterranean Wildlife Fund; FVSM), created in Mallorca in 2002 to conserve biodiversity in the Balearic Islands, reckons the population has since multiplied by at least 10: an estimated 200 cinereous vultures fly in Mallorca's skies today, including 35 breeding pairs in the wildest realms of the Serra de Tramuntana.

X MARKS THE SPOT

Platja des Coll Baix Only accessible by boat or forest trail, this isolated cove on pine-draped Cap des Pinar cooks up pristine white sand, cliffs and cobalt-blue water.

Sa Calobra Expect drama at every hairpin turn along this spectacular 12km (7.4-mile) road built between Sa Calobra and Cala Tuent in 1932.

Deià The cream of a rich hilltop village crop, Deià teeters high above the iridescent Med in the shade of Mallorca's Serra de Tramuntana mountains.

Parc Natural de S'Albufera Birdwatchers' paradise: two-thirds of species that live permanently in (or winter on) Mallorca are here.

Festes de la Verema Cavort with fire-breathing devils and join in the grape fight at this iconic harvest festival in Binissalem, in the centre of Mallorca.

❶

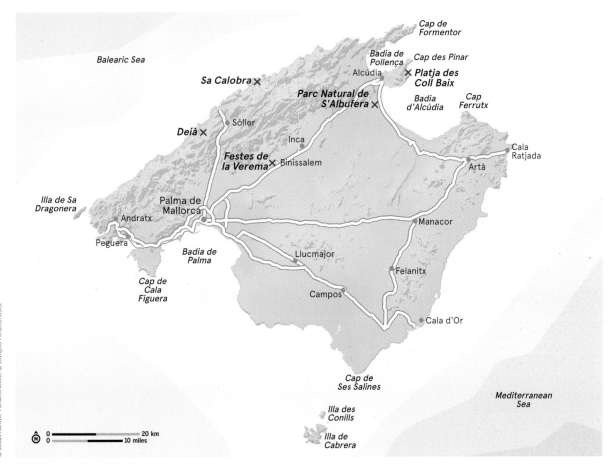

2

Balearic Sea

Cap de Formentor

Badia de Pollença *Cap des Pinar*

Alcúdia ✕ **Platja des Coll Baix**

Sa Calobra ✕

Parc Natural de S'Albufera ✕

Badia d'Alcúdia *Cap Ferrutx*

Sóller

Deià ✕

Inca

Cala Ratjada

Festes de la Verema ✕ Binissalem

Artà

Illa de Sa Dragonera

Palma de Mallorca

Andratx

Manacor

Peguera

Badia de Palma

Llucmajor

Felanitx

Cap de Cala Figuera

Campos

Cala d'Or

Cap de Ses Salines

Mediterranean Sea

Illa des Conills

Illa de Cabrera

0 ——— 20 km
0 ——— 10 miles

〜〜〜〜〜〜

1. Hilltop Deià village

2. Two-wheel touring to Cap de Formentor

English Channel

0   200 m
0   0.1 miles

La Merveille
×

Abbaye du Mont-Saint-Michel
×

Pont Passerelle

FRANCE

River Couësnon
×

X MARKS THE SPOT

River Couësnon These rushing waters empty into La Manche (the Channel) at the foot of Mont Saint-Michel, after travelling 100km (62 miles) across northern France.

Abbaye du Mont St-Michel The Mont's historic hilltop abbey was built between the 11th and 16th centuries.

La Merveille The precariously perched, history-rich buildings of 'the Marvel' cling to the northern part of the island.

Ramparts These formidable bastions were originally constructed as a defence against the countless English attacks from across the Channel.

The Bay Sweeping wide around Mont St-Michel, it's said to have the most extreme tidal variations in Europe.

Mont St-Michel

COUNTRY FRANCE • **COORDINATES** 48.636° N, 1.511° W • **AREA** 0.04 SQ KM (0.1 SQ MILES)

For centuries before today's tourist crowds began to trickle in, this hauntingly beautiful tidal island off the Brittany and Normandy coast was a major Christian pilgrimage destination. Once a month or so, Mont St-Michel rises out of the sea like a vision reflected in the glimmering waters of the Couësnon estuary; at other times, a swirl of silvery sand stretches for miles all around the bay. Check the tides in advance if you like, but either way, it will inevitably take your breath away. Around 40 monks and nuns still live here, amid narrow cobbled alleys and sky-reaching spires encircled by imposing ramparts, above which awaits a spectacular medieval abbey that traces its origins back more than a thousand years. The Mont is one of the most-visited attractions in France, luring around 2.5 million tourists each year; you can help with conservation efforts by staying overnight (rather than daytripping), directly supporting the island's businesses and exploring the surrounding region.

A LITTLE HISTORY

When the Bishop Aubert of nearby Avranches had a vision of the Archangel Michael, back in the early 8th century (or so the story goes), he set about building a chapel on the crown of Mont St-Michel, surrounded by the rolling sea. A Benedictine abbey was established here from 966 onwards, under the watch of the dukes of Normandy, and the fortified island grew into an unrivalled centre of knowledge and learning, reeling in astronomers, scientists, manuscript illuminators and other scholars from all over Europe (as well as souvenir sellers and an ever-growing number of pilgrims). In the 17th century, it was turned into a political prison by Louis XIV, a role that only grew further with the French Revolution, which led to an estimated 14,000 prisoners being locked up here. In 1979, the entire island and its surrounding bay were designated a Unesco World Heritage Site.

1. Mont St-Michel lit up at dusk

2. The soaring Abbaye du Mont St-Michel

3. Abbey adornments: 16th-century bas-relief of the Four Evangelists

❶

Îles d'Hyères

COUNTRY FRANCE
COORDINATES 43.001° N, 6.221° E • AREA 29 SQ KM (11.1 SQ MILES)

Military camp, nudist colony, national park, ancient fruit orchard and snorkelling micro-paradise. Hands down one of the Mediterranean's zaniest archipelagoes, this oddball island collection off the southern French coast in Provence blends natural beauty with whimsical stories.

Three toasters and a towel set just weren't enough for one Mrs Fournier, who received the beach-laced island of Porquerolles – the largest in the archipelago – as a wedding present from husband François in 1912. The couple's descendants still own a large chunk of the land.

Across the water on Port-Cros, Barbary pirates tyrannised islanders until the 1630s when Richelieu had defensive forts and towers built to protect them. The tiny island's overwhelming serenity piggybacks on its exceptional fauna and flora, protected by France's first marine national park. Diving, snorkelling or boating offshore are marvellous and moving in equal measure.

Then there is the military-zone isle of Île du Levant, only a teeny slice of which is open to civilians – nudists to boot, although baring all is only obligatory on its sliver of sandy beach.

FORGOTTEN FRUIT

Few islands evoke a Garden of Eden quite like Port-Cros and Porquerolles, both of which fall within the Parc National de Port-Cros. This is a landscape of pine woods, aromatic maquis (herbal scrubland), eucalyptus and a huge variety of indigenous and tropical flora, including Requien's larkspur, said to grow nowhere else in the world.

So pristine is this island environment that, in 1979, Porquerolles was selected as the perfect spot to safeguard France's national collection of ancient varietals – a powerful rendition of lost biodiversity. Dozens of different types of olives, peaches, figs, apples, date palms, mulberries for silk worms and other forgotten fruits that once grew in abundance in France's hot south are now only found in carefully tended orchards on the island. To visit is to witness the traditional landscape of Provence a century ago.

X MARKS THE SPOT
Jardin Emmanuel Lopez, Porquerolles A horticultural oasis of green exotica, planted with wisteria, prickly pear, yucca and 26 varieties of palm tree.

Plage de la Courtade, Porquerolles The island's most glorious crescent of sand.

Sentier Sous-Marin, Port-Cros The golden ticket to uncovering 500 seaweed species and 180 types of fish along an underwater snorkelling trail; buy a waterproof 'what-to-spot' sheet before diving in.

Circuit de Port-Man, Port-Cros Forts, forests and dramatic coastline along a four-hour, beach-to-beach hiking trail on Port-Cros' northeastern tip.

Domaine de l'Île, Porquerolles How can rosé produced on this winegrowing estate owned by French fashion house Chanel be anything other than excellent?

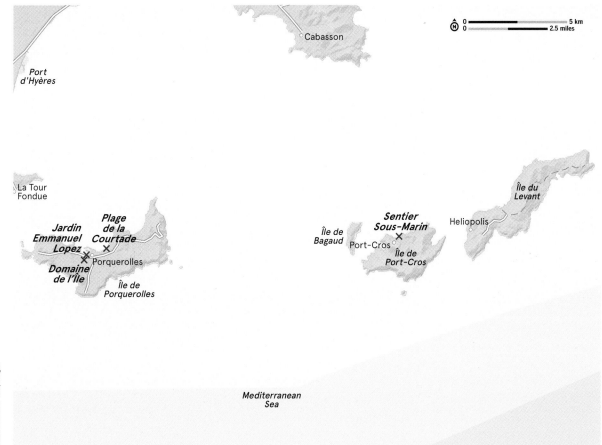

Cabasson

Port
d'Hyères

La Tour
Fondue

Jardin
Emmanuel
Lopez
Plage
de la
Courtade
Porquerolles
Domaine
de l'Île
Île de
Porquerolles

Île de
Bagaud
Sentier
Sous-Marin
Port-Cros
Île de
Port-Cros
Heliopolis
Île du
Levant

Mediterranean
Sea

1. Fruits of France

2. Maquis along the
Porquerolles coast

Île de Ré

COUNTRY FRANCE

COORDINATES 46.191° N, 1.394° W • **AREA** 85 SQ KM (33 SQ MILES)

The call of the wild harks back centuries on this chic Breton island, scattered with whitewashed villages in hues of aqua-green and eggshell blue. This might be the hobnobbing hotspot of weekending Parisians in summer, but the roots of tradition run deep in salt-of-the-earth Brittany: *sauniers* harvest *sel* from ancestral salt pans, farmers toil in family potato fields and new-gen artisans distil gin and vodka with homegrown fingerling potatoes and organic seaweed gathered along the shore. Grab a bicycle in the quaint fishing port of St-Martin-de-Ré and enjoy the ride!

SALT-MARSH OYSTERS

To know on first taste if an oyster has been bred in sea or salt marsh – hints of hazelnut and almond, a silky texture, are giveaways – is an epicurean skill born-and-bred islanders on Île de Ré share. Oyster farming has shaped the island's shoreline since the Middle Ages, with 60 *ostréiculteurs* today producing some 10,000 tonnes of oysters a year in 550 hectares (1359 acres) of oyster beds at sea. Many offer *dégustation* (tasting) in situ – a privileged experience, shared around rough wooden tables facing the water.

At La Ferme des Baleines, oyster farmer Benjamin Courtadon takes Île de Ré's fierce short-circuit ethic one step further with his plump, salt-marsh *huîtres* reared exclusively from spat to edible oyster in roomy clay pans previously used for salt. His oysters thrive on the extra space and richer, phytoplankton diet. Wild samphire and sea purslane grow on the pond banks and migratory birds fly overhead. Backbreaking artisanal techniques – lifting kilos of lantern nets, brimming with oysters, in and out of the water or tumbling the nets to mimic waves – recreate life at sea. The farm only produces about 30 tonnes a year, compared to some 300 at a traditional farm at sea, but the difference in taste – to every islander at least – is quite extraordinary.

Phare des
Baleines
✕

Les Portes-
en-Ré

Conche des
✕ Baleines

Banc de
✕ Bucheron

Saint-Clément-
des-Baleines

Cabane de
✕ la Patache

Loix

Ars-en-Ré

St-Martin-
de-Ré

La Couarde-
sur-Mer

La Flotte

Le Bois-
Plage-en-Ré

Rivedoux-Plage

Sainte-Marie-
de-Ré

ATLANTIC
OCEAN

X MARKS THE SPOT

Banc du Bucheron An ephemeral sand-beach island, magically rising from the ocean at low tide and accessible only by boat.

Phare des Baleines The island's scarlet-tipped lighthouse rewards those who scale its dizzying heights with a 360-degree coastal panorama.

Cabane de la Patache What began as a beach shack selling waffles is now the dress circle from which to watch fiery sunsets over oysters and a glass of island white.

Fleur de Sel Île de Ré's rose-tinged 'flower of salt' has been hand-harvested in shimmering salt marshes since the 7th century.

Conche des Baleines Nothing to do with '*baleines*' (whales): rather, a sweep of sand hued a kaleidoscope of changing colour by the tide, weather and time of day.

1. Île de Ré beach

2. Harbour at La Flotte

3. A pretty patchwork of saltpans on Île de Ré

ATLANTIC OCEAN

× *Macalla Farm*

× *Knockmore Mountain*

× *St Bridgit's Abbey*

N 0 — 2 km
0 — 1 miles

Ireland (2km) ↘

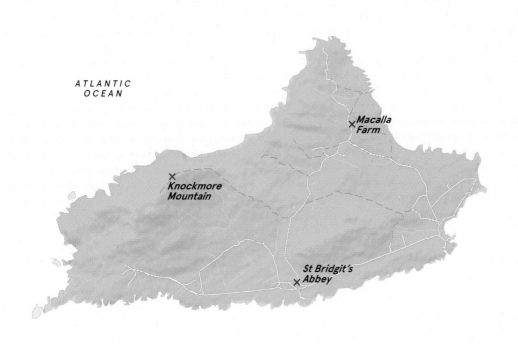

X MARKS THE SPOT

Knockmore Mountain Offering sweeping views of Clew Bay and the mainland pilgrimage mountain of Croagh Patrick, this is the island's highest peak (461m/1512ft).

Macalla Farm Regeneration is key at this organic farm and retreat centre where you can unwind with yoga, mindfulness and vegetarian-cooking courses.

Birdlife The dramatic northern coast ends in steep cliffs home to gannets, kittiwakes, fulmars and, most recently, great skuas.

St Brigid's Abbey Pay homage to the O'Malley clan and admire the unusual medieval paintings at this 12th-century abbey.

Fulachta Fiadh (fol-akta fia) Scattered across the island, these Bronze Age cooking sites are surrounded by semi-circular mounds of stones.

1. Mountains of Clare

2. Granuaile Castle, a stronghold of Grace O'Malley in the 16th century

3. Cliffs of Clare Island

Clare Island

COUNTRY IRELAND
COORDINATES 53.804° N, 9.995° W • **AREA** 16 SQ KM (6 SQ MILES)

Once home to a 16th-century pirate queen, this small, mountainous island 5km (3 miles) off the shore of Louisburgh in County Mayo is known for its dramatic cliffs, sandy beaches and great walking and climbing. Set out on foot and explore its raw beauty along the course of two looped trails that take in some of the many heritage sites littered across the island, which has been inhabited for over 5000 years. You'll come across megalithic tombs, ancient field systems, promontory forts and, at Clare's Cistercian abbey, some of Ireland's best medieval wall paintings. Temper it all with a dram of local whisky, a yoga or weaving course, some excellent diving, or a few wild nights at one of the regular summer festivals.

GRACE O'MALLEY

Occupying a strategic position at the mouth of Clew Bay, Clare Island became a stronghold for Grace O'Malley, Ireland's most notorious pirate queen. When her father refused to let her sail with him as a child, she cut off all her hair to stow away on his boat, a trick which earned her the lifelong nickname of Gráinne Mhaol (Bald Grace). Her skill, determination and ruthlessness quickly became apparent and she was soon levying taxes on all who passed the island. She became renowned as a great leader and fighter, and at one point controlled most of the western seas from her castle on Clare Island. She was so feared and respected that even Queen Elizabeth I agreed to meet her at Greenwich Palace in 1593, to discuss the release of family members and the control of the west of Ireland. Grace reputedly refused to bow to the monarch, yet they still came to agreement. Grace O'Malley is said to be buried in the island's abbey in a tomb bearing the family motto: 'Invincible on land and sea'.

Inis Mór

COUNTRY IRELAND
COORDINATES 53.128° N, 9.719° W • **AREA** 31 SQ KM (12 SQ MILES)

The largest of the three Aran Islands in Galway Bay, Inis Mór (Big Island) is a thriving community where Irish is the spoken language and traditional music, culture and heritage go hand in hand with a lively calendar of festivals and events. A vast network of hand-built stone walls criss-cross the fissured limestone landscape, the island's one road joined by countless lanes and pathways leading to ancient monuments, medieval churches, high crosses, holy wells and stalwart lighthouses. Come to walk, ride or cycle along the edge of Europe, to join a yoga retreat or learn to weave a traditional basket, play a bodhrán (goat-skin drum) or sing in the traditional *sean-nós* style. Or you could feast on fresh lobster, celebrate the summer solstice or just marvel at the unique light and culture here that have attracted artists and writers for centuries.

THE ARAN JUMPER

Marilyn Monroe, Steve McQueen, Grace Kelly and, more recently, Taylor Swift have all been spotted in the traditional Aran jumper over the years. Made from undyed wool to retain its natural water-repellent lanolin, the off-white chunky knit is blanketed with complex patterns. Although often marketed as a traditional island craft in which each family developed its own stitch to identify drowned fishermen washed up on shore, the truth is more prosaic, with the knits a crafty way to bring increased income to the islands after a fisheries improvement project in the early 20th century. Popularised in the 1940s and '50s with a hard sell to the American heritage market, the Aran *geansaí* (gahn-zee) supported about 500 home-knitters at its peak, although today, many examples are machine knit. What is true, however, is that the patterns hold deep symbolism here: the honeycomb for hard work, the plaited cable for family connections, diamond stitch for success and the basket stitch for a plentiful catch.

X MARKS THE SPOT

Dún Aonghasa A massive, semicircular prehistoric fort; it's thought the other half fell away as the Atlantic eroded the cliffs.

Music & Dance Renowned for its traditional music, Inis Mór is a great place to join an impromptu pub session or dance.

The Fields With no topsoil, fields were created from a mix of sand, seaweed and manure, and protected from the winds by stone walls.

The Worm Hole A natural blowhole on the island's southwest shore, where the sea sinks and swells.

Teampall Chiaráin Draw a handkerchief through the hole in the decorated stone slab at this 12th-century church for luck or fertility.

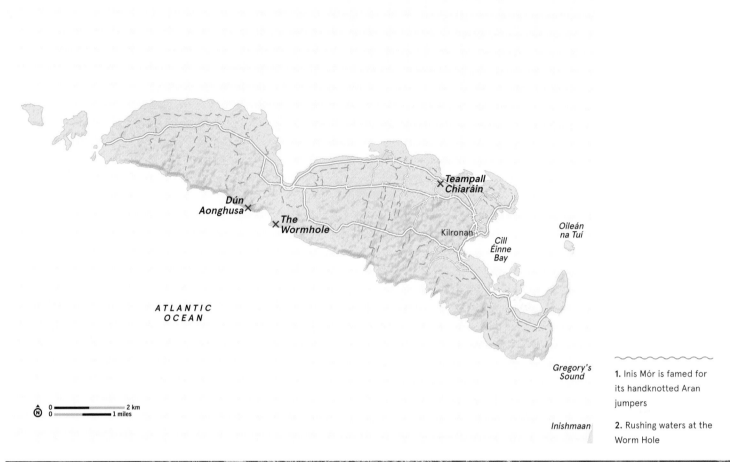

ATLANTIC OCEAN

Dún Aonghusa ✕

✕ *The Wormhole*

✕ Teampall Chiaráin

Kilronan

Cill Éinne Bay

Oileán na Tuí

Gregory's Sound

Inishmaan

0 — 2 km
0 — 1 miles
N

1. Inis Mór is famed for its handknotted Aran jumpers

2. Rushing waters at the Worm Hole

Portmagee (Co Kerry, Ireland)
(15km)

Little
Skellig

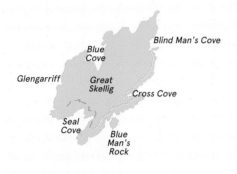

Blind Man's Cove

Blue
Cove

Glengarriff

Great
Skellig

Cross Cove

Seal
Cove

Blue
Man's
Rock

| N | 0 | | | | 1 km |
| | 0 | | | 0.5 miles | |

1. The ruined remains
of Skellig Michael
monastery

2. Gannets speckling
the Skellig shoreline

Skellig Islands

COUNTRY IRELAND
COORDINATES 51.770° N, 10.540° W • **AREA** 0.33 SQ KM (0.1 SQ MILES)

Flung out into the Atlantic, 12km (7 miles) off the Kerry coast, the jagged pyramids of rock known as the Skellig Islands have long been spiritual outposts for those seeking solace and isolation. Playwright George Bernard Shaw dubbed the larger of the two islands, Skellig Michael, the 'most fantastic and impossible rock in the world'. Here, up a roughly hewn stone staircase over a thousand years old, is a monastic settlement dating back to the 6th century. The long, hard climb up the 618 steps rewards with glorious views and a sense of wonder at the tenacity and determination of the monks who made their home here. Now a Unesco World Heritage Site, it is among the most inhospitable of monastic sites in Europe and the final stop on the Apollo/St Michael Axis that links sacred sites all the way to the Middle East. The sea swells make it difficult to land here even today but you may recognise its otherworldly landscape as a location in several *Star Wars* films.

LITTLE SKELLIG'S GANNETS

The sound of the waves pounding at the base of Little Skellig is almost drowned out in summer by the deafening noise of gannets cackling and calling. The steep-sided slopes of the island are inundated with these birds between May and September, when up to 35,000 breeding pairs nest here – making it one of the largest gannet colonies in the world. At times, the birds can be seen queueing for a place to lay their eggs, while many others wheel overhead, their black-tipped wings making them easy to identify. Landing is not permitted here, but a boat trip to the island will also offer the chance to spot Manx shearwaters, puffins, kittiwakes and fulmars, and, as your boat circles the pinnacle of rock, possibly grey seals, dolphins, porpoises or basking sharks.

X MARKS THE SPOT

Monastic Latrine A small 'beehive' hut constructed over a steep ravine; the monks had a dramatic setting to tend to the calls of nature.

Water Cisterns An ingenious system collected and stored water from the sloping rocks to overcome the monastery's lack of fresh water.

Retaining Walls Protective drystone walls constructed from huge slabs of rock created flat, sheltered terraces for building.

Vegetable Garden Sheltered behind stone walls, a milder microclimate was created allowing the monks a space to cultivate vegetables.

Cell A This domed and corbelled two-floor communal living space remains watertight centuries after it was built.

Islay

COUNTRY SCOTLAND
COORDINATES 55.736° N, 6.177° W · **AREA** 620 SQ KM (239 SQ MILES)

Known as the Queen of the Hebrides, Islay (*eye*-lah) is a whisky lover's dream. The island sits in the Southern Hebrides in Scotland and, despite its small size, supports nine working distilleries and is internationally renowned for the quality of its smooth, peaty spirits. Along with visiting the distilleries, Islay offers the chance to walk along sea cliffs, turquoise bays and sandy beaches, spotting seals and shipwrecks on headlands and wild goats on the moors, as well as heading out onto the water to spy dolphins, porpoises and basking sharks. Although the landscape isn't quite as dramatic as some of its neighbours, Islay's western beaches are superb and the Oa Peninsula offers a steely, rugged charm. There's wildlife in abundance, stellar seafood and the chance to visit the very source of a treasured late-night dram.

WATER OF LIFE

In the early 14th century, monks fleeing Ireland arrived on Islay and are credited with bringing the art of distilling with them. No one knows for sure if this is true, but the abundance of barley, peat and fresh water meant that the island was fertile ground for whisky production, and at its height 23 distilleries operated here. The 1644 Excise Act levied a tax on whisky and production quickly went underground, with illicit home stills and a brisk smuggling trade emerging. Today, *uisge beatha* (water of life) is again the island's most important export, with the single malts produced here prized as some of the best in the world, lent a distinctive flavour by the peaty soil and water, and by the sea salt driven inland on winter storms.

The southern distilleries – Laphroaig, Lagavulin and Ardbeg – are known for their potently peaty, smoky spirits, while the northern distilleries – Bruichladdich and Bunnahabhain – use natural spring water to produce a lighter, milder spirit with a mossy finish.

1. The means for making the 'water of life'

2. Barrels await at Bunnahabhain distillery

3. Ardbeg distillery

X MARKS THE SPOT

Museum of Islay Life Barrels, beds and bathchairs fill this former church in an illustration of life on the island from Mesolithic times.

Finlaggan A ritual meeting place and stronghold of the Lords of the Isles, this scenic islet witnessed many twists in Islay's history.

Loch Gruinart Nature Reserve Follow the trails through mudflats, moorland and woods to spot lapwings, corncrakes and curlews.

Kildalton Cross A monolithic stone cross carved with biblical scenes, this is one of Scotland's best-preserved early Christian monuments.

Islay Ales If you tire of all that whisky, this microbrewery offers free tours and samples of its hand-crafted real ales.

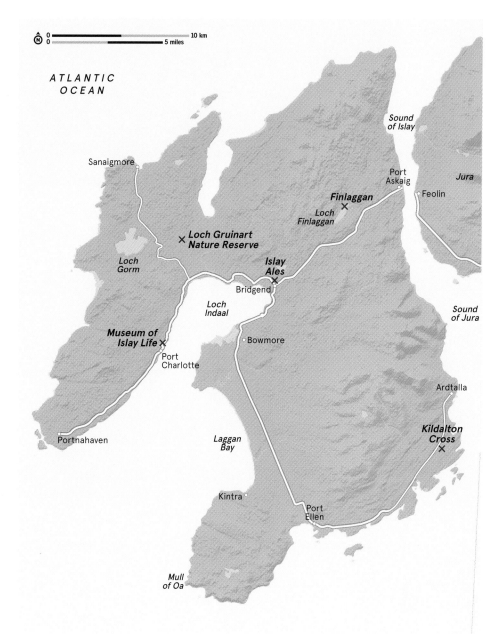

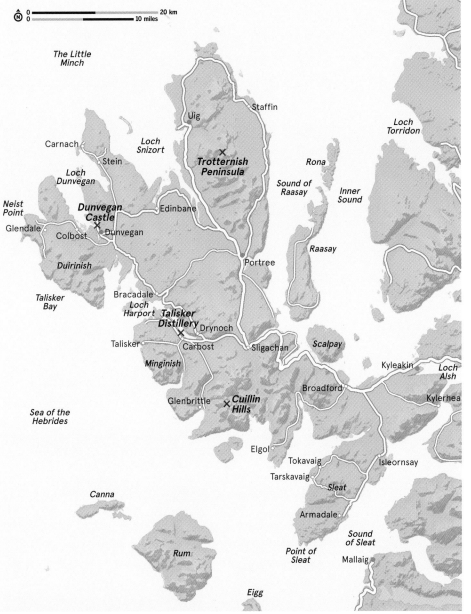

X MARKS THE SPOT

Cuillin Hills A dramatic playground for rock climbers, these knife-edge ridges and jagged peaks give the island a stunning backdrop.

Dunvegan Castle The oldest continually inhabited castle in Scotland and home to the chiefs of the McLeod clan for 800 years.

Talisker Distillery Skye's oldest distillery is set on the shores of Loch Harport, with dramatic views of the Cuillins.

Trotternish Peninsula Arresting rock outcrops dot this spectacular landscape where the steep cliffs are strewn with dramatic buttresses.

Sea Kayaking Take to the water to view the island's rugged mountains from the sea and catch a glimpse of seals, porpoises and white-tailed eagles.

Isle of Skye

COUNTRY SCOTLAND • **COORDINATES** 57.273° N, 6.215° W • **AREA** 1656 SQ KM (639 SQ MILES)

The second-largest of Scotland's islands, in the Inner Hebrides, is its most spectacular, with a landscape that lurches from quiet coves and inky lochs to jagged pinnacles, tumbling waterfalls and pleated cliffs. Skye's dramatic mountains and undulating moors are easily reached by a bridge from the mainland, but to access the remotest corners and most impressive views you'll need to take to the high moorland on foot, cycle precipitous mountain roads or kayak along the puckered and indented coast. Temper it all with a visit to fairy-tale castles, colourful fishing villages and a host of museums, galleries and craft shops in the island's lively towns. Bring a raincoat, though: the name Skye comes the old Norse *sky-a*, meaning 'cloud island'. The weather here is unpredictable at best, but the scudding clouds and brooding skies only heighten the drama.

SKYE'S EAGLES

Large enough to carry off a full-grown sheep, Scotland's eagles didn't endear themselves to farmers and gamekeepers and were eventually hunted to extinction over a century ago. A successful reintroduction programme began in 1975 and the wild uplands and coastline of Skye now serve as a favoured home for the country's largest birds of prey. About 30 pairs of golden eagles and 16 pairs of white-tailed (sea) eagles nest here and can be easily spotted from public roads. The cliffs near Portree offer reliable sightings of white-tailed eagles, a massive bird with a 2m (6.5ft) wingspan easily identified by the 'fingers' at its wing tips. Golden eagles are more easily seen in the mountains, where you may spot them diving at speeds of up to 320km/h (199mph). The eagles are still critically endangered and continue to be threated by human persecution. They're sensitive to disturbances, particularly during the breeding season from February to September, so stick to well-trodden paths and give them plenty of space.

1. Traditional thatched-roof crofters' cottages

2. White-tailed eagle

3. Broody skies over the Isle of Skye's emerald interior

Lindisfarne

COUNTRY ENGLAND
COORDINATES 55.680° N, 1.800° W • **AREA** 4 SQ KM (1.5 SQ MILES)

An ancient pilgrims' path runs over steely grey mudflats to the Holy Island of Lindisfarne off the northeast coast of England. Submerged at high tide, the path – as well as the narrow, modern-day causeway – only offer intermittent access to this bleak but enchanting place, where abbey ruins and a fairy-tale castle top the craggy rocks. St Aidan established a monastery in this strategically located but isolated spot in 635 but it fell prey to a series of Viking raids. The monks departed for good in 793, but not before they had completed one of the most celebrated illustrated manuscripts of the time, the Lindisfarne Gospels. The evocative ruins of a later 12th-century priory survive, while elsewhere upturned boats act as sheds, stone lime kilns dot the landscape and waterfowl flock to the mudflats and dunes. The island is cut off twice a day, so make sure to check the tide tables as rescue from the rapidly flooding causeway or path is an expensive option.

HOLY SPIRITS

Legend has it that it was the 7th-century Irish monks who came to Lindisfarne with St Aidan who first established a distillery on the island, and mead – hot contender for the world's oldest alcoholic drink – was probably among their artillery. A staple of the Greeks, Romans and Vikings, mead is a sweet honey wine long associated with good health and vitality. It was also claimed to be a potent aphrodisiac and newlyweds were traditionally gifted a month's supply. Today, St Aidan's Winery has re-established Holy Island's place in the annals of distillation and its flagship mead, made in the Roman style from white grapes, honey and herbs, is silky smooth and easy on the palate. You can visit the distillery for a sample, and if mead's not your thing, pick up some Holy Island beer or rum instead.

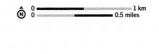

*Lindisfarne
National
Nature Reserve*
×

*Holy
Island*

*The
Lough*

← *Beal; Berwick-upon-Tweed
(3km)*

*North
Sea*

*St Mary
the Virgin
Church* ×

×*Lindisfarne
Museum*

×*Lindisfarne
Castle*

St Cuthbert's ×
Isle

ENGLAND

X MARKS THE SPOT

Lindisfarne Castle A 16th-century fort remodelled as a castle, this stronghold became an English socialite's historic holiday home.

Lindisfarne Natural Nature Reserve These salt marshes and marram-covered dunes support 11 species of orchid, plus wintering waterfowl and harbour seals.

St Cuthbert's Isle Unbelievably, this tiny islet cut off from Lindisfarne by the high tide was where St Cuthbert once lived as a hermit.

Lindisfarne Museum Brutal Vikings raids, medieval cults and illustrated manuscripts are explored in the island's interpretive centre.

St Mary the Virgin Church A long nave lit by lancet windows, a fisherman's altar and modern sculptures adorn the island's 12th-century parish church.

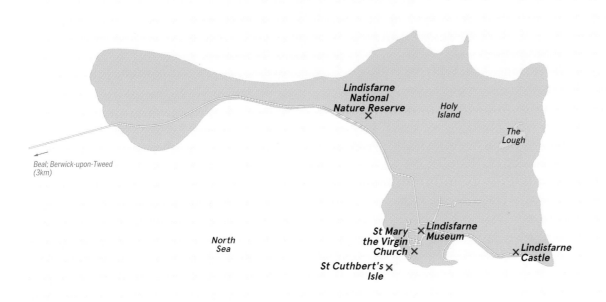

1. Lindisfarne's ruined 12th-century priory

2. Lindisfarne Castle

3. Statue of St Cuthbert

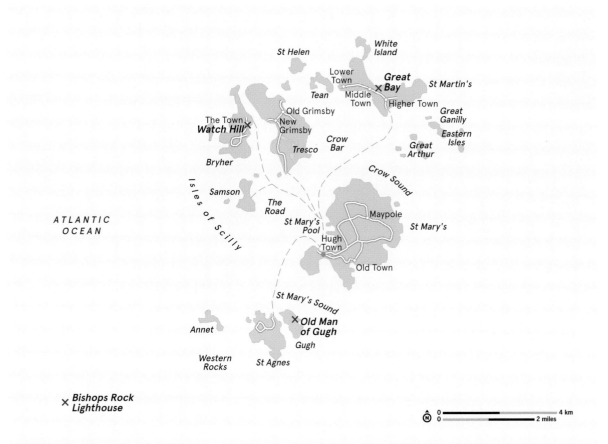

Map of the Isles of Scilly showing: St Helen, White Island, Lower Town, Great Bay, St Martin's, Tean, Middle Town, Higher Town, Great Ganilly, Old Grimsby, The Town, Watch Hill, New Grimsby, Eastern Isles, Tresco, Crow Bar, Great Arthur, Great Ganilly, Bryher, Crow Sound, Samson, The Road, Maypole, St Mary's, St Mary's Pool, Hugh Town, St Mary's, Old Town, St Mary's Sound, Old Man of Gugh, Annet, Gugh, Western Rocks, St Agnes, Bishops Rock Lighthouse, ATLANTIC OCEAN, Isles of Scilly

0 — 4 km
0 — 2 miles

X MARKS THE SPOT

Bishops Rock Lighthouse A 19th-century engineering marvel, teetering on a sliver of rock in the notorious cluster of shipwreck-strewn skerries called Western Rocks.

Watch Hill The archipelago panorama atop this hill on Bryher is sublime – even more so at sunset when sky and sea blaze flame-red.

Old Man of Gugh This 3m-tall (10ft) menhir lies on the deserted isle of Gugh, accessible on foot from St Agnes at low tide.

Swimming with Seals Don snorkel and mask to eyeball Atlantic grey seals in crystal-clear waters offshore from St Martin's.

Great Bay Turquoise water, white sand and scarcely a soul to be seen on the remote north side of St Martin's.

1. Lighthouse on St Agnes

2. Lobster catch

3. Sailing the crystal-clear waters off Tresco

Isles of Scilly

COUNTRY ENGLAND • **COORDINATES** 49.923° N, 6.296° W • **AREA** 16 SQ KM (6 SQ MILES)

Given Britain's unexotic and often bleak weather, it is all the more extraordinary to think that the country squirrels away an ecological Eden where subtropical succulents, desert cacti and Seychelles-esque palm trees grow like weeds. But then again, the Isles of Scilly, 45km (28 miles) off Cornwall's southwest shore in the Atlantic Ocean, have always been cut off from mainland Britain, ensuring a unique ecosystem blissfully undisrupted by invasive plant or animal species.

This paradisal string of 200-odd islands – five are inhabited – belongs to the Duchy of Cornwall, an ancient royal fiefdom where every local is a tenant of the Prince of Wales. This Scillonian anomaly aside, British tradition is tantalisingly alive and well, from crab sandwiches or fish and chips to creamy ice-cream whipped up from island milk and flowers, or farmhouse fudge cooked on an Aga in the farm kitchen.

A NATURALIST'S HAVEN

Breaking waves, cawing gulls, the whistle of Scilly shrews and occasional buzz of endangered moss carder bees is as noisy as it gets on the pristine island of Tresco. Wandering round its abbey gardens, lush with lipstick-red flame trees and 20,000 other exotic species, it's hard to believe that the island – the second largest in the archipelago after St Mary's – was barren when horticultural visionary Augustus Smith arrived in 1834 as Lord Proprietor and leaseholder of the Isles of Scilly.

Choosing Tresco as his home, he planted exquisite subtropical gardens nurtured by the temperate Gulf Stream. He introduced hardy Monterey cypresses and pines to protect seedlings in the breezy, salt-heavy environment – and after his death in 1872, his successors continued his grand vision, introducing new plant species collected from across the globe. Free of natural predators, the gardens are a haven for native British red squirrels and other fauna. Along the Scillonian coastline – leased, along with Scilly's many uninhabited rocks and islands, by the Isles of Scilly Wildlife Trust for an annual peppercorn rent of one daffodil – you can spy colonies of puffins, shearwaters and grey seals.

NORTH
ATLANTIC
OCEAN

× Ward
Hill

George Waterston
Memorial Centre
and Museum ×

South ×
Lighthouse

North
Sea

0 ———————— 1 km
0 ———————— 0.5 miles

X MARKS THE SPOT

George Waterston Memorial Centre & Museum This small museum tells the story of the island's history, from crafts and crofting to soldiers and shipwrecks.

Ward Hill Hike above coastal cliffs to the island's highest point for superb views.

Fair Isle Crafts Seek out the island's makers to learn how they knit the intricate designs for which Fair Isle is renowned.

Ranger Walks Join a free ranger-led walk to see puffins, tag birds or go rockpooling in this key stopover for migrating seabirds.

South Lighthouse You'll be treated to dramatic views from this remote outpost, the last lighthouse in Scotland to be automated.

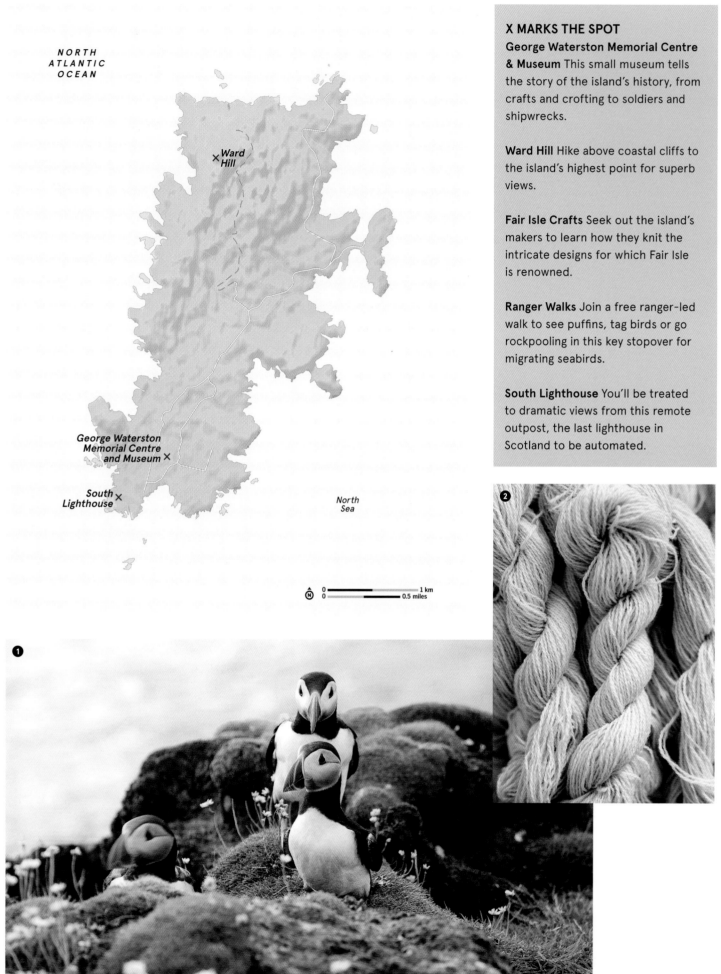

❶

❷

Fair Isle

COUNTRY SCOTLAND
COORDINATES 59.533° N, 1.633° W • **AREA** 8 SQ KM (3 SQ MILES)

Best known for its distinctive knits, Fair Isle, which lies halfway between Orkney and Shetland, is the most remote inhabited island in Scotland, and although the voyage here is often rough, the arrival is dramatic. Flanked by a lighthouse at each end, ringed by rugged cliffs and home to crofters, crafters and conservationists, Fair Isle was known to Norse settlers as Friđarey (the 'island of peace'). It's a place renowned for its varied birdlife, but you'll also find Iron Age settlements, shipwrecks, secluded coves, wonderful hiking and a way of life that relies less on the outside world than its own innovation, creativity and determination.

ATLANTIC PUFFINS

From May to August each year, puffins become one of the star attractions on Fair Isle. These instantly recognisable birds with their black-and-white feathers and colourful beaks spend most of their life at sea and only come ashore to breed. In Fair Isle they return in late March, lay a single egg in late April and leave once their chicks are fledged in August. Once airborne, the chicks don't return to land for two years. Although there has been a dramatic fall in puffin numbers in recent years, they can still be easily spotted on the island, their clumsy, comical antics providing plenty of entertainment for birdwatchers. Whether gathering to watch a fight, making crash landings at sea or excavating burrows and showering each other in soil, they are one of the most characterful birds to observe. At times their gestures seem to mirror those of humans, with dominant birds strutting deliberately through the colony and submissive ones scurrying past, heads held low. The puffins are most active in the evening before they go to sea to feed and are often seen on the cliffs around the ferry terminal and at the North Lighthouse.

1. Atlantic puffins

2. Yarn made from Shetland wool

3. Boats docked at Fair Isle Harbour

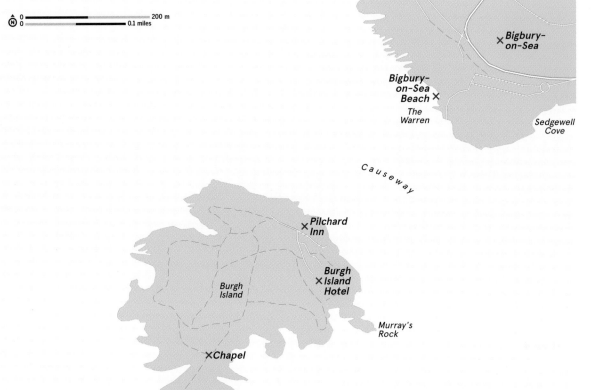

Bigbury-on-Sea

Bigbury-on-Sea Beach

The Warren

Sedgewell Cove

C a u s e w a y

Pilchard Inn

Burgh Island Hotel

Burgh Island

Murray's Rock

Chapel

1. Burgh Island: just a pub, a hotel, a chapel and a golden-sand beach

2. Burgh Island Hotel

❷

Burgh Island

COUNTRY ENGLAND
COORDINATES 50.279° N, 3.899° W • **AREA** 0.105 SQ KM (0.04 SQ MILES)

When the tide is high, the only way to reach grass-green Burgh Island is aboard a lumbering, mid-20th-century hydraulic creation known as a sea tractor. With its wild beauty and near-yet-far seclusion, this enigmatic tidal island sits in the heart of the South Devon Area of Outstanding Natural Beauty, between Salcombe and Plymouth and just off the long-distance South West Coast Path. Its mysterious tale takes in pirates, smugglers, fisherfolk, celebrities and adventurers, and it's thought that a monastery may have once existed here. As the waters recede, a golden-hued sandy strand paves the way to a single, glamorous hotel known for its art deco style and high-profile clientele, which once included Devonian author Agatha Christie. The only neighbours here are an old fishing hut and a lively historical pub. You could hire the whole island if you fancied it these days, but Burgh is still a place where days move with the gentle ebb and flow of the tide.

A LITERARY PILGRIMAGE

In the 1941 novel *Evil Under the Sun*, by beloved mystery writer Agatha Christie, Belgian detective Hercule Poirot heads off on a well-deserved break to coastal Devon, where he is drawn into solving the murder of a fellow hotel guest whose body is found face down on a sandy beach. It's widely believed that Burgh Island, a favourite landmark in Christie's home county, inspired the novel's setting, with the author having spent time here on various trips over the years. In another fictional rendition of this breezy little isle, Christie's bestselling *And Then There Were None* (published in 1939), sees 10 strangers lured to eerie Soldier Island off the Devon coast, where a series of mysterious deaths take place. Modern-day visitors can follow in Christie's footsteps (quite literally) with a stay at Burgh Island Hotel's elegant Beach House, originally built as a writer's retreat in the 1930s.

X MARKS THE SPOT

Sark Lighthouse Perched atop cliffs on the east coast at Point Robert, the island's octagonal, whitewashed lighthouse dates from 1913.

Little Sark Dangling off Great Sark, this rocky peninsula has tempting tidal swimming pools and rugged scenery.

La Coupée One of the most spectacular sights around: the spine-tinglingly narrow, 80m-tall (262ft) isthmus linking Little Sark to the main island.

Gouliot Headland Over on the west coast, opposite Brecqhou island, sits this grassy outcrop known for its sprawling sea caves and rich ecosystems.

Dixcart Bay A peaceful woodland path leads down to a golden-sand beach with perfect swimming.

~~~~~~~~

1. La Coupée

2. Sark Lighthouse

3. Horse-drawn cart

Sark

COUNTRY CHANNEL ISLANDS
COORDINATES 49.430° N, 2.366° W • **AREA** 5 SQ KM (2 SQ MILES)

Scattered out in the English Channel, between Guernsey and Jersey, there's a sun-soaked island where the roads have no cars and people get around by bike, on foot or even in tractors and horse-drawn carts. Like its neighbouring sister isles, Sark (the fourth-largest island in the archipelago) sits closer to Normandy in France than to British shores, and the local population numbers only around 500. Sheer cliffs cascade into sand-and-pebble coves along the rugged coastline, while flower-sprinkled meadows, peaceful country lanes and woodland walking paths stretch inland. For adventure lovers, this is a paradise made for kayaking, coasteering, diving and other adrenaline-addled pursuits. And when night falls, the deliciously clear sky bursts into a swirl of faraway stars. It might take a flight to Guernsey or Jersey and then a ferry ride to get here, but Sark's slow-down charm makes it a thrill at any time of year – just make sure you prebook your bike!

STARRY NIGHTS

Gaze up on any crisp, clear night as you amble along Sark's narrow vehicle-free lanes with just a head torch for company, and you'll catch distant stars, blazing meteors, the hazy Milky Way and perhaps even the moon's craters glinting across the spectacularly unpolluted sky. It's a magical sight, easily visible to the naked eye. With no streetlights, floodlit buildings or motorised vehicles, serene Sark was named the world's first ever Dark Sky Island back in 2011, and the wonderful stargazing here is attracting growing numbers of visitors to its shores, particularly outside the summer beach season. There's now even an officially named 'Sark' star in the Corona Borealis constellation, spotted high above during springtime. For anyone keen to delve deeper, Stark Observatory, built in 2015, leads stargazing sessions at the heart of the island and is staffed by enthusiastic volunteers who will happily show you the ropes. After all, these star-studded skies are Sark's most beloved local personalities.

3

Skjoldnæs
× Lighthouse

Drejø

Hjortø

Skovballe

Tåsinge

Søby

Birkholm

Vitsø
Nor
×

Store
Egholm

Revkrog

Dejrø

Bredholm

Strynø
Kalv

Skovby

Leby

Bregninge

Ærøskøbing

Halmø

Vindeballe

Ommel

Voderup ×
Klint

× Olde Mølle

Kragnæs

Marstal

Store Rise

Dunkær

Gråsten

Marstal Bugt

0 ————————— 5 km
0 ————————— 2.5 miles
N

X MARKS THE SPOT

Olde Mølle Take a pew on 'Peace Bench', an artwork by Erik Brandt, and ponder world peace over soul-stirring island and Baltic Sea views.

Skjoldnæs Lighthouse The island's sturdy, 22m-tall (72ft) granite-stone lighthouse has guided seafarers since 1881. Views from the top are glorious.

Vitsø Nor Nature reserve of restored wetland and 50-hectare (123-acre) lake with trio of artificial 'bird islands' to attract breeding waterfowl.

Voderup Klint On the south coast, tall banks of grassy moraine double as dreamy sunset-viewing spot – or nip down the steps to the quiet pebble beach below.

Kyststien Ærø's serene coastal path follows the coast 30km (19 miles) from Øhavsstien, near main town Marstal in the south, to Vitsø in the north.

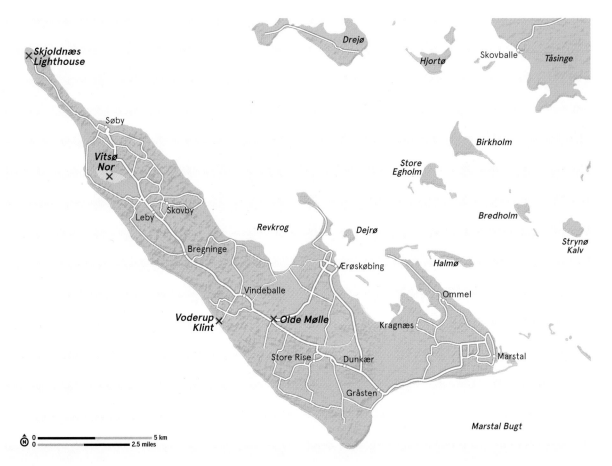

1. Coastal living in Ærø

2. Bed down in an Ærø beach house

3. The Ærøskøbing ferry

Ærø

COUNTRY DENMARK · COORDINATES 54.858° N, 10.387° E · AREA 88 SQ KM (34 SQ MILES)

Its name alone (pronounced 'air-rue') piques an island adventurer's natural curiosity. One step removed from modern-day toil or trouble, in Denmark's remote South Funen Archipelago, this tiny Baltic Sea island measures no more than 30km (19 miles) or so long by 4km to 8km (2-5 miles) wide, and is a model of clean living.

From the little port town of Ærøskøbing, rural roads roll into pristine green countryside peppered with thatched-roofed, half-timbered houses and vintage windmills. Photogenic bathing huts fringe beaches, and a sprinkling of basic huts inspired by traditional fishing shacks promise an unusual overnight for nature lovers venturing off grid to Ærø's abundant wild and untouched beauty spots. Looking out to sea, the Baltic teems with teeny deserted islands begging to be explored.

Sea-kayak, bicycle, one's own two feet – or a free public bus servicing the length of the island – is how islanders choose to get around. Cars on the island are few: Ærø is one of a handful of Denmark's thousand-plus islands with no tunnel or road bridge linking it to the mainland or other islands.

CLEAN ENERGY

Ærø has long been prized for its pristine environment, and ambitious sustainable-energy initiatives are rapidly rebranding the forward-thinking Danish island as a world pioneer in renewable energy. Ærø already produces more renewable energy than it uses: heating is solar powered and wind turbine farms generate 130% of the island's electricity needs. Surplus power is notably used to recharge *Ellen*, the world's first e-ferry (a fully electric ferry), which yo-yos between its home port on Ærø and the neighbouring isle of Als. The e-ferry is near-silent, has none of the stink or smoke of a traditional diesel vessel, and transports up to 200 passengers and 30 cars at a time. Powered by 56 tonnes of hi-tech lithium-ion batteries, it can sail up to 22 nautical miles (around 38km/26 miles) before recharging, and reduces CO_2 emissions by an estimated 2000 tonnes per year – a happy thought, given that marine traffic is currently responsible for around 12% of all CO_2 emissions in Europe.

Gotland

COUNTRY SWEDEN

COORDINATES 57.468° N, 18.486° E • **AREA** 3184 SQ KM (1229 SQ MILES)

Known as the 'Queen of the Baltic', Gotland is a magical island where medieval towns and churches butt up to sandy beaches and dunes, sculptural sea stacks, lush meadows and sleepy villages. It is Sweden's largest island and sits in the Baltic Sea roughly halfway between mainland Sweden and Estonia – a strategically important location which has seen it inhabited for some 8000 years. Gotland is home to the narrow, cobbled lanes and quaint cottages of Visby, its Unesco World Heritage–listed capital, with wonderful early Gothic architecture and the most alluring of long summer evenings. Outside the capital and away from peak season, it's a serenely tranquil spot, sparsely populated and best explored by bike. Come for the medieval week in August to see jousters and jesters; the truffle festival in November; or just to wander from flea market to beach to remote hamlet, soaking up the views as you go.

SWEDEN'S CULINARY CAPITAL

Holding a strategic position on a northern merchant route, the busy trading post of Gotland was often the first place in Sweden to get hold of spices and delicacies from afar; the combination of these exotics with its own traditional produce saw the development of a well-deserved reputation for fine food. Today, Gotland is something of a gourmet hotspot, and it's a great place to sample contemporary Swedish food, whether lamb fed on grass whipped by a sea breeze, an abundance of fresh fish, seafood, wild garlic and asparagus, or truffles unique to the island. Saffron plays a leading role in local desserts – look out for the traditional *saffranspannkaka*, a saffron-infused rice pancake served with whipped cream and dewberry jam. Juniper flavours local ales such as Gotlandsdricka, a smoky-sweet brew made here for centuries and now joined by a slew of microbreweries churning out their own take on craft beers.

1. Cycling on Gotland

2. Fårö coastline

3. Visby's flower-filled Old Town

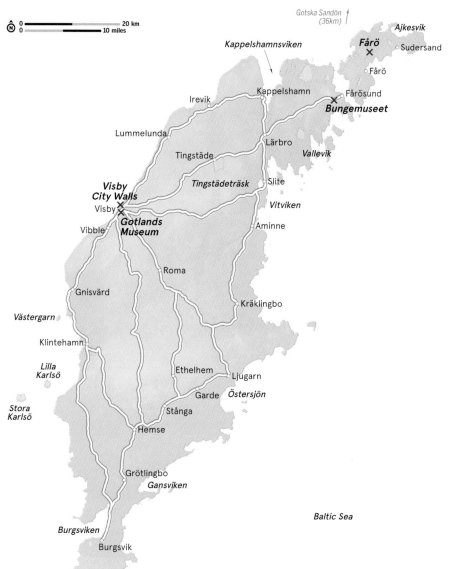

Gotska Sandön
(36km)

Ajkesvik

Fårö

Sudersand

Fårö

Kappelshamnsviken

Fårösund

Kappelshamn

Irevik

Bungemuseet

Lummelunda

Lärbro

Vallevik

Tingstäde

Visby
City Walls

Tingstädeträsk

Slite

Visby

Vitviken

Gotlands
Museum

Vibble

Aminne

Roma

Gnisvärd

Kräklingbo

Västergarn

Klintehamn

Lilla
Karlsö

Ethelhem

Ljugarn

Garde

Östersjön

Stora
Karlsö

Stånga

Hemse

Grötlingbo

Gansviken

Baltic Sea

Burgsviken

Burgsvik

X MARKS THE SPOT

Visby City Walls Walk the city's 13th-century protective walls, which remain almost intact and reach six storeys high in places.

Gotlands Museum One of Sweden's best regional museums, where you'll learn about the 'hedgehog girl', Norse religion, the Black Death and Viking jewellery.

Gotska Sandön Splendid isolation joins white-sand beaches, dunes, seals and birdlife in this remote island national park.

Bungemuseet Step into the 17th century in this open-air museum where you can wander through historic housing and see pre-Viking picture stones.

Fårö Fans of film director Ingmar Bergman should make their way to his adopted home, a small, sleepy island just north of Gotland.

X MARKS THE SPOT

Tórshavn The Faroes' capital city is a pint-sized delight extending from a turf-roofed historical core, Tinganes, on a peninsula jutting out into the crashing bay.

Vestmanna Sea Cliffs Reason alone to seek out the Faroes, these 700m-high (2297ft) cliffs are home to thousands of seabirds every summer, including puffins, razorbills and fulmars.

Skansin Fort Built in 1580 by order of the Faroese explorer Magnus Heinason, to protect Tórshavn from pirate attacks.

Kirkjubøur Guarded by the unfinished medieval St Magnus Cathedral, this impossibly scenic southwest-coast village was once the Faroes' main religious hub.

Nólsoy Streymoy's slender neighbouring island makes a splash with its end-of-the-world lighthouse and astonishing storm petrel colony, said to be the world's biggest.

Streymoy

COUNTRY FAROE ISLANDS (DENMARK)
COORDINATES 62.152° N, 7.075° W • **AREA** 373 SQ KM (144 SQ MILES)

In the magical, isolated Faroe Islands – a self-governing Danish archipelago lost in the North Atlantic between Iceland, Scotland and Denmark – an endless band of spectacularly elemental landscapes fires up the imagination. As the salt-swirled air whooshes around, plunging fjords, wide-open moorlands and sheer-edged sea cliffs begin to emerge from the mist. There are no trees, in summer the sun barely sinks, and sheep famously outnumber people. Streymoy, home to the Faroese capital Tórshavn, is the largest and longest of these 18 far-flung isles, whose fantastical natural spaces and edge-of-the-Earth intrigue have inspired adventurers since the Vikings first arrived over a thousand years ago.

FAROESE CUISINE

When Faroese chef Poul Andrias Ziska began crafting deliciously daring 17-course tasting menus rooted in local produce at Streymoy's Koks restaurant, two Michelin stars swiftly followed, along with hundreds of bookings. Now, while the raw, windswept landscapes might steal the headlines, the Faroe Islands sit firmly on the world's foodie map, too.

Menus here change with the seasons, with traditional cooking techniques and beloved age-old recipes taking centre stage alongside boundless creativity. Foraging, fermenting and preserving are all key to the Faroe Islands' distinctly Nordic yet highly regional culinary scene, which is just as likely to see you diving into the world of *raest* (wind-drying meat and fish in a wooden shed called a *hjallur*) as settling in for a boundary-pushing multi-course gastronomic experience. Few vegetables survive in the Faroes' harsh North Atlantic climate. Potatoes, turnips and rhubarb are the local staples, as well as lamb, seaweed, in-season fish and seafood and even seabirds.

A highly memorable Faroese activity for food-loving travellers is to join a local family over *heimablídni* (home hospitality), a traditional, intimate home-cooked meal that also weaves in tales about the islands' folklore and history.

3

1. Faroese fishing sweater made in Tórshavn

2. Kirkjubøur

3. Primary hues along Tórshavn's waterfront

Lofoten Islands

COUNTRY NORWAY
COORDINATES 68.471° N, 13.863° E • **AREA** 1227 SQ KM (474 SQ MILES)

The fabled maelstrom and fire-engine-red fishing huts on stilts in Lofoten that French novelist Jules Verne evoked in his classic sci-fi adventure novel *Twenty Thousand Leagues Under the Sea* were no flights of fancy. This end-of-the-Earth archipelago, linked by ferry or a series of road tunnels and bridges to mainland Norway, is straight off a cinema screen. The raw natural beauty – not to mention the celestial Arctic light – is simply staggering.

Fishing, farming and tourism chart out the seasons on this rugged string of islands where the flow of the Gulf Stream ensures a soft warmth unmatched elsewhere in the Arctic Circle. On white summer nights, the Midnight Sun bathes the islands' shark-fin chiselled mountains in gold and turns the Norwegian Sea a pale violet no painter can truly capture. The coveted winter chase – in a kayak or husky sled, on snowshoes or horseback – to watch the godlike Northern Lights tango purple and emerald-green across the dark sky is majestic, unmatched and utterly unforgettable.

GLORY BE TO COD

The local culinary delicacy – crispy fried cod's tongue – is an instant giveaway as to the lifeblood of this extreme-north archipelago: cod, or rather the giant migrating cod (*skrei*), up to 180cm (70 in) long and weighing up to 55kg (121lb), that swim from the Barents Sea to Vestfjorden each winter to spawn.

Early Viking islanders hung their catch out to dry to make stockfish – eaten raw, salted or reconstituted with water, edible for years and the perfect trading commodity. From the Middle Ages, fishermen from all over Norway sailed to Lofoten each winter to spend the season catching, drying and preserving cod: saltfish is filleted, salted and dried for about three weeks (unlike stockfish which is hung decapitated but otherwise whole, in pairs, over wooden drying racks to lose 80% of its weight). Some 50,000 tonnes (30,000 minus the heads) are fished annually.

Then there's the liver, which produces cod-liver oil, rich in vitamin D that has long been known to prevent rickets and assuage the depression brought on by mad-long, dark-all-day Arctic winters.

X MARKS THE SPOT

Svolværgeita There's a reason this mountain is called 'Svolvær geita' (Svolvær goat). Daredevils leap from its two 'horns' or rock pinnacles, teetering high above Svolvær town on Austvågøy island.

Moskenstraumen One of the world's most treacherous whirlpool chains, up to 50m (164ft) deep, offshore from Moskenesøy island.

Reine The village to snap Lofoten's signature red *rorbuer* (fishing huts), built atop stilts from the 12th century for wintering fishermen.

Nrsk Fiskeværsmuseum Uncover Europe's oldest cod-liver-oil factory and a smithy which crafts cod-liver-oil lamps in the tiny village of Å, on Moskenesøy's southern tip.

Røst Reef The world's largest cold-water coral reef – a riot of yellow, pink and orange-red lophelia coral, 35km (22 miles) long and 3km (1.8 miles) wide – lies west of Røst island.

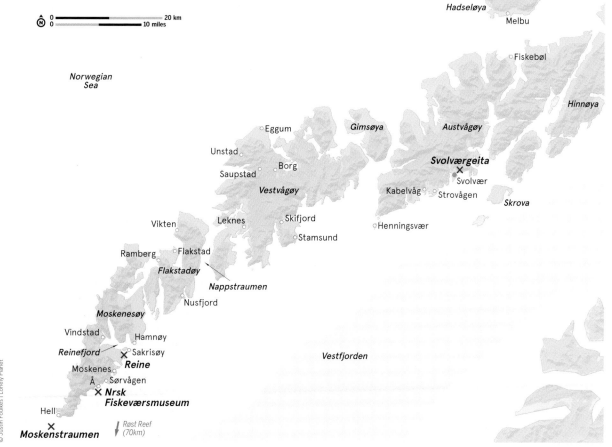

❷

0 _____ 20 km
0 _____ 10 miles

*Norwegian
Sea*

Hadseløya
○ Melbu

○ Fiskebøl

Hinnøya

○ Eggum
Gimsøya   *Austvågøy*

Unstad ○
○ Borg   *Svolværgeita*
Saupstad ○   ✕
                         ○ Svolvær
Vestvågøy   Kabelvåg ○   ○ Strovågen
                              ○
Vikten ○   Leknes ○   ○ Skifjord   *Skrova*
                      ○ Stamsund
Ramberg ○ ○ Flakstad   ○ Henningsvær
        Flakstadøy

      Nappstraumen
            ○ Nusfjord

Moskenesøy
Vindstad ○   ○ Hamnøy
Reinefjord ✕ ○ Sakrisøy   *Vestfjorden*
Moskenes ○   **Reine**
      Å ○ ○ Sørvågen
         ✕ *Nrsk*
         Fiskeværsmuseum
Hell ○
      ✕
Moskenstraumen
         ↓ *Røst Reef
         (70km)*

~~~~~~~~~~~~~~~~

1. Stockfish drying on
wooden racks

2. Hamnøy port and
waterfront

Texel

COUNTRY THE NETHERLANDS
COORDINATES 53.054°N, 4.797°E • **AREA** 463 SQ KM (179 SQ MILES)

Sweeping white-sand beaches, wildlife-rich nature reserves, sun-dappled forests and quaint villages are just some of the highlights of Texel (pronounced 'tes-sel'), the largest and most visited of the Wadden Islands, which stretch along Holland's northeast coast.

Once a main stop for ships en route to Asia, Africa and North America (the first trade mission to the East Indies began and ended here), Texel's typically flat Dutch landscape makes it idyllic for cycling, and sheep are everywhere: the local wool is highly prized and lamb is always on the menu. During lambing season around Easter, you'll see bouncy lambs aplenty; join the locals in taking a Lammetjes Wandeltrocht (a 'walk to look at the lambs').

With enough diversions to keep you entertained for days on end, Texel is popular with Dutch and German visitors but is otherwise little-known, making it feel like a real find.

TEXEL DUNES NATIONAL PARK

The patchwork of dunescape running along the island's western coast is a prime reason for visiting Texel. Salt fens and heath alternate with velvety, grass-covered dunes; plants endemic to the habitat include the dainty marsh orchid and orange-berried sea buckthorn.

Much of the area is a bird sanctuary and accessible only on foot. Set out for a wander with your binoculars, or book a ranger-led walk at the Ecomare visitor centre, which also supplies maps. The De Slufter section became a brackish wetland after an attempt at land reclamation failed; after a storm breached the dykes in the early 1900s, the area was allowed to flood and a unique ecosystem developed. To the south, De Muy is renowned for its colony of spoonbills. A stone's throw from the windswept beach lies the dark, leafy forest of De Dennen. Originally planted as a source of lumber, today it has an enchanting network of walking and cycling paths.

❶

1. Texel sheep with lamb

2. Texel Lighthouse

3. Maritime and Beachcombers Museum

0 ———— 5 km
0 ———— 2.5 miles
N

Klimpstraat

De Cocksdorp

North
Sea

De Slufter

De Muy

De Koog

Oosterend

Ecomare✕

De Dennen

De Waal

Den Burg

*Bulb
Fields*

Oudeschild ✕ **Kaap Skil Museum
Van Jutters
& Zeelui**

Den
Hoorn

Waddenzee

't Horntje

Hors

X MARKS THE SPOT

Beaches by Numbers Lining the
western shore, beaches are numbered
by the kilometre from south to north.
Prepare for nudity on #9 and #27.

Artisan Produce Along with local
cheese, ice cream and even wine,
look out for Texel-distilled spirits.

Ecomare Don't miss this impressive
nature centre devoted to the
preservation of local wildlife.

**Kaap Skil Museum Van Jutters &
Zeelui** The superb Maritime and
Beachcombers Museum is packed
with flotsam and jetsam recovered
from sunken ships and the shore.

Maritime Disaster On Christmas Day
1593, hurricane-force winds battered
a merchant fleet moored off Texel's
coast; 44 vessels sank, and about a
thousand seamen lost their lives.

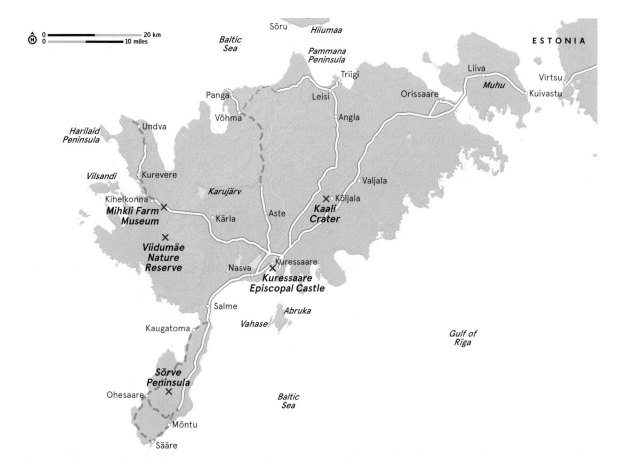

Map Labels

Sõru
Hiiumaa
Baltic Sea
Pammana Peninsula
ESTONIA
Triigi
Liiva
Virtsu
Muhu
Panga
Leisi
Kuivastu
Võhma
Angla
Orissaare
Harilaid Peninsula
Undva
Vilsandi
Kurevere
Valjala
Karujärv
Kihelkonna
X Kõljala
Mihkli Farm Museum X
Kärla
Aste
Kaali Crater X
Viidumäe Nature Reserve X
Nasva
X Kuressaare
Salme
Kuressaare Episcopal Castle
Abruka
Kaugatoma
Vahase
Gulf of Riga
Sõrve Peninsula X
Ohesaare
Baltic Sea
Mõntu
Sääre

Scale: 0 — 20 km / 0 — 10 miles

X MARKS THE SPOT

Kuressaare Episcopal Castle
Built in the 14th century, the mighty Dolomite fortress stages thought-provoking art exhibitions and summer concerts.

Kaali Crater At Kaali, a misty forest rings a 100m-wide (328ft) curiously round lake formed by a meteorite some 4000 years ago. Eight smaller craters are nearby.

Sõrve Peninsula A long pine-backed coastline reaches a dramatic end at Sääre, with a lighthouse and a narrow sandspit extending out to sea.

Viidumäe Nature Reserve Short nature trails take in different habitats for rare plant species, while an observation tower offers panoramic views of western Saaremaa.

Mihkli Farm Museum This well-preserved early-18th-century farm has thatched-roof wooden farmhouses, a sauna, a windmill and a traditional village swing.

1. Rural cabin at NamiNamaste, Simisti

2. Beachcombing bounty, Saaremaa

3. Viirelaid Lighthouse Island Resort

❸

Saaremaa

COUNTRY ESTONIA

COORDINATES 58.485° N, 22.613° E • **AREA** 2670 SQ KM (1031 SQ MILES)

If you're looking for the soul of Estonia, skip the medieval turrets of Tallinn and the university fervour of Tartu and head instead to the vast open spaces of Saaremaa. The largest island in the country is home to oak and juniper forests, craggy sea cliffs and small villages that still follow the ancient rhythms of rural life. For Estonians there's an ineffable magic to Saaremaa's old windmills, flower-strewn meadows and folkloric history that dates back many centuries. One of the country's most impressive castles rises above the picturesque town of Kuressaare – the island's biggest settlement – and the mazelike corridors within are packed with Estonian treasures. Saaremaa is also known for its earthy cuisine, from rye bread made from old family recipes to smoked fish sold from tiny markets, alongside some of the best farmhouse beer brewed in the Baltics.

JAANIPÄEV

The roaring bonfire sends sparks high into the sky as flames dance on the logs. A violinist and a pair of guitar-playing crooners belt out folk tunes, while couples twirl barefoot across the grass. A group of children scamper through the woods nearby in search of the fern flower, said to bloom only on this night. Though it's just after 10pm, the sun hangs low over the horizon on this warm June evening. It's Jaanipäev, Midsummer's Eve, which brings friends and families together during one of the most important holidays in Estonia. Here on Saaremaa, it is a night full of magic, symbolism and unbridled possibility. Earlier, when the bonfire was smaller, daring souls took turns leaping over the flames – a way of guaranteeing prosperity for the year ahead (assuming you didn't fall in). Some believe that the bonfire celebration dates back to ancient times, when meteorites landed on the island – part of the Baltic mythology of the sun falling onto the Earth.

Bled Island

COUNTRY SLOVENIA • **COORDINATES** 46.362° N, 14.090° E • **AREA** 1.45 SQ KM (0.55 SQ MILES)

Starlet of many an Instagram mood board, tear-shaped Bled Island is insanely good-looking – and one of its biggest thrills is travelling to it, by old-fashioned rowing boat or traditional *pletna* crafted by an artisan shipwright across the water in Bled town.

Slovenia's natural majesty is legendary, and the setting for this green-thinking country's smallest speck of an islet is no exception: the serene, shimmering emerald and cobalt-blue water of Lake Bled, against a godlike backdrop of medieval castle clinging to rocky cliff and the soaring peaks of the Julian Alps and Karavanke mountains. Tourists swarm here in July and August, for undeniably good reason.

Bled Island itself is steeped in folkloric belief: this is where ancient pagans built a temple to Živa, the Slavic goddess of fertility. Since the 17th century, gallant grooms carry their bride up the 99 stone steps leading from the water's edge to the island's inland Church of the Assumption, while anyone keen to see their desires come true rings the 'wishing bell' inside the baroque chapel's 52m-tall (171ft) bell tower.

BOATING LAKE BLED

Cruising across silky lake waters aboard a traditional wooden *pletna* (a flat-bottomed boat with a colourful candy-striped awning) has been the only way to access Bled Island since the 16th century. Evocative of a Venetian gondola, these silent hand-crafted boats with wide stern and pointed bow are navigated by a *pletnar* who rows with two oars standing up. Each *pletna* is typically 7m (23ft) long and 2m (6.5ft) wide, and carries up to 20 passengers.

Pletna are built by hand in artisan boatyards in Bled, can't be sold, and belong to a handful of multigenerational boating families. The profession of oarsman has been hereditary – and exclusively male – since 1740 when Empress Maria Theresa granted 23 local families the right to transport religious pilgrims across the lake to worship on Bled Island. Those same families ferry snap-happy tourists today.

1. A traditional *pletna* ferries passengers to Bled Island

2. Paddleboading silky-smooth Lake Bled

3. Phytoplankton algae in crimson bloom around Bled Island

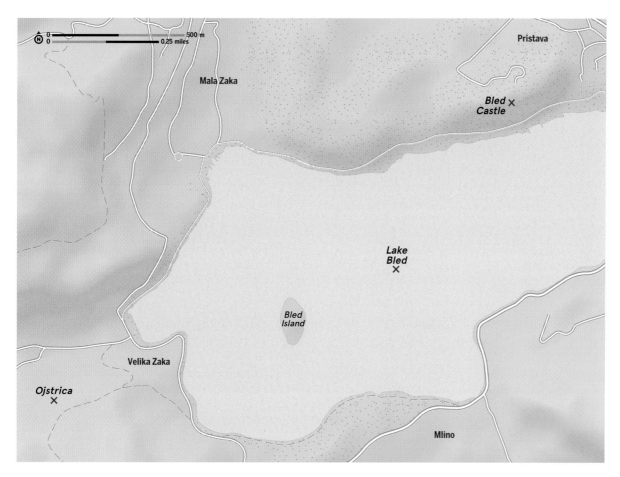

X MARKS THE SPOT

Bled Castle Gorge on dress-circle views from the island of Bled's iconic, 11th- to 16th-century fortress, towering high on a cliff above Lake Bled.

Lake Bled Admire the island from every angle: along the 6km (3.7-mile) footpath encircling Lake Bled, or take to a stand-up paddleboard or old-fashioned rowing boat.

Algal Blooming See Lake Bled turn red each March, when phytoplankton algae in the water blossoms. The milder the winter, the 'redder' the sun-blazed water appears.

Ojstrica Hike up this pointy peak (611m/2004ft) for spectacular bird's-eye views of Bled Island – sunrise or sunset are particularly phenomenal.

White Water Lily From June to September, endangered water lilies bathe Lake Bled in a profusion of exquisite white blooms.

Sicily

COUNTRY ITALY

COORDINATES 37.600° N, 14.015° E • AREA 25,711 SQ KM (9927 SQ MILES)

The largest island in the Mediterranean has long been at the centre of history, with the Greeks, Romans, Arabs and Normans just some of the cultures that have influenced its coastal cities, hilltop villages and rugged and mountainous interior. In the 21st century, Palermo and Catania are diverse and cosmopolitan cities, and still at the centre of European and world history with their acceptance of more recent refugee arrivals fleeing war and social deprivation in nations to the south. Forever the eternal crossroads of the Med, the cuisine, culture and history of the island all combine to make it a unique part of Italy. Welcome to a place where most people will definitely say they're 'Sicilian first and Italian second'.

SICILY'S MOORISH MENU

At the strategic and trading heart of the Mediterranean, Sicily has long been washed over and conquered by different civilisations, and this ongoing interaction and influence has ensured the development of one of Europe's most interesting culinary scenes. Ingredients, cooking styles and recipes all provide echoes of past centuries, with the use of mint and almonds both descended from the island's Arab rule in the 9th and 10th centuries. Spicy couscous, infused with saffron and local seafood, is a popular dish in the western city of Trapani, while even the names of iconic Sicilian desserts like *cannoli* and *cassata* can be traced back to Arab words. Venture to the food and produce markets of Catania, and the industrious ambience is equal parts Southern Europe and North Africa, with stallholders conversing and bartering in a local slang laced with a few archaic Arab phrases. Order *pasta con le sarde* (pasta with sardines) in a simple Palermo trattoria, and your relaxed lunch will come with pine nuts, raisins and fennel. Welcome to a seamless fusion of Italian and Arabic cuisine.

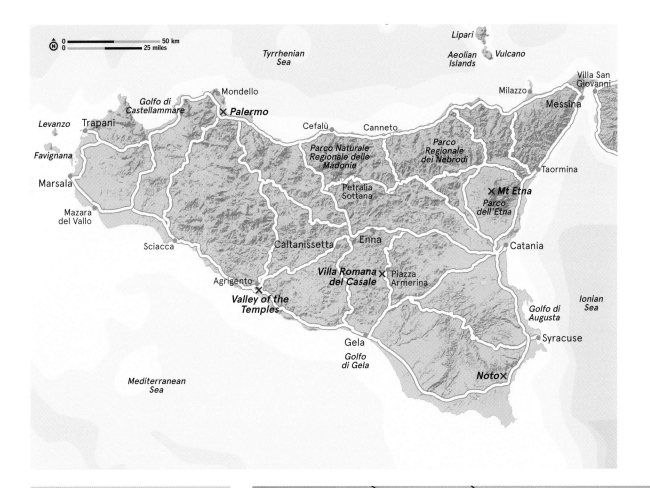

0 — 50 km
0 — 25 miles

Tyrrhenian Sea

Lipari
Aeolian Islands
Vulcano

Levanzo
Favignana
Trapani
Golfo di Castellammare
Mondello
✕ *Palermo*
Cefalù
Canneto
Milazzo
Villa San Giovanni
Messina

Marsala
Mazara del Vallo
Parco Naturale Regionale delle Madonie
Parco Regionale dei Nebrodi
Taormina

Sciacca
Petralia Sottana
✕ *Mt Etna*
Parco dell'Etna

Caltanissetta
Enna
Catania

Agrigento
Villa Romana del Casale ✕ Piazza Armerina

✕
Valley of the Temples

Golfo di Augusta
Ionian Sea

Gela
Golfo di Gela

Syracuse

Mediterranean Sea

Noto ✕

© Jonathan Stokes | Lonely Planet; © Alexander Nikiforov | Getty Images

X MARKS THE SPOT

Palermo Centuries of cultural exchanges influence the markets and street food of Palermo's gritty and fascinating capital.

Mt Etna From the world's finest pistachios to an excellent wine scene, Mt Etna's stop-start schedule of volcanic activity ensures a fertile agricultural hinterland.

Valley of the Temples Located high above the Mediterranean, Agrigento's Valley of the Temples is a legacy of Sicily's Greek period, some 2500 years ago.

Villa Romana del Casale With artworks depicting hunting and chariot races, history comes alive in the superbly restored floor mosaics of this former Roman emperor's mansion.

Noto Competing purveyors of the finest gelato and granita vie for visitors' attention amid the honey-coloured architecture of this baroque hill town.

1. Ragusa Ibla in southern Sicily

2. Funivia dell'Etna cable car to Etna volcano

3. Palermo market

Elba

COUNTRY ITALY

COORDINATES 42.778° N, 10.192° E • **AREA** 224 SQ KM (86 SQ MILES)

According to legend, the islands of the Tuscan archipelago are jewels dropped from Aphrodite's necklace. Elba, just 10km (6 miles) offshore, is the largest in the chain, set between Corsica and the mainland. Although Napoleon wasn't too entranced when he was exiled here in 1814, Elba's combination of sandy beaches and coves, translucent waters, rugged interior and traditional villages is magical nonetheless. You can spend your day hiking along paths through chestnut woods where wild boar and mouflon snuffle in the scrub before descending along rocky paths to a secluded cove lapped by azure water, where you can reward yourself with a swim and a homemade pistachio ice-cream from a traditional gelateria. Laze on the beach, kayak, dive, mountain-bike or tour the vineyards and olive groves: this is quintessential Tuscany.

FESTA DELL'UVA

The iron-rich hillsides, rich variety of soils and sunny slopes provide ideal conditions for the cultivation of grape vines, grown on Elba since Etruscan times. Pliny the Elder described the island as *'insula vini ferax'* (the 'island that produces a lot of wine') and although only a fraction of the original vineyards remain, those that do have been lovingly brought back to life by small-scale vintners intent on producing the finest quality wines. The whole process is celebrated in spectacular style in the handsome village of Capoliveri during the first weekend of October, when the harvest festival sees the town's four districts working with stage designers and actors to create a little cinema-style history. The lavish sets, costumed events and trade and craft demonstrations transform the medieval streets, but only when the winning district is crowned do the real festivities commence. A parade featuring a giant statue of Bacchus acts as a signal for the wine to flow, a feast of local dishes to emerge and the music and dancing to begin.

❶

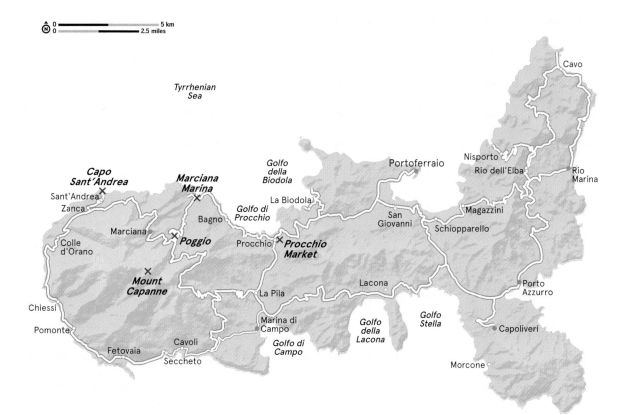

0 — 5 km
0 — 2.5 miles

Tyrrhenian Sea

Cavo

Capo Sant'Andrea

Sant'Andrea
Zanca

Marciana Marina

Golfo della Biodola

Portoferraio

Nisporto
Rio dell'Elba

Rio Marina

La Biodola

Bagno

Golfo di Procchio

Marciana

Colle d'Orano

Poggio

Procchio

Procchio Market

San Giovanni

Magazzini

Schiopparello

Mount Capanne

Lacona

Porto Azzurro

Chiessi

La Pila

Pomonte

Marina di Campo

Golfo della Lacona

Golfo Stella

Fetovaia

Cavoli

Golfo di Campo

Capoliveri

Seccheto

Morcone

X MARKS THE SPOT

Mt Capanne A network of trails winds up the island's highest peak, offering views as far as Corsica on a clear day.

Procchio Market Twice a week this village springs to life with a showcase of Elba's finest wine, oil, cheese and honey.

Capo Sant'Andrea This wild, mountainous corner of the island has steep chestnut forests for hiking and pinnacles, reefs and wrecks for diving.

Poggio Steep, cobbled laneways lined by tall stone houses lead to sweeping views of the shoreline in the island's prettiest mountain village.

Marciana Marina Calm waters, rugged cliffs and secluded coves make this an excellent spot for kayaking trips.

1. Napoleon's bicorne

2. Elba coastline

3. *Pelagia noctiluca* jellyfish in Elba's gin-clear waters

Burano & Mazzorbo

COUNTRY ITALY
COORDINATES 45.485° N, 12.416° E • **AREA** 0.5 SQ KM (0.2 SQ MILES)

It's said that the vibrant houses strung along the slender canals in Burano and Mazzorbo were washed in eye-popping colours to help Venetian fishermen find home safely on deeply, eerily misty days. Across this delightful twinset of islands in the northern Venice lagoon, tiny bridges criss-cross shimmering canals and a swirl of mango-yellow, dusty-red, sky-blue and pearly pink buildings glint back from the water. Beautiful Burano is known for its hand-stitched lace, still crafted here by around a hundred local women, while the less-visited former agricultural hub of Mazzorbo is awash with vineyards that include the rare Dorona grape. As in other parts of Venice, growing depopulation and uncontrolled tourism have become major concerns, with island residents leaving for the city's mainland in their droves. Show your support for on-the-ground initiatives by learning all about traditional crafts with a local expert (from fishing to lacework to gastronomy) and exploring outside peak times, perhaps with an overnight stay.

MAZZORBO WINES

Years ago, Venice's islands were filled with fragrant vineyards, vegetable crops and fruit orchards, and life revolved around the lagoon's ancient northern settlements. Struck by disease and, later, by the devastating 1966 Venice flood, many local families abandoned their ancient crops, and Mazzorbo's agricultural and winemaking heritage fell into decline. Now, thanks to the groundbreaking work of winemaker Gianluca Bisol at his Michelin-starred hotel-restaurant Venissa (venissa.it), the almost-extinct Dorona di Venezia grape is being ingeniously revived in a 800-year-old waterside estate specialising in traditionally made macerated wines. Over the centuries, these autochthonous vines have adapted to the salty lagoon waters, and yield earthy whites with a strong resemblance to red wines. The walled Venissa vineyard is open for visitors to stroll around; better yet, book into one of the handful of freshly styled, wood-beamed guestrooms and wake up to sprawling early morning views across the glowing lagoon.

X MARKS THE SPOT

Piazza Baldassarre Galuppi Burano's main square is home to the 16th-century Chiesa di San Martino, with its leaning Pisa-style tower.

Bridge From the northwest tip of Burano, a wood-panelled walkway stretches across to Mazzorbo just over the water.

Chiesa di Santa Caterina One of the oldest bell towers on the lagoon awaits at Mazzorbo's 13th-century church, built in Romanesque style.

Venissa This forward-thinking Mazzorbo winery is credited with rescuing the Dorona grape from extinction.

Mazzorbetto Get a glimpse of Mazzorbo's agricultural past at this sparsely populated neighbouring island.

1. Burano lace

2. Canalside colour in Burano

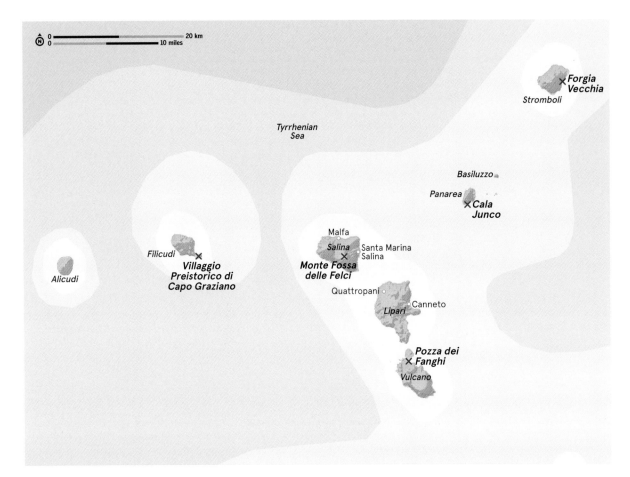

Forgia
Vecchia
Stromboli

Tyrrhenian
Sea

Basiluzzo

Panarea
Cala
Junco

Malfa
Salina
Santa Marina
Salina
Monte Fossa
delle Felci

Quattropani
Canneto
Lipari

Filicudi
Villaggio
Preistorico di
Capo Graziano

Alicudi

Pozza dei
Fanghi
Vulcano

1. Shimmering Aeolian
views: Vulcano Island
from Lipari

2. Crater on Vulcano

Aeolian Islands

COUNTRY ITALY
COORDINATES 38.493° N, 14.927° E • **AREA** 115 SQ KM (44 SQ MILES)

It's only fitting that a string of islands named after Greek god Aeolus, keeper of the winds and king of the mythical floating island of Aeolia, are as otherworldly as their divinity-inspired name implies. Aeolians – the inhabitants of the Aeolian Islands that rise out of the cobalt-blue seas off Sicily's northeastern coast – certainly seem to have mastered the enviable Italian life concept of *dolce far niente* (meaning 'sweet idleness' or 'pleasure in the moment') admirably well.

The landscape of these seven Mediterranean islands – Lipari, Vulcano, Salina, Stromboli, Filicudi, Alicudi and Panarea – mirrors a marvellous picture-book universe of black-sand beaches, wild moors, cliff-cradled coves and magical blue waters. Hissing volcanoes (Stromboli), hot mud (Vulcano), Greek and Roman shipwrecks (Filicudi), donkey-fuelled villages (Alicudi) and five millennia of history create sufficient drama and suspense to keep island explorers happy for days.

LIGHTHOUSE OF THE MEDITERRANEAN

Stromboli has been lighting up the night sky with its volcanic rumblings, explosive fireworks and lava bombs for the last 200,000 years, hence its evocative moniker 'Lighthouse of the Mediterranean'. Volcanic activity scars much of the same-name island, the northeastern corner of which is dotted with black beaches and the whitewashed town of Stromboli on the volcano's lower slopes. But despite the picture-postcard appearance, life here is tough: food and drinking water are ferried in, there are no roads across the island, and until relatively recently Ginostra,

the diminutive second settlement on Stromboli's isolated west coast, had no electricity.

During active periods volcanic explosions occur every 20 minutes or so and are preceded by a humongous belly-roar as gases force hot magma into the air. A hike from Stromboli's port up to the Sciara del Fuoco viewpoint unveils a dramatic perspective of the blackened laval scar running down Stromboli's northern flank. Cascades of red-hot rock crash down the mountainside into the sea and, come dark, the volcano's powerful flame-orange beacon lights up the night sky.

X MARKS THE SPOT

Monte Fossa delle Felci, Salina The Aeolians' highest point (962m/3156ft) on Salina, with jaw-dropping views of the archipelago's second-largest island and its extinct volcano twinset.

Forgia Vecchia The best of Stromboli's black-pebble volcanic beaches.

Cala Junco A crystalline cove on the island of Panarea, with dramatic headlands and ruins of a Bronze Age village.

Pozza dei Fanghi Warm mud baths on Vulcano, stinking of rotten eggs and the perfect partner to neighbouring hot-bubbling springs and crystal-clear seawater pool.

Villaggio Preistorico di Capo Graziano These lichen-covered stone foundations of 27 Bronze Age huts, on a terraced hillside on Filicudi, date to 1700 BCE.

Corsica

COUNTRY FRANCE • **COORDINATES** 42.039° N, 9.012° E • **AREA** 8722 SQ KM (3367 SQ MILES)

It has been part of France for more than 200 years, but wild and fiercely proud Corsica (Corse or L'Île de Beauté, meaning the 'Island of Beauty') is dramatically different from the mainland. Be it customs, culture, cuisine or language, a unique Corsican identity oozes out of every last pretty hilltop village, harmonious polyphonic song and haunting *lamentu* (lament) listened to over a glass of blood-red Cap Corse Mattei.

Corsica's natural landscape is kaleidoscopic. Its sandy beaches and gold-crescent coves, thick forests and verdant valleys, sawtooth mountain ridges and rocky promontories are heaven for outdoor explorers. Immense geographical diversity is also the backbone of the island's compelling multifaceted history. Begin at ground zero with the enigmatic 'Sea People'.

MEGALITHIC ART

Ducking and diving around granite monoliths dotting the countryside around Filitosa in southern Corsica is a lesson in megalithic history. The archaeological site remains shrouded in mystery, but it offers living proof that humans have inhabited the island since the dawn of civilisation.

Why the menhirs (standing stones) here are carved with human faces or armed with crude daggers and swords remains an enigma. Prehistoric peoples erected stone monuments along Europe's entire Mediterranean and Atlantic coastlines, but Corsica is the only place to boast 2m- to 3m-tall (6.5ft to 9.8ft) menhirs bearing individual human likenesses or entire human figures armed with weapons.

Archaeologists believe the island's megalithic artists could have been the 'Sea People' – long-standing enemies of the ancient Egyptian pharaohs – who sailed west across the Mediterranean to Corsica during the Bronze Age, and re-carved already-ancient monuments in their own image before slipping back into obscurity. Some they destroyed to build their own *torri* (circular monuments), the purpose of which is unclear: to mark a communal tomb, to delineate territory or to commemorate a warrior or chieftain?

1. Hillside town of Corte

2. Switchback road in Les Calanques de Piana

3. Corsica coastline

X MARKS THE SPOT

Îles Lavezzi *Oui*, more islands – but these uninhabited white-sand isles off Corsica's southern shore have more than a hint of the Seychelles.

Escalier du Roi d'Aragon A daredevil staircase of 187 steps, cut spectacularly into a southern cliffface dangling above the sea, in Bonifacio.

Les Calanques de Piana Bring sunglasses. The blazing red glare of these extraordinary and fantastical rock formations is dazzling.

Réserve Naturelle de Scandola A boat is the only way into this majestic wilderness of russet-hued cliffs, clandestine coves, precious red coral and intoxicating maquis (herbal scrub).

Aiguilles de Bavella A ribbon of serrated 'needles' in the L'Alta Rocca mountain wilderness, soaring up to 1600m (5249ft) in endless hypnotic shades of grey.

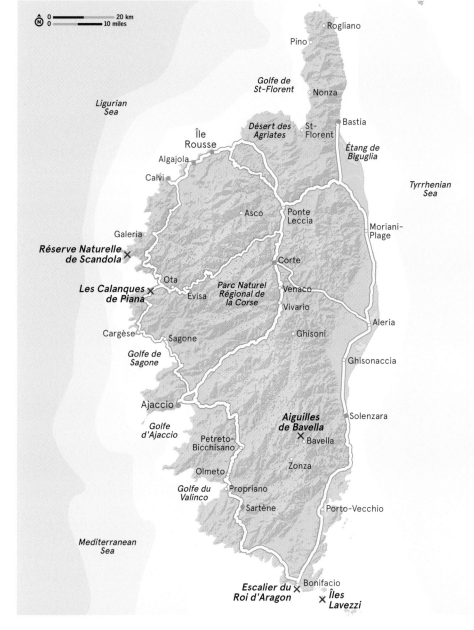

Sardinia

COUNTRY ITALY • **COORDINATES** 40.120° N, 9.012° E • **AREA** 24,090 SQ KM (9301 SQ MILES)

The largest island in the Mediterranean after Sicily, Sardinia is the feisty, brilliantly moody and charismatic offspring of conquest and occupation. Power-hungry masters were numerous prior to the island becoming part of unified Italy in 1861, yet the Sards never let time or the elements erase their brilliant story. The fierce passion and pride in Sardinian culture and heritage, the stubborn fraternity, the infectious zeal for *la festa* (party) and the slow food ethic that every islander shares is compelling. Think beyond flopping on the dreamiest white beaches on European shores. Exploring this natural habitat is a wild adventure, with vertiginous coastal paths and spectacular cliff-cradled bays, rugged mountains and sheep-specked hinterland, remote hilltop villages, Neolithic tombs and medieval cities riddled in mystery.

NURAGHI CIVILISATION

The 7000-odd *nuraghi* scattered across Sardinia like pieces of a jigsaw puzzle waiting to be discovered are the tip of the iceberg. Archaeologists believe at least the same number again of these unfathomable stone towers and 'fortresses' from the Bronze Age remain buried underground. Watchtower, sacred temple, communal meeting place: their precise purpose is unknown. But the precision with which these archaic structures were constructed from cut stone and zero mortar between 1800 and 500 BCE is testimony to the sophistication, skill and mettle of Sardinia's highly cultured Nuragic civilisation.

The island's most prized Nuraghi sight, the Unesco-listed Nuraghe Su Nuraxi, lies in voluptuous green hills of La Marmilla in southwestern Sardinia. Its signature stone tower, 18.6m (61ft) tall with three floors upon completion in 1500 BCE, originally stood alone but was subsequently incorporated into a fortified compound, with huge defensive walls and multiple towers. A beehive of circular interlocking buildings tumbling down the hillside date to the Iron Age. Equally enigmatic are the island's *pozzi sacri* (sacred wells) and *tombe dei giganti* (giants' tombs), megalithic mass graves sealed off by stone stele.

1. The north-coast town of Castelsardo

2. Sardinian vineyard

3. Cala Goloritze on the Golfo di Orosei

X MARKS THE SPOT

Golfo di Orosei Where the mountains collide with the sea, this sweeping crescent forms the seaward section of the Parco Nazionale del Golfo di Orosei e del Gennargentu.

Gola Su Gorropu Europe's Grand Canyon, this ravine transcends space and time with its 400m-high (1312ft) rock walls, eerie light and giant boulders strewn like marbles.

Parco Nazionale dell'Asinara Natural habitat of the blue-eyed albino donkey, this wildlife-strewn national park is one of Sardinia's richest coastal wildernesses.

Spiaggia del Principe A perfect moon of pearl-white sand and emerald water on Sardinia's sensational Costa Smeralda.

Mamoiada Stone-and-stucco village host to Sardinia's most eccentric carnival parade: ghoulish *mamuthones* don sheepskins and beastly wooden masks to banish winter demons.

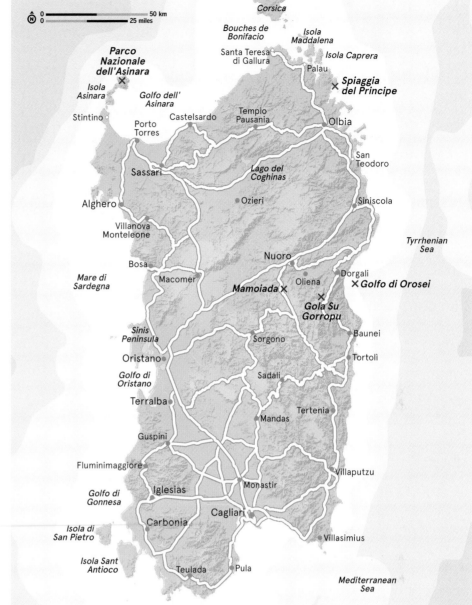

Crete

COUNTRY GREECE

COORDINATES 35.240° N, 24.809° E • **AREA** 8450 SQ KM (3262 SQ MILES)

A mythical island closely tied to Greek legend, Crete is both the birthplace of Zeus and the home of the minotaur. Sitting about 160km (100 miles) south of the mainland, it is the largest of the Greek islands: a rocky, mountainous place, fringed by sandy coves and beaches, riven by canyons and littered with architectural glories. The Bronze Age Minoans built a sophisticated civilisation here and the remains of their temples, palaces and cities date back almost 4000 years. They're joined by Byzantine churches, Venetian harbours and Turkish baths in atmospheric port towns once key to Mediterranean trade. But it's the sheer variety of things to do here which is most impressive: in a single day you can cycle between vineyards, orchards and olive groves; hike to deserted beaches; gorge on sardines and raki; or tackle corkscrew roads that rise into wild mountains then drop into deep-blue bays.

HIKING SITIA GEOPARK

Hot, dry and rugged, the wild and remote landscape around Sitia in eastern Crete is riddled with fossils, extensive cave systems, underground rivers and limestone karsts. As you hike its rocky trails the scent of thyme, broom, sage and juniper fill the air, while the landscape unfolds in a blanket of golds, greens and blues. Traditional stone houses and small chapels dot the trails that lead to Minoan quarries and palaces, deserted beaches and steep ravines and canyons. Follow coastal trails to arrive at dunes covered in cedar groves and forests of carob, hike down craggy gorges to isolated coves or trace the trail of the dry riverbed flanked by steep slopes pitted with ancient cave-burial sites. It's a region of Crete little-visited by others where the small villages, warm welcome and deliciously simple food seem to embody the very soul of the island.

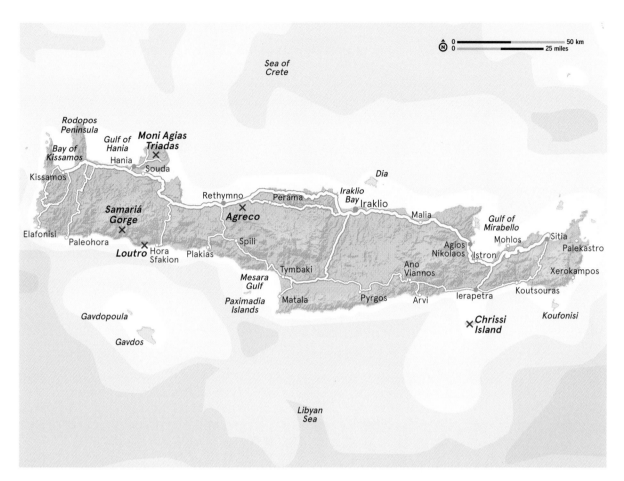

0   50 km
0   25 miles

Sea of Crete

Rodopos Peninsula
Gulf of Hania
Moni Agias Triadas ✕
Bay of Kissamos
Hania
Souda
Kissamos
Dia
Rethymno   Perama
Iraklio Bay
Iraklio
Elafonisi
Samariá Gorge ✕
Agreco ✕
Malia
Gulf of Mirabello
Paleohora
Mohlos
Sitia
Loutro ✕   Hora Sfakion
Spili
Plakias
Agios Nikolaos
Istron
Palekastro
Tymbaki
Ano Viannos
Ierapetra
Xerokampos
Mesara Gulf
Matala   Pyrgos   Arvi   Koutsouras
Paximadia Islands
Koufonisi
Gavdopoula
Chrissi Island ✕
Gavdos
Libyan Sea

X MARKS THE SPOT

Loutro Basking between sapphire seas and steep mountains, this scenic fishing village is only accessible on foot or by sea.

Samaria Gorge Tackle this tough 16km (10-mile) hike through a striking canyon where sheer cliffs soar 300m (984ft) above.

Agreco Tread grapes, press olives or milk the goats at this organic farm built in 17th-century style.

Moni Agias Triadas Convene with holy spirits of one kind or another at this Venetian-influenced monastery where the monks make and sell their own wine, oil and raki.

Chrissi Island Golden beaches, cedar forests and Minoan ruins face dappled waters on this uninhabited island.

1. View out to the Aegean from Hania's port

2. Cretan vineyards

3. Traditional taverna lunch

Ionian Islands

COUNTRY GREECE • **COORDINATES** 38.249° N, 20.624° E • **AREA** 2307 SQ KM (891 SQ MILES)

A chain of islands along the west and south coast of the Greek mainland, the Ionians combine lush valleys and mountains with deep blue seas and a rich history that has left them strewn with Greek temples, Venetian forts, Parisian-style arcades and picture-pretty fishing villages. The Greeks, Romans, Byzantines, Venetians, Neapolitans and even the British ruled here over the years and the islands are quite distinct in culture, architecture and cuisine, making them wonderfully varied to explore. Kefallonia and Corfu are probably the best known, and much loved for their vineyards, mountains and architecture. The sandy beaches of Lefkada and the Italianate fishing villages of Paxi see far fewer visitors, while the Ithaki wilderness is great for hiking and climbing. Zakynthos is known for its sea caves and turtles, and off-the-beaten-track Kythira has green valleys, spectacular gorges and bright-blue seas.

THE HORSES OF AINOS

On the high, rocky slopes of Mt Ainos in Kefallonia, a herd of semi-wild horses roams the forests. Descended from the ancient Greek mountain pony, the Pindos, but now thought to have evolved into a separate breed, they were brought here from the mainland by villagers but abandoned after WWII. Today, only a small group survives. The lack of water, food and shelter, and the harsh winters mean their numbers have rapidly dwindled to a point where they're considered endangered. The horses are shy but extremely surefooted – if you spot them running across the slopes you'll marvel at their ability to navigate the rocky terrain. Their small number and reserved nature make them difficult to see, but your best chance is to go to the Zoodohos Pigi Monastery near the village of Arginia at sunset when the horses often go to drink from a freshwater spring, the only one in the area.

X MARKS THE SPOT

Petani Beach, Kefallonia Cradled by cliffs and lapped by glittering waters, this is one of Greece's finest beaches.

Logothetis Organic Farm, Zakynthos Discover how olive oil is extracted, take a cooking lesson, or stay overnight to explore the island by bike or on horseback from this idyllic organic farm.

Mon Repos, Corfu The wooded site of Corfu's most important ancient settlement, Palaeopolis, with ancient ruins and a clifftop Doric temple.

Gidaki, Ithaki This white-pebble beach with sapphire waters is accessible only on foot or by boat.

Windsurfing, Lefkada Fly on the dependable thermal winds that make Lefkada one of Europe's top wind- and kite-surfing hubs.

1. Ancient Greek temple

2. Assos village, Kefallonia

3. Olives ripening in the Ionian sunshine

© Szymon Mucha | Alamy Stock Photo. © Paweł Kazmierczak | Shutterstock

Milos

COUNTRY GREECE
COORDINATES 36.691° N, 24.393° E • **AREA** 160 SQ KM (62 SQ MILES)

Despite being fringed by some of the finest beaches in the Aegean and littered with geological wonders, Milos receives less attention than some of the other Cyclades islands, a chain sitting southeast of the Greek mainland. Its unusual geology has made it an attraction since Neolithic times when obsidian was mined here, and along with a ruined amphitheatre, you'll find labyrinthine early Christian catacombs, hot springs, rock arches, coastal caves and about 70 glorious beaches with sands that range from white to pink, orange and gold. Milos' most famous export is the *Venus de Milo*, now in the Louvre in Paris, but stay here for even a few days and you'll be smitten by its quintessential island charm, vivid colours, varied landscape and complete lack of pretension.

SLOW FOOD MILOS STYLE

Slow food is no trendy fad in Milos, it's just how things have always been done. Cross the hills on foot and you'll be hit by the scent of sage, thyme and oregano; linger by the waterfront to see the fishing boats pour in with fresh octopus, shrimp and lobster; or pluck a juicy red tomato and you'll find the long sunny days make them some of the sweetest you'll ever have tasted. The island's many family-run tavernas are now attracting attention from Athenians once lured by the gourmet glitz of Santorini or Sifnos, and there's no better place to try traditional Melian food than the legendary O! Hamos, where homemade bread hangs from a string bag on your chair and all the meat, cheese, fruit and vegetables come from their own farm. You may have to queue, but it's worth it to sample the *aginares miliotikes* (fried artichoke with eggs, onion and dill), the *gourounopoulo metimezako* (slow-roasted piglet in molasses-mustard) or *melitzana boulouka* (lamb- and goat-stuffed aubergine with tomato, garlic and local cheese).

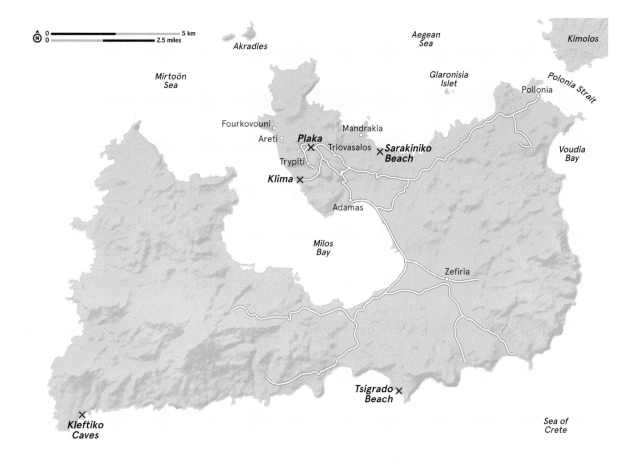

X MARKS THE SPOT

Sarakiniko Beach A lunar-like landscape of bleached and weathered rock frames sparkling waters in this narrow inlet.

Plaka Far-reaching views reward those who make it to this Venetian hilltop fortress in the island's car-free capital.

Kleftiko Caves Hop in a boat to swim through sapphire waters in the tunnels and caves of the dazzling white rock here.

Klima Colourful fishermen's *syrma* (boathouses topped by living quarters) are dug into the cliffs here above perfectly clear seas.

Tsigrado Beach It's worth the squeeze down a narrow rock channel and a descent-by-ladder to reach this crescent beach flanked by high cliffs.

1. The Agios Nikolaos chapel in Pollonia, at Milos' northeast tip

2. Swimming at sun-baked Sarakiniko

3. Checking the nets in Pollonia

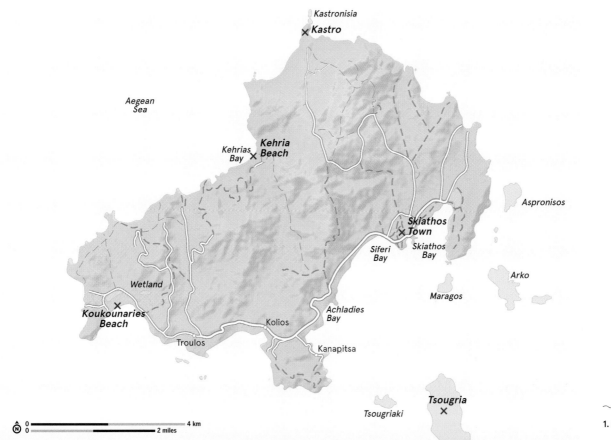

Kastronisia
× **Kastro**

*Aegean
Sea*

Kehrias
Bay × **Kehria
Beach**

**Skiathos
Town** ×
Skiathos
Bay

Siferi
Bay

Aspronisos

Arko

Maragos

Wetland

×
**Koukounaries
Beach**

Kolios

Troulos

Achladies
Bay

Kanapitsa

Tsougriaki

Tsougria
×

0   4 km
Ⓝ 0   2 miles

~~~~~~~~~~
1. Skiathos waterfront

2. Skiathos Town

Skiathos

COUNTRY GREECE
COORDINATES 39.163° N, 23.490° E • **AREA** 50 SQ KM (19 SQ MILES)

Eyes closed, picture the Greek beach of your dreams. A glinting pebble-studded cove? A luscious stretch of powdery white sand? A rocky sea-hugging outcrop at sunset? Skiathos is all this, and much more. Birthplace of the great 19th-century Greek writer Alexandros Papadiamantis and a key location during the Greek War of Independence, this history-rich pine-scented island sits just off mainland Greece, halfway between Athens and Thessaloniki, in the glittering Sporades. The small and relaxed capital, Skiathos Town, reveals a jumble of white-walled streets and traditional island architecture, while ancient monasteries lie tucked away in the hushed mountains and the unbelievably beautiful coastline unfolds in a series of blissful strands backed by rolling olive groves. Escape to the cliff-edged northern coast, whose craggy hills sweep down to secluded silver-pebble coves where family-owned tavernas have been serving up feta-loaded salads, crisp golden chips and platters of super-fresh seafood for years.

SKIATHOS MONASTERIES

Long before its beachy tourism scene kicked off, Skiathos was an island inhabited by wandering monks, skilled shipbuilders and freedom fighters, as well as remote mountain monasteries where winemaking was considered an essential chore. The island fell under Ottoman rule in the early 16th century, but throughout the 1820s, during the Greek War of Independence, it became an important refuge for Greek resistance fighters seeking self-rule. It was at the 18th-century Moni Evangelistrias, hidden in the lush mountains near Skiathos Town, that the Greek flag was first raised back in 1807 by key revolutionaries including Theodoros Kolokotronis and Andreas Miaoulis. Today's serene monastery, with its local-crafts shop and view-laden vineyards, feels worlds away from its turbulent past. Further afield, in the forested heart of the island, peaceful Moni Panagias Kounistras dates from the 17th century and is filled with swirling frescoes; according to legend, a local monk found a figure of the Virgin Mary swinging from a tree here.

X MARKS THE SPOT

Skiathos Town The island's whitewashed, pebble-floored capital, with lively tavernas, boho-chic boutiques and the former home of the Greek novelist Alexandros Papadiamantis.

Koukounaries Beach Backed by a protected lagoon, this pale-gold pine-studded sandy beauty is Skiathos' most beloved beach.

Kastro Byzantines, Venetians and Turks once inhabited the ruined former capital, perched on the northwest tip of the island.

Kehria Beach A jewel of a pebble cove clinging to the north coast, with its own fabulous taverna.

Tsougria Seasonal taxi-boats sail out from Skiathos Town to this delightful beach-fringed islet.

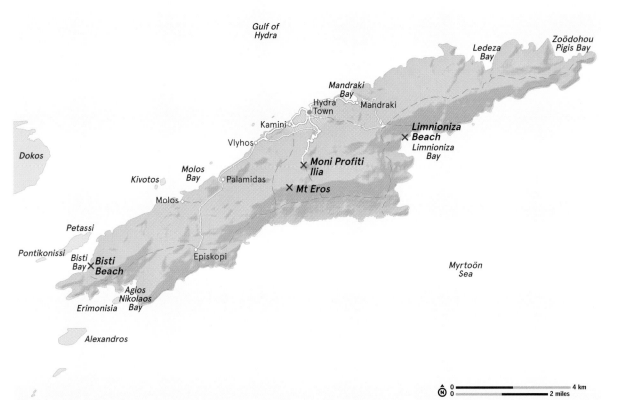

Gulf of Hydra

Zoödohou Pigis Bay

Ledeza Bay

Mandraki Bay

Mandraki

Hydra Town

Kamini

Limnioniza Beach

Limnioniza Bay

Vlyhos

Dokos

Molos Bay

Kivotos

× Moni Profiti Ilia

Palamidas

× **Mt Eros**

Molos

Myrtoön Sea

Petassi

Pontikonissi

Bisti Bay × **Bisti Beach**

Episkopi

Agios Nikolaos Bay

Erimonisia

Alexandros

0 —— 4 km
Ⓝ 0 —— 2 miles

1. Sunset over Hydra's picture-perfect port

2. Hydra harbour

Hydra

COUNTRY GREECE
COORDINATES 37.328° N, 23.471° E • **AREA** 64 SQ KM (25 SQ MILES)

It is not without deep irony that this idyllic Greek island, named after its abundance of freshwater springs and streams in antiquity, should now need to import drinking water – all 3.5 to 4 million litre bottles a year.

Sitting pretty in the Aegean Sea, a conveniently short boat-hop from Athens and the mainland, the island of Hydra otherwise ticks all the right boxes: no mucky cars, no screeching scooters, a wealth of tranquil cobbled trails winding into the arid mountain interior and an irresistible gaggle of locally bred donkeys, mules and horses.

Streets and local landmarks don't have names here: there is just the 'clock tower at the harbour' or the 'cafe at the port where Leonard Cohen and cronies spun tunes in the 1960s'; and the 'taverna where Mrs Christina and her children cook up the island's finest fresh fish' or the 'hotel that used to be a sponge factory'.

Yes, life on this enchanting Greek isle of whitewashed houses, turquoise waters and teeny pebble beaches is that simple.

TIME-HONOURED ARCHITECTURE

Unlike many touristed spots in Europe, strict preservation orders on Hydra have protected the entire island as a national monument since the 1950s. New swimming pools and vehicles are outlawed, while rigorous building laws ensure that island architecture remains faithful to tradition and reflects the distinctive Hydriot style that first appeared on the island in the 1800s. The beautifully preserved *archontiko* (mansions), built in grey stone on the waterfront of Hydra's town for wealthy ship owners, date from this period. Some famously appear in the 1957 Hollywood classic *Boy on a Dolphin*, starring Italian starlet Sophia Loren as an impoverished Greek sponge diver on Hydra.

X MARKS THE SPOT

Mt Eros The island's highest point at 588m (1929ft), with heart-singing island, coast and sea panoramas.

Moni Profiti Ilia A wonderful hilltop monastery complex, founded by 13 monks in 1813 and dedicated to the Prophet Elias. Views to die for.

Bisti Beach Emerald waters, pine forest, bijou pebble beach and a disproportionately large summer crowd.

Limnioniza Beach Dramatically deep waters not far from shore make this quiet pebble beach a favourite with scuba divers.

Greek Tortoise May and October – mating seasons – are the best months to spot Hydra's favourite reptile.

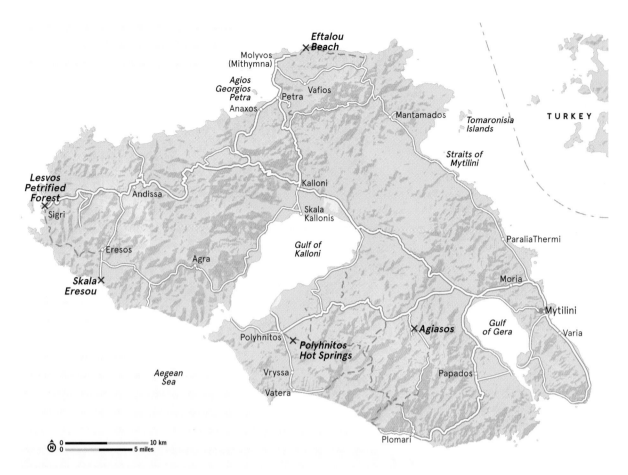

TURKEY

Eftalou
✕ *Beach*
Molyvos
(Mithymna)
Vafios
Agios
Georgios
Petra
Petra
Anaxos
Mantamados
Tomaronisia
Islands

Straits of
Mytilini

Kalloni

Lesvos
Petrified
Forest
Andissa
✕
Sigri

Skala
Kallonis

ParaliaThermi

Gulf of
Kalloni

Eresos
Agra

Skala ✕
Eresou

Moria

Mytilini

Gulf
of Gera
Varia

Polyhnitos
✕ *Polyhnitos*
Hot Springs

✕ *Agiasos*

Aegean
Sea
Vryssa
Papados

Vatera

Plomari

0 _____ 10 km
N 0 _____ 5 miles

1. Fisher prepping his
nets at Lesvos' Skala
Kallonis harbour

2. Classic Greek salad at
Cavo Doro, Sigri

Lesvos

COUNTRY GREECE
COORDINATES 39.264° N, 26.277° E • **AREA** 1633 SQ KM (630 SQ MILES)

Tucked in on the southeast fringe of the EU and separated from Turkey by narrow straits, Greece's third-largest island is an historical melting pot of Christians and Muslims – a former Ottoman Empire outpost and cultural frontier in the Aegean Sea. More recently, Lesvos (also Lesbos in English) made headlines when a devastating fire in 2020 destroyed an overcrowded refugee camp on the island – Europe's largest – leaving 12,000 refugees without canvas above their heads.

Nature's tapestry here is electric. Quiet beaches, serene Byzantine monasteries and rolling hills stitched from pine forests and olive groves dominate the soulful north. The south raises the bar with Lesvos' best beaches and highest peak, Mt Olympus (968m/3176ft), as well as the birthplace of one of Greece's most famous lyric poets, Sappho, dubbed the 10th muse by Plato. Adventurers travelling west find themselves embroiled in a stark primeval landscape, scattered with the giant trunks of fossilised sequoia trees, pistachio nuts and other ancient flora petrified during the Miocene era by violent volcanic eruptions.

OUZO CENTRAL

The island's deep south is a sizzling hot agricultural oasis where production of prized olive oil, wine and ouzo easily outshine tourism: farmers here produce half of the ouzo sold worldwide. The characteristically milky, aniseed-flavoured aperitif has its roots in the grape-based spirit *tsipouro*, made by monks on mainland Greece in the 14th century. Five centuries later Lesvos islanders used copper sills to distil the modern ouzo consumed far beyond island tavernas today. Plomari on Lesvos' southern coast is Greece's ouzo central. Multigenerational distilleries here blend locally grown anise (anise cultivated on organic farms in the hillside village of Lisvori is considered the world's finest) with cinnamon, rosemary, coriander and other herbs to create their own – closely guarded – secret recipes.

When sampling ouzo, look for '100%' written on the label, indicating the quality of the distillate.

X MARKS THE SPOT

Polyhnitos Hot Springs Southern Lesvos' therapeutic hot springs gush with some of the warmest mineral waters in Europe.

Eftalou Beach Cliff-ensnared pebble beach on the northern Lesvos shore, with a vintage Ottoman bathhouse.

Agiasos Religious pilgrims pour into this quirky hamlet of cobbled lanes and traditional *kafeneia* (coffee houses) on 15 August to venerate the miraculous icon dedicated to the Virgin Mary in its church.

Skala Eresou The sensuous poetry of ancient Greek poet Sappho (c 630 BCE) draws lesbians from around the world to the village where she was born.

Lesvos Petrified Forest A patch of petrified forest is preserved inside Sigri's natural history museum in western Lesvos.

Hvar

COUNTRY CROATIA
COORDINATES 43.154° N, 16.652° E • **AREA** 297 SQ KM (115 SQ MILES)

A favourite of the smart set who flock here in summer, Hvar is the sunniest and most glamorous of Croatia's Dalmatian islands. Just 90 minutes from Split by ferry, it's easy to understand why it has such a favourable international reputation. From the marble streets and Gothic and Renaissance palaces of handsome Hvar Town to quiet fishing villages, hidden coves lapped by crystalline waters and a reputation for fine food and wine, it's a glorious place to hang out. Inland, the fields are blanketed in lavender, rosemary and heather, while olives, figs and grapes hang off the trees; and outside the busy summer months, it's easy to find deserted beaches and explore the island's rich Greek, Roman, Byzantine and Venetian influences. Settle down in a whitewashed town, tour the wineries and beaches, dine like a king and soak up some sun – it doesn't get much better than this.

SUMMER SCENTS

In early summer, the rocky fields of Hvar are blanketed in a shimmering purple haze of lavender, which has been cultivated here for about 2500 years. Hvar's long, sunny days and dry soil produce highly prized plants, which are grown in terraces along the island's rocky slopes.

It's a landscape that has remained largely as it was when the island was first colonised by Ionian Greeks in the 4th century BCE; plants are still harvested by hand in traditional ways,

as the terraces are too steep and rugged for modern machinery.

The lavender harvest in late June or early July fills the air with a heady aroma, and is celebrated with a festival in the 14th-century village of Velo Grablje. Join a workshop on lavender-oil distillation, feast on artisan foods, listen to traditional music and browse markets selling everything from freshly picked lavender to scented soaps, and lavender-infused honey, ice-cream or even kombucha.

X MARKS THE SPOT

Hvar Town Marble streets lined with 16th-century palaces, a Renaissance cathedral and a Spanish fort await in the island's capital.

Jelsa Wineries Tour the local vineyards and wine cellars to sample Prošek, a traditional Dalmatian dessert wine.

Pakleni Islands Kayak through turquoise waters around this group of wooded islands known for their secluded coves and beaches.

Stari Grad Plain Cleared and constructed by the ancient Greeks, the stone walls and agricultural terraces here are still in use today.

Vrboska Boats bob in a long, narrow inlet surrounded by Renaissance and Gothic houses in this fishing village on the island's north coast.

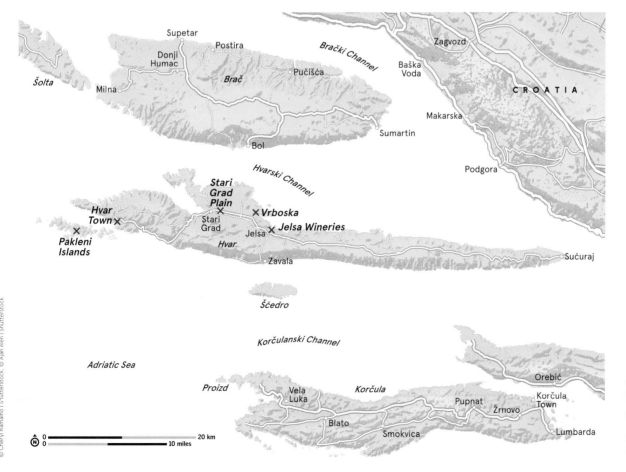

2

Supetar

Postira

Donji Humac

Brački Channel

Zagvozd

Baška Voda

Šolta

Milna

Brač

Pučišća

C R O A T I A

Makarska

Bol

Sumartin

Podgora

Hvarski Channel

Stari Grad Plain

×

Vrboska ×

Hvar Town ×

Stari Grad

Jelsa × **Jelsa Wineries**

×
Pakleni Islands

Hvar

Sućuraj

Zavala

Šćedro

Korčulanski Channel

Adriatic Sea

Proizd

Vela Luka

Korčula

Orebić

Korčula Town

Pupnat

Žrnovo

Blato

Smokvica

Lumbarda

0 — 20 km
0 — 10 miles
N

1. Stone buildings of Stari Grad

2. A bird's-eye view of the Pakleni Islands

Hvar

CROATIA

Šćedro

Ploče

Korčulanski Channel

Neretvanski Channel

Trpanj

Proizd ×

Orebić

Vela Luka

Korčula

Moreška Sword Dance × Korčula Town

Pupnat

Blato

Žrnovo

Smokvica

Pupnatska Luka ×

Lumbarda

Trstenik

Mljetski Channel

Lastovski Channel

Adriatic Sea

Mljet

Pomena

Mrčara

Lastovo

Pasadur

Mljet National Park ×

Kopište

Krućica

0 ___ 10 km
Ⓝ 0 ___ 5 miles

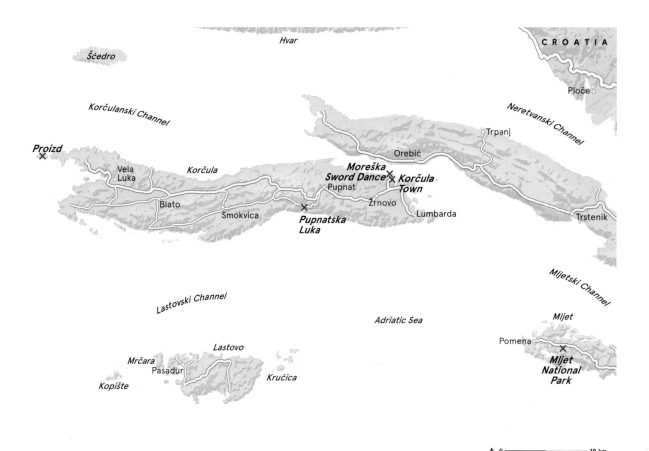

X MARKS THE SPOT

Korčula Town The island's medieval capital is dubbed 'Little Dubrovnik' thanks to its elaborate churches, grand squares and Venetian palaces.

Pupnatska Luka The country's best beach offers white sands and cerulean waters backed by forested slopes.

Mljet National Park Hop on a boat to this nearby park for scenic walking in the forests and kayaking on the lakes.

Moreška Sword Dance One of the island's most colourful traditions lives on as costumed kings duel to music over the love of a princess.

Proizd A small islet off the coast near Vela Luka, Proizd is known for its dazzling white stones and glassy waters.

Korčula

COUNTRY CROATIA • COORDINATES 42.958° N, 17.134° E • AREA 279 SQ KM (108 SQ MILES)

A tapestry of vineyards, olive groves and dense forests blankets Korčula, the greenest of the Dalmatian islands. It lies just 3km (1.8 miles) from the mainland and is understandably busy in summer, but outside the peak season it's a serenely beautiful place to visit. The island's well-preserved medieval towns and villages are awash with historic architecture, from the Gothic, Renaissance and Baroque palaces of Korčula Town to the simple stone cottages and farmhouses of the interior. It's a place to hike or bike to small-scale wineries and olive mills; see traditional folk dances, religious processions and musical performances; or better still, laze on a sandy beach, an attraction almost unheard of in Croatia.

NATIVE WINES

Wine has been produced on Korčula for over 2000 years – but unlike in the rest of Dalmatia, it is the quality of its whites that attracts the accolades here. Complex and aromatic with a high alcohol content and low acidity, Korčulan wines are made from native grape varieties. Around the hamlets of Čara and Smokvica in the island's heartlands you'll find Croatia's finest whites made from the indigenous Pošip grape. Lumbarda, on the eastern side of the island, with its sandy soil, cultivates the native Grk grape (meaning bitter in Croatian) which produces a rich, tart wine that goes well with seafood. Croatia's best-known red, the rich, full-bodied Plavac Mali is produced on the island's southern slopes; as Grk vines have only a female flower, Plavac Mali is also interspersed with Grk vines, which allows pollination to take place. Hop between wineries to sip the crisp dry whites alongside platters of local cheese, ham or seafood; or linger longer in one of the vineyard restaurants over a traditional meal of *Žrnovski makaruni* (handmade pasta), *popara* (fish stew) or *Korčulanska pašticada* (beef stew said to have its roots in antiquity).

1. Korčula Town from above

2. Pebbled shores along Korčula's coast

3. Korčula wine

3

1. Aerial view of Stiniva beach

2. Fort George, near Vis Town

3. Harvesting grapes in Vis

X MARKS THE SPOT

Blue Cave A sea cave bathed in an unearthly blue light, on the island of Biševo off Vis' southwestern tip.

Stiniva The island's most perfect cove; a blazing-white pebble beach encircled by sky-high cliffs.

Boeing B-17 Wreck The remains of one of the USA's WWII fleet of 'Flying Fortress' heavy bombers, hit by German air missiles en route to Vienna on 6 November 1944, is today one of the world's premier wreck-dive sites.

Mt Hum With glorious views over the small town of Komiža, Vis' highest mountain (587m/1926ft) also holds a cave used by partisan leader Tito as his HQ during WWII.

Podšpilje A cluster of hamlets where Vis' unique white grape varietal Vugava has been cultivated for winemaking since ancient times.

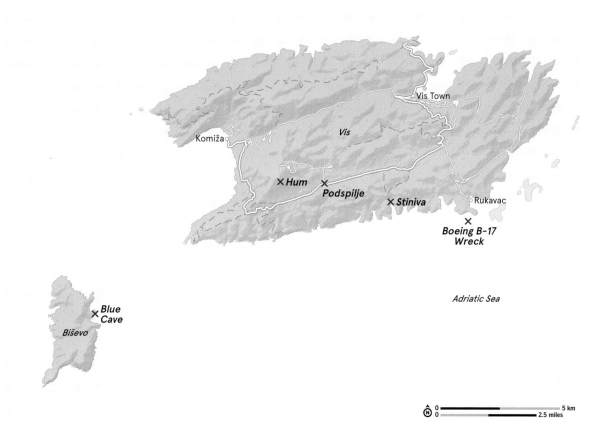

Vis

COUNTRY CROATIA • COORDINATES 43.045° N, 16.154° E • AREA 90 SQ KM (35 SQ MILES)

Cut off from the rest of the world from the 1950s until 1989, this former Yugoslav military base is bliss for island-lovers seeking peace, tranquillity and untouched natural beauty in spades. Pristine forests, citrus groves, pebble beaches, clandestine nudist coves and dazzling sea caves evoke an island idyll of yesteryear – before tourism was born.

Incongruously, some of Vis' most beautiful natural spots squirrel away rocket shelters, bunkers, weapon chests and submarine pens – abandoned by the Yugoslav National Army when it packed up camp and left the island in 1992. Remains of Greek and British naval cemeteries, Roman baths and an English fortress are further witness to this enigmatic island's curious history.

A GEOLOGICAL WONDER

While most islands in the Adriatic are formed from sedimentary rock, the inland chunk of Vis and much of its same-name archipelago are volcanic. It was for this very reason that ancient Greeks arriving in the Adriatic chose to settle Vis first: water springs in the volcanic rock formed 220 million years ago assured fertile land, ideal for planting vines and crops.

Protected as a Unesco Geopark, the volcanic rocks of Vis Archipelago are the oldest of their kind in the Adriatic. Unique caves and rock formations in the northeast were formed by sand deposits during the Ice Age. Natural lakes and black-rock shorelines characterise the islets of Brusnik and Jabuka – traditionally feared by fishermen, who would steer well clear of the black volcanic pyramids rising out of the sea here: magnetite in the magmatic rock sent their compasses in a spin. Both islets are uninhabited, leaving ample space for the endemic black karst lizard, easy to spot with its distinct turquoise spots, to roam unhindered.

Unsurprisingly perhaps, exceptional biodiversity on land and underwater scores a spot for the Vis Archipelago in the World Wildlife Fund's sacred Adriatic Blue Corridor – the zone in the Mediterranean with the largest biodiversity.

Lokrum

COUNTRY CROATIA
COORDINATES 42.631° N, 18.117° E
AREA 0.8 SQ KM (0.3 SQ MILES)

Myth and mystery run wild on thickly forested Lokrum, a pinprick of an Adriatic Sea island within taxi-boat distance from Dubrovnik's old town harbour in southern Croatia. That the island was used as a stand-in for the fictional city of Qarth near the Jade Sea in Season 2 of the TV fantasy drama *Game of Thrones* only adds to Lokrum's natural drama.

Inland forests stitched from holm oaks, flowering ashes, Aleppo pines and olive trees provide a green escape from Dubrovnik's touristed walled city. Prides of colourful peacocks strut beneath gigantesque agaves and Brazilian palms in prized botanical gardens, and Mediterranean long-eared and lesser horseshoe bats haunt the medieval attics of Lokrum's showpiece 11th- to 15th-century Benedictine monastery. The short coastline is distinctly rocky: sea caves pocket rugged karst cliffs.

THE LOKRUM CURSE

Ask any Croat about Lokrum and you'll invariably get the same response: Lokrum is cursed! The tale began on St Benedict's Day in 1023 when fire swept through Dubrovnik, decimating the town's wooden houses and prompting locals to build a monastery on Lokrum in thanks for their spared lives. All too soon Benedictine monks on the island were caring for the sick and needy, even taking in – so legend says – a shipwrecked Richard the Lionheart after his ship was tossed off course by tempestuous waters during a November storm in 1192.

All remained well on the paradisal island until 1798 when the monks were evicted and the island sold. Before leaving the monks, dressed in black and bearing candles, placed a curse on anyone who dared possess their island. Within days, one of the Dubrovnik councillors overseeing the sale hung himself, another threw himself out of a window and the third fell into the sea and drowned.

1. Wild peacocks roam Lokrum

2. View to Lokrum over red-roofed Dubrovnik Old Town

3. Lokrum's Benedictine monastery

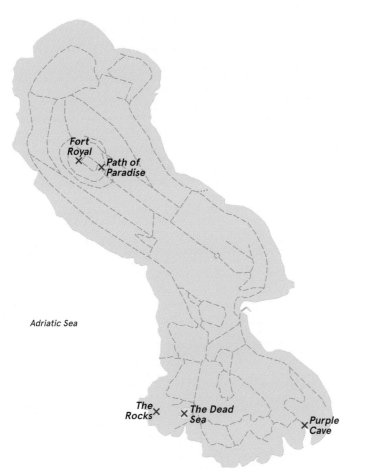

Dubrovnik (750m)

0 — 500 m
0 — 0.25 miles

Fort Royal
✕

✕ *Path of Paradise*

Adriatic Sea

The Rocks ✕

✕ *The Dead Sea*

✕ *Purple Cave*

X MARKS THE SPOT

Dead Sea A crystal-clear salt lake in the south of the island, hemmed in by rocks and linked to the Adriatic by a hole in one rock. Swimmers' nirvana.

The Rocks Hotspot for coasteering. Ladders allow easy access into the ocean – or jump!

Path of Paradise A footpath to 'paradise', aka the highest point on the island, 96m (315ft) above sea level. Cypress trees flank the route, landscaped by Maximilian I of Habsburg who purchased the island in 1859.

Purple Cave One of several sea caves specking Lokrum's rocky shore, covered in purple seaweed and accessible by boat, kayak or stand-up paddleboard.

Fort Royal Built by the French after seizing Dubrovnik in 1806, Fort Royal affords dreamy views across the water to Dubrovnik old town.

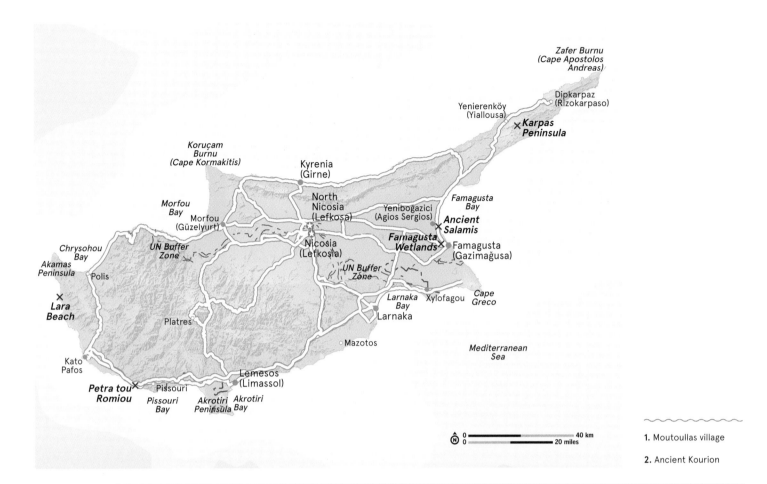

Zafer Burnu
*(Cape Apostolos
Andreas)*

Dipkarpaz
(Rizokarpaso)

Yenierenköy
(Yiallousa)

× **Karpas
Peninsula**

*Koruçam
Burnu
(Cape Kormakitis)*

Kyrenia
(Girne)

*Famagusta
Bay*

*Morfou
Bay*

Morfou
(Güzelyurt)

North
Nicosia
(Lefkoşa)

Yeniboğazici
(Agios Sergios)

**Ancient
Salamis** ×

*Chrysohou
Bay*

*UN Buffer
Zone*

Nicosia
(Lefkosia)

**Famagusta
Wetlands** ×

Famagusta
(Gazimağusa)

*Akamas
Peninsula*

Polis

*UN Buffer
Zone*

× **Lara
Beach**

Platres

*Larnaka
Bay*

Xylofagou

*Cape
Greco*

Larnaka

Mazotos

*Mediterranean
Sea*

Kato
Pafos

Lemesos
(Limassol)

**Petra tou
Romiou** ×

Pissouri

*Pissouri
Bay*

*Akrotiri
Peninsula*

*Akrotiri
Bay*

⊿N 0 ————————— 40 km
    0 ————————— 20 miles

1. Moutoullas village

2. Ancient Kourion

❶

Cyprus

COUNTRY CYPRUS

COORDINATES 35.126° N, 33.429° E • AREA 9251 SQ KM (3572 SQ MILES)

An ophiolite (uplifted chunk of ocean crust) that rose from the sea 20 million years ago, this swordfish-shaped island is the Mediterranean's third-largest. Its rich biodiversity draws nature lovers like bees to a honeypot: where else are beach-bums urged to plant their sun parasols by the shoreline, to avoid crushing eggs buried by nesting green and loggerhead turtles in the gloriously golden, powder-soft sand? Steeped in myth and coveted by every conqueror, Cyprus' tumultuous and multi-layered past has strewn ancient riches across the entire island. Cypriot culture is an intoxicating mix of Med and Middle East, with a sun-scorched capital city incongruously split since 1974 by the infamous Green Line, a UN-patrolled buffer zone. The country's seductively beautiful beaches are of Aphrodite ilk, but dig into the past here and you'll unearth the entire story of the Mediterranean.

ISLAND OF SAINTS

Griffon vultures, falcons, Cyprus warblers and nightingales swoop through the skies above the iconic peak of Mt Olympus (1952m/6404ft), the highest point of Cyprus in the Troödos Mountains. In the most remote corners of this vast range, Cypriot mouflons run wild and rare giant and woodcock orchids flower.

These mountains also saw a flowering of the arts during the 12th and 15th centuries. After France's Lusignan Catholic dynasty took control of Cyprus in 1197, repressed Orthodox Greek Cypriot clergy, artisans and artists retreated to the secluded northern slopes of the Troödos, building isolated ecclesiastical retreats embellished with some of the most extraordinary frescoes of the late- and post-Byzantine periods. Inside what was often little more than a barn, with steep overhanging roofs to protect from accumulated snow, frescoed walls dazzle with vivid imagery painted in spectacular colour and detail. Later, didactic-style frescoes were painted like a movie strip to teach illiterate villagers the rudiments of the gospels. Ten such chapels here are Unesco World Heritage Sites.

X MARKS THE SPOT

Lara Beach A spectacular powder-sand beach on the Akamas Peninsula, cupped by limestone rocks and awash at night with hatching turtles.

Karpas Peninsula Uncover rare orchids on this skinny peninsula with a spine of cliffs, dune-laced beaches and a scattering of traditional villages.

Petratou Romiou This romantic pebble beach on Cyprus' south coast is where Greek goddess of love Aphrodite emerged from the sea to embark on her bed-hopping romps.

Famagusta Wetlands Rife with waterbirds (pelicans, flamingos, demoiselle cranes, spoonbills), and home to the island's only glossy ibis breeding site.

Ancient Salamis The debris of all who set their sights on Cyprus bejewels this vast archaeological site by the sea.

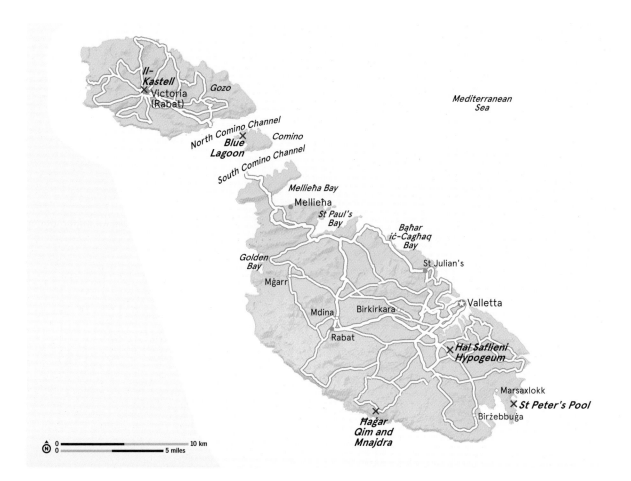

Mediterranean
Sea

Gozo

Il-
Kastell
Victoria
(Rabat)

North Comino Channel
Comino
Blue
Lagoon
South Comino Channel

Mellieħa Bay
Mellieħa
St Paul's
Bay
Baħar
iċ-Cagħaq
Bay
Golden
Bay
St Julian's
Mġarr
Valletta
Mdina
Birkirkara
Rabat
Ħal Saflieni
Hypogeum
Marsaxlokk
St Peter's Pool
Birżebbuġa
Ħaġar
Qim and
Mnajdra

N
0   10 km
0   5 miles

1. Fortified city of
Senglea, near Valletta

2. Snorkelling Comino's
Blue Lagoon

Malta

COUNTRY MALTA
COORDINATES 35.937° N, 14.375° E • **AREA** 316 SQ KM (122 SQ MILES)

From the Romans to the Arabs to the Knights of St John, and more recently the French and the British, Malta's long list of rulers have all made their mark on this intriguing Mediterranean island nation, which has a culture, language and cuisine all of its own.

Around 190km (118 miles) south of Sicily, Malta – which gained its independence from the UK in 1964 – comprises three main islands: the buzzy administrative centre of Malta; smaller and more relaxed Gozo; and tiny Comino, sandwiched in between. Built on a peninsula, the capital Valletta's 16th-century elegance is a top draw, but there's plenty more to discover beyond, from mysterious megalithic temples to pretty villages and some of the dreamiest swimming (and best diving) spots in the Med.

The sole survivor of the Arabic dialects spoken in Spain and Sicily in the Middle Ages, the Maltese language is particularly unique. English is the other official language, though more than half the population also speak Italian.

MYSTERIOUS ANCIENTS

About a thousand years before the construction of the Great Pyramid of Cheops in Egypt, the people of Malta were manipulating megaliths that weighed up to 50 tonnes and creating elaborate buildings that appear to be oriented in relation to the winter solstice sunrise. Constructed between 3600 and 2500 BCE, these mysterious temples on both Malta and Gozo are the oldest surviving free-standing structures in the world.

It's a mystery why the temple's builders died out: theories include drought and famine, an epidemic or an attack from overseas – or perhaps a combination of these afflictions. Whatever the reason, temple building appears to have come to a sudden stop around 2500 BCE.

X MARKS THE SPOT

Ħal Saflieni Hypogeum Just south of Valletta, this 5000-year-old rock-carved necropolis is amazingly well preserved. Book tickets well in advance.

Blue Lagoon Dive into a living postcard at this idyllic lagoon in a sheltered cove on Comino.

Ħaġar Qim & Mnajdra These megalithic temples in southern Malta are the nation's best-preserved and most evocative prehistoric sites, with an unparalleled location atop sea cliffs.

Il-Kastell Enjoy superb views over Gozo and towards the Med from this splendid citadel in Victoria, which has a fascinating backstory.

St Peter's Pool Jump off the rocks into the azure water at this hidden cove on Malta.

AFRICA

Lanzarote

COUNTRY SPAIN • **COORDINATES** 29.046° N, 13.590° W • **AREA** 862 SQ KM (333 SQ MILES)

Around 1000km (62 miles) southwest of mainland Spain, out in the Atlantic off the Moroccan coast, lies an endlessly entrancing, volcano-studded island put on the map by the 20th-century artist, architect and conservationist César Manrique. Sun-soaked Lanzarote defies all the Canary Islands stereotypes. One minute you're feasting on a platter of just-grilled fish on a near-deserted black-sand beach; the next you're admiring wandering vines at a sleekly designed winery; and then you're twisting and turning down a mountain lane between whitewashed low-rise villages. The island's powerfully creative spirit is felt everywhere, from the locally crafted ceramics to the sky-blue seaside shutters to the avant-garde restaurants paying homage to Canarian gastronomy.

VOLCANIC VINEYARDS

Late into the night on 1 September 1730, a series of catastrophic eruptions began to rumble around the Volcán de los Cuervos in Lanzarote's heartland. For a staggering six years they continued, destroying around 20 villages and forcing the local population to flee to distant parts of the island. Once the eruptions subsided, however, it wasn't long before the forward-thinking *lanzaroteños* turned this natural disaster to their own advantage – repurposing the freshly created volcanic ash to grow exceptional Canarian wine-producing grapes. Today, much of Lanzarote's

volcanic centre and north-facing coast is protected by the unmissable Parque Nacional de Timanfaya, with the cutting-edge DO Lanzarote wine region extending around its fringes in La Geria, Tinajo and Masdache.

According to Oliver Horton, founder of Wine Tours Lanzarote: 'Lanzarote wine is unique, from its origins nestled in lava fields covered with a deep layer of volcanic ash, to the five grape varietals that have adapted to arid conditions where winemaking shouldn't even be possible. The Malvasía Volcánica grape is the star, native to the island, where its fresh, crisp notes match those of our endless summer.'

1. Punta Mujeres

2. Parque Nacional de Timanfaya

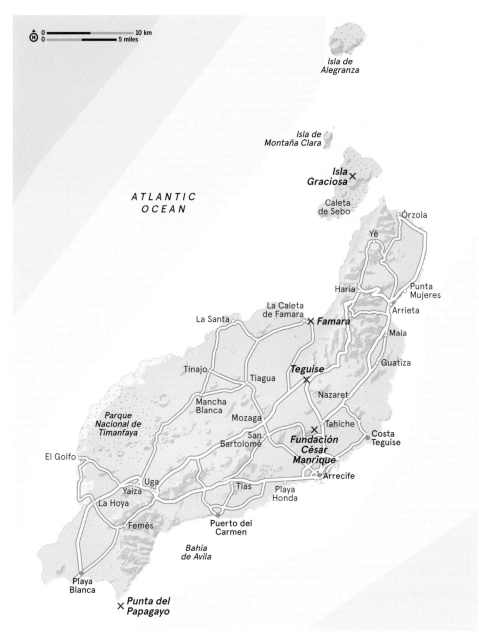

0 10 km
0 5 miles
N

Isla de Alegranza

ATLANTIC OCEAN

Isla de Montaña Clara

Isla Graciosa ✕
Caleta de Sebo

Órzola

Yé

Haría
La Caleta de Famara
La Santa
✕ *Famara*

Punta Mujeres
Arrieta
Mala

Tinajo
Tiagua
Teguise ✕
Guatiza

Mancha Blanca
Mozaga
Nazaret

Parque Nacional de Timanfaya
San Bartolomé
✕ Tahíche
Fundación César Manrique
Costa Teguise

El Golfo
Uga
Yaiza
Tías
Arrecife

La Hoya
Playa Honda

Femés
Puerto del Carmen

Bahía de Avila

Playa Blanca

✕ *Punta del Papagayo*

X MARKS THE SPOT

Teguise Lanzarote's evocative original capital reveals centuries-old mansions, shady plazas and a creative design scene best enjoyed at its wildly popular Sunday market.

Punta del Papagayo Rugged golden-sand beaches, rust-red sea cliffs and dusty walking paths dot this unbelievably beautiful nature reserve.

Isla Graciosa Just off northern Lanzarote, this road-free, sparsely populated island encompasses a jumble of sandy trails, dreamy Atlantic beaches and bare volcanic cones, all protected as a *parque natural*.

Famara A perfect sweep of powdery beach framed by cascading cliffs, famous for its fabulous surf and white-walled fishing village.

Fundación César Manrique Lanzarote's identity is tightly linked with the legacy of César Manrique, whose former home is built into Tahíche's lava fields.

❷

El Hierro

COUNTRY SPAIN · **COORDINATES** 27.725° N, 18.024° W · **AREA** 269 SQ KM (104 SQ MILES)

Few parts of Spain feel as thrillingly remote as the volcanic, Unesco-protected island of El Hierro, strewn out in the Atlantic to the southwest of Tenerife and La Gomera in the luscious Canary Islands. Just to get here, you'll be hopping on a bumpy three-hour ferry or a one-hour flight from Tenerife – but even so, you won't be able to help falling instantly under the island's slow-going spell. All over this windswept Spanish outpost, towering coastal cliffs give way to twinkling natural sea pools, while steeply stacked vineyards sit below wind-sculpted juniper groves, electric-green pines sweep down lava-flow hills and silent pastoral paths disappear among whispering laurel forests. The diving is dreamy, the local gastronomy is a delight and, most importantly, responsible tourism has been key for decades. El Hierro was declared a Unesco Geopark in 2014 and runs mostly on renewable-powered electricity, with ambitious future plans to become the world's first self-sufficient island.

A GREEN FUTURE

Just outside El Hierro's capital, Valverde, stands a string of looping wind turbines, gazing out on the craggy coast and rugged hills like an army of sentinels. But these aren't just any old turbines. This is the game-changing Gorona del Viento power plant, launched in 2014 to provide green electricity from exclusively renewable sources such as wind and water, and a key player in El Hierro's drive towards becoming a 100% sustainable island. The site is even open for expert-led visits, showing that sustainability sits at the core of this warm-hearted island, where around 60% of all electricity already comes from renewable sources. Elsewhere, rural wineries are reviving ancient local grape varieties, organic farming is taking centre stage, the endangered El Hierro giant lizard is being reintroduced, and there are plans for the Mar de las Calmas marine reserve to (eventually) be upgraded to national park status.

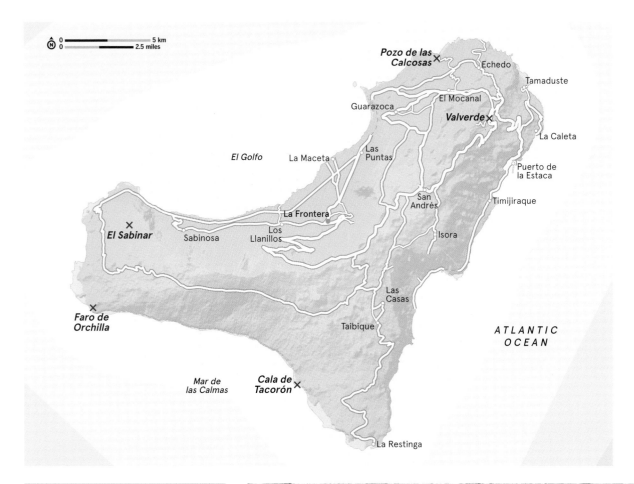

0 — 5 km
0 — 2.5 miles

Pozo de las Calcosas ✕
Echedo
Tamaduste
El Mocanal
Guarazoca
Valverde ✕
La Caleta
El Golfo
La Maceta
Las Puntas
Puerto de la Estaca
San Andrés
Timijiraque
El Sabinar ✕
Sabinosa
Los Llanillos
La Frontera
Isora
Faro de Orchilla ✕
Las Casas
Taibique
ATLANTIC OCEAN
Mar de las Calmas
Cala de Tacorón ✕
La Restinga

X MARKS THE SPOT

Faro de Orchilla An isolated lighthouse, surrounded by lava-formed cliffs and the crashing Atlantic, makes up the evocative southwest tip of the island.

Cala de Tacorón Natural sea pools are a local speciality: dive in at these divinely turquoise volcanic coves.

El Sabinar Remote even by El Hierro standards, the island's eerie juniper groves have been pummelled into spectacularly extreme shapes by the Atlantic winds.

Pozo de las Calcosas With its distinctive lava-rock houses, this 300-year-old village sits tucked into the island's north coast.

Valverde El Hierro's wind-lashed, landlocked capital traces its origins back to the 16th century.

1. Volcanic cone

2. La Maceta rock pool, near Las Puntas

3. Faro de Orchilla

0   20 km
0   10 miles

N

Porto
Santo ✕
Vila
Baleira

Ilhéu
de Baixo

ATLANTIC
OCEAN

Porto
Moniz ✕
Santa
Ribeira
da Janela
Ponta do
Pargo
São
Vicente
Ponta
Delgada
Pico
Ruivo ✕
Santana
Porta da Cruz
Serra
de Água
Curral
das
Freiras ✕
Caniçal
Calheta
Machico
Ponta
do Sol
Cabo
Girão ✕
Santa
Cruz
Ribeira
Brava
Câmara
de Lobos
Funchal
Caniço

Ilhas
Desertas

〜〜〜〜〜

1. Risco Waterfall

2. Jardins Botânicos da
Madeira

3. Rural Madeira

Madeira

COUNTRY PORTUGAL
COORDINATES 32.760° N, 16.959° W • AREA 801 SQ KM (309 SQ MILES)

Breeze in your hair, you zoom sharply downhill on a toboggan-like wicker sledge, just the latest convert to this beloved white-knuckle tradition going back at least a hundred years on the spectacular volcanic island of Madeira. Flung out in the Atlantic, 300km (183 miles) off the Moroccan coast and over 1000km (621 miles) away from mainland Portugal, this endlessly fascinating isle was first settled in the 15th century by the Portuguese. Today it serves up black-sand beaches lapped by the Atlantic, soothing subtropical gardens, delightful terracotta-roofed towns and low-key artisanal markets alongside adrenaline-fuelled adventure sports and fabulous hiking through terraces of banana palms and sugar-cane. Throw in a thriving local crafts scene, the urban buzz of lively capital Funchal and a distinctive cuisine rooted in home-grown ingredients (and famously fortified wines), and there's no resisting Madeira's charms.

MADEIRA'S LEVADAS

The story of the ancient, narrow irrigation canals that swoop across Madeira's mountainous interior begins long ago, with the Portuguese arrival here in the 15th century. Faced with the dry south of the island, early settlers began to carve out *levadas* to help channel and redistribute freshwater to farms, crops and villages; some were wedged through tight spaces, others opened up along precariously perched seaside cliffs. Little did their builders know

that this ingenious idea would spiral all the way into the 20th century. Today, Madeira has around 2500km (1553 miles) of waterways, and many of them double up as inspiring hiking trails, with paths tracking alongside the canals. Dive into the Unesco-listed laurisilva forest, walk between spine-tingling peaks, wander through eerily lit tunnels, zip beneath rushing waterfalls, clamber along thrilling coastal cliffs – always accompanied by a slice of island history and the blissful soundtrack of trickling water.

X MARKS THE SPOT

Cabo Girão Some of the highest sea cliffs in the world sweep 580m (1903ft) down to disappear into the swirling, whirling Atlantic.

Curral das Freiras A dramatically set speck of a village, surrounded by tempting walking trails in a lush valley.

Porto Moniz Plunge into the Atlantic at these gorgeous volcanic rock pools at the northwest end of the island.

Pico Ruivo Madeira's tallest peak soars to 1861m (6106ft), and can be reached only by way of a demanding hike.

Porto Santo Boat across to tiny Porto Santo island, with its wonderfully wild coral beach; this was the first spot spied by Portuguese colonisers back in the 15th century.

Djerba

COUNTRY TUNISIA

COORDINATES 33.807° N, 10.845° E • **AREA** 514 SQ KM (198 SQ MILES)

To the Ancient Greek poet Homer, Djerba was the 'Land of the Lotus Eaters', a place so seductive that none who visited could ever bear to leave. These days, it's not difficult to see what he meant, thanks to the combination of beautiful beaches, fascinating history and a beguiling modern Tunisian story. Much of the island is an open-air museum, while the excellent museums bring so many of these stories into focus. Mosques and a synagogue, beaches and bazaars, shops and galleries: this North African gem really is so much more than just a pretty face.

SOMETHING ELEMENTAL

Connected to the mainland by a 6km-long (3.7-mile) causeway and not far from the border with Libya, Djerba rises gently from the ocean off Tunisia's southeastern coast. Away from built-up areas, there is something elemental about Djerba, where the yellows of the arid North African coast – pale under a midday sun, golden at sunset – meet the deep blues of the southern Mediterranean. It is the call to prayer carrying out across the whitewashed rooftops, or the murmur of Talmudic scholars in the synagogue in Erriadh. Or it is the cries of fishmongers at Houmt Souk's Marché Central, offset by smells to savour

from island specialities like grilled kebabs, stuffed calamari and great steaming platters of rice.

The Zone Touristique could be any resort-heavy coastal strip along the Mediterranean's southern shore. But the island is unmistakeably Tunisian, drawing on the experience of welcoming visitors down through the centuries, even as it holds fast to its culinary and other cultural traditions. The museums here are the best in Tunisia's south and the street art brings a fresh approach to old neighbourhoods. But it's when you lose yourself in the tangle of cobblestone lanes of an ancient Djerba medina that you'll most likely decide that you never want to leave.

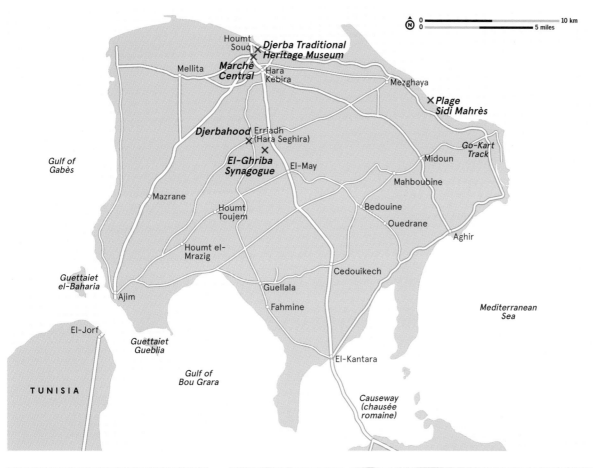

0 | 10 km
0 | 5 miles

Houmt Souq

X Djerba Traditional Heritage Museum

Mellita

X Marché Central

Hara Kebira

Mezghaya

X Plage Sidi Mahrès

Djerbahood X Erriadh (Hara Seghira)

Go-Kart Track

Gulf of Gabès

X El-Ghriba Synagogue

El-May

Midoun

Mahboubine

Mazrane

Houmt Toujem

Bedouine

Ouedrane

Aghir

Houmt el-Mrazig

Cedouikech

Mediterranean Sea

Guettaiet el-Baharia

Guellala

Ajim

Fahmine

El-Jorf

Guettaiet Gueblia

El-Kantara

Gulf of Bou Grara

TUNISIA

Causeway (chausée romaine)

X MARKS THE SPOT

Plage Sidi Mahrès From Ras Remel Peninsula (home to winter flamingos) to Taguermes Lighthouse, this glorious stretch of sand is an indulgent meeting of sand, sea and sky.

El Ghriba Synagogue This current incarnation dates to the 19th century, but a synagogue has stood here since ancient times.

Djerba Traditional Heritage Museum Go on an enlightening journey through every aspect of Djerba's history in a stunning architectural setting.

Marché Central This atmospheric fish market is a window on Djerba's traditional fishing culture.

Djerbahood This 2014 street-art project illuminates whitewashed village walls with artworks by 150 local and international artists.

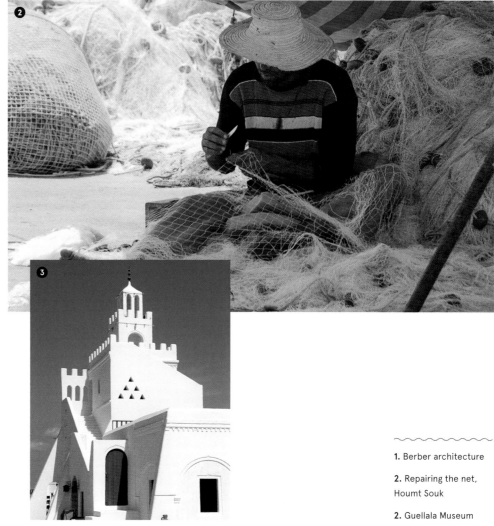

1. Berber architecture

2. Repairing the net, Houmt Souk

2. Guellala Museum

ATLANTIC OCEAN

IFAN Historical Museum

Dakar-Gorée Ferry

Hostellerie du Chevalier de Boufflers

Botanical Garden

La Maison des Esclaves

Jardin Public Adanson

Castel Hill

0 — 200 m
0 — 0.1 miles

X MARKS THE SPOT

Castel Hill The view from the top of the Castel, on the island's south, are some of the best on the island, with artists' workshops nearby.

IFAN Historical Museum Visit this museum for an informative overview of the island's story; there are also great views across the water to Dakar from the roof.

La Maison des Esclaves One of the most thought-provoking, emotive museums of its kind in all of Africa.

Hostellerie du Chevalier de Boufflers This elegant colonial-era Gorée home has a stunning garden restaurant.

Dakar-Gorée Ferry This short ferry ride connects two vastly disparate worlds, with fine views on the way over and back.

Île de Gorée

COUNTRY SENEGAL

COORDINATES 14.667° N, 17.398° W • **AREA** 0.28 SQ KM (0.1 SQ MILES)

Île de Gorée is a soulful, haunting place, at once uplifting and profoundly disturbing: it's a symbol of the Atlantic slave trade that saw millions of enslaved African people shipped across the sea in chains, never to return. Barely a 20-minute ferry ride off the coast of Dakar, the roiling, modern Senegalese capital, Gorée is a peaceful place to ponder this darkest period of African history. There are a number of historical sites to anchor your visit, but the quiet beauty of this tragic place also leaves its mark on all who visit.

'DOORWAY TO NOWHERE'

Île de Gorée has seen it all. It was ruled over by the Portuguese, Dutch, English and French, but its modern, eerily calm aspect – there are no sealed roads and no cars, just narrow alleyways with trailing bougainvilleas and colonial-era brick buildings with wrought-iron balconies – does little to mask its brutal past. The island's history is best told at La Maison des Esclaves (the 'Slave House'), among the few surviving 18th-century buildings on Gorée. Built in 1786, renovated in 1990, its most famous feature is the chilling 'doorway to nowhere', opening directly from the lower-floor storeroom onto the sea and the ships that once carried the enslaved away. As you explore the dimly lit dungeons, it's easy (and yet at the same time impossible) to imagine the terrible suffering that people endured here.

It's not so much that La Maison des Esclaves was any more significant than many other such historical sites strung out along the West African coast. But something intangible about this place brings the horror and the cruelty of what happened here into sharp and challenging focus. And from the midst of it all, new shoots have sprouted: Gorée is now home to an active artists community, with small studios found all across the island.

1. La Maison des Esclaves

2. Île de Gorée shore

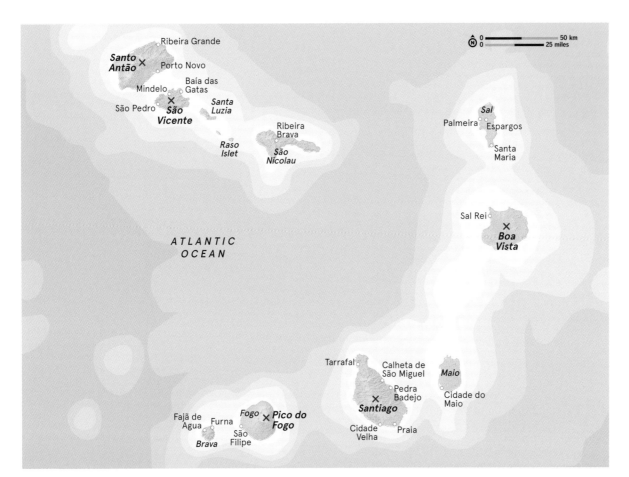

0 — 50 km
0 — 25 miles

Ribeira Grande
Santo Antão ✕
Porto Novo
Baía das Gatas
Mindelo
São Pedro
São Vicente ✕
Santa Luzia
Raso Islet
Ribeira Brava
São Nicolau

Sal
Palmeira
Espargos
Santa Maria

Sal Rei
Boa Vista ✕

ATLANTIC OCEAN

Tarrafal
Calheta de São Miguel
Maio
Pedra Badejo
Santiago ✕
Cidade do Maio
Cidade Velha
Praia

Fajã de Agua
Furna
Fogo
Pico do Fogo ✕
São Filipe
Brava

1. Paul Valley, Santo Antão

2. Skimboarding

Cabo Verde

COUNTRY CABO VERDE (CAPE VERDE)
COORDINATES 16.538° N, 23.041° W • **AREA** 4033 SQ KM (1557 SQ MILES)

Rising from the Atlantic 500km (311 miles) west of Senegal, this glorious island chain has a captivating blend of mountains, beaches and tranquil seaside villages. On Santo Antão, craggy peaks hide piercing green valleys of flowers and sugar cane, ideal for epic hikes. São Vicente is home to the cultural capital of the islands, Mindelo, which throbs with bars and music clubs. On Sal and Maio, undulating windswept dunes merge with indigo-blue seas on unspoilt beaches of powdery white sand. Meanwhile, far-flung Fogo and Brava in the southwest offer their own enchantments, from surreal volcanic landscapes to sparkling bays framed by towering peaks.

BAREFOOT DIVA

Cabo Verdean music evolved as a protest against the horrors of slavery, and today, two kinds of song dominate the islands' traditional music: *mornas* and *coladeiras*, both built on the sounds of stringed instruments like the fiddle and guitar. As the name suggests, *mornas* (melodic, melancholic music) are mournful songs of *sodade* – an unquenchable longing, often for home. With faster, more upbeat rhythms, *coladeiras*, in contrast, tend to be romantic love songs or more active expressions of protest.

Undisputed queen of the *morna* and Cabo Verde's most famous citizen, Cesária Évora (known as the 'barefoot diva') wowed the world with a voice at once densely textured and disarmingly direct. She began to gain an international audience in the mid-1990s but vaulted to stardom in 1997 when she won best female vocalist at the second annual All African Music Awards. Suddenly people around the world were swaying to the rhythms of Cabo Verde's music, even if they couldn't point the country out on a map. When she died at 70 in 2011, after a bout of illness, Cabo Verde declared two days of national mourning and the Mindelo airport was renamed in her honour. Her musical legacy very much lives on.

X MARKS THE SPOT

Santo Antão Misty pine-clad ridges, sheer canyons and verdant valleys on Cabo Verde's most spectacular island.

Pico do Fogo Admire the views from the summit of the country's only active volcano, a cinder-clad 2829m-high (9281ft) stunner.

São Vicente Follow the melodic sounds of *morna* and *coladeira* to festive, open-air spots scattered around this music-loving seaside town.

Boa Vista Relax on the beach and feast on delicious seafood at this wondrously laid-back island.

Santiago Explore the colonial-era ruins of the picturesque Cidade Velha, followed by seaside drinks and dancing in Praia.

Bioko Island

COUNTRY EQUATORIAL GUINEA
COORDINATES 3.619° N, 8.748° E • **AREA** 2017 SQ KM (779 SQ MILES)

Off the coast of Cameroon but very much a part of Equatorial Guinea, Bioko is Central Africa's quintessential tropical island. A refuge for pirates in not-so-ancient times, Bioko now hosts Malabo, Equatorial Guinea's capital, which is at once oil-boom town and a languid tropical outpost with a Gothic, Gaudí-inspired cathedral close to the island's Gulf of Guinea shore. Despite being the national seat of power, Bioko has some of the most important wildlife habitats anywhere in West or Central Africa, and its mountainous and densely forested interior is home to the volcanic Pico Basile (3012m/9882ft).

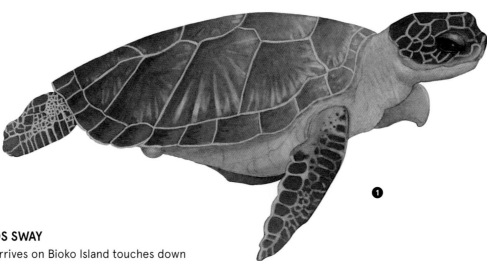

NATURE HOLDS SWAY

Everyone who arrives on Bioko Island touches down in Malabo, and it's a fascinating experience, from the older port area and its Spanish colonial architecture in the east, to the garish bright lights and skyscrapers of the aspirational oil city in the west. In between, expect the country's best restaurants and live music, as well as tin-roofed shanty towns home to those yet to benefit from Equatorial Guinea's newfound riches. It's a sometimes thrilling, often disconcerting combination.

But for all the bustle and business deals of Malabo, nature holds sway on Bioko. Not far beyond the rather scrappy city limits, rainforest takes over and never really lets go, carpeting most of the island's largely trackless interior in the deepest of greens. Filled with the primates for which Bioko is famed, these forests are only interrupted by the occasional small village and encircled by an often-pristine coastline with white or chocolate-coloured sands; the island's southern and western reaches in particular have a wonderfully remote wilderness quality.

The beaches and lookouts of Luba, on the southwestern coast, are simply superb, but to really fall off the map, Ureca is where rainforest meets the sea, with the added attraction of nesting sea turtles thrown in for good measure.

1. Sea turtle

2. Bioko's untrammelled shoreline

0   20 km
0   10 miles

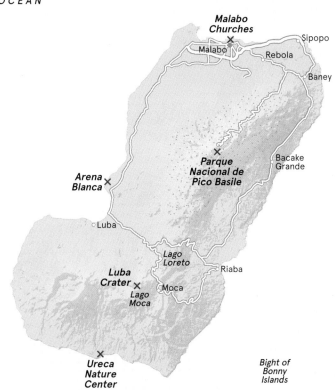

ATLANTIC OCEAN

Malabo Churches
×

Malabo

Sipopo

Rebola

Baney

Parque Nacional de Pico Basile
×

Bacake Grande

Arena Blanca ×

○Luba

Lago Loreto

Riaba

Luba Crater ×

Moca

Lago Moca

× *Ureca Nature Center*

Bight of Bonny Islands

X MARKS THE SPOT

Malabo Churches Catedrál de Santa Isabel is the centrepiece of Malabo's decadent, peeling-pastel architectural story, a Spanish outpost transplanted onto African soil.

Luba Crater This dramatic forested crater has Bioko's famed primate populations, including the gloriously named putty-nosed guenon and the golden-bellied crowned guenon.

Arena Blanca Here at one of Bioko's most beautiful white-sand beaches, you'll see more butterflies than people if you visit on a weekday.

Ureca Nature Centre Learn about the amazing conservation work being done to protect Bioko's biodiversity, see monkeys and sea turtles, and support local communities.

Parque Nacional de Pico Basile Climb the slopes of Bioko's highest peak for astonishing views.

Robben Island

COUNTRY SOUTH AFRICA
COORDINATES 33.807° S, 18.371° E • **AREA** 5.18 SQ KM (2 SQ MILES)

Transformed from a place of infamy into a monument to the resilience of the human spirit, Robben Island is a fantastic place to learn about apartheid. Nelson Mandela was imprisoned here for 27 long years, but he wasn't alone – the stories of other apartheid-era prisoners offer similarly humbling learning experiences. With its fine views of the mainland, it's a beautiful spot, which only highlights the appalling conditions in which the prisoners were held. Perhaps Robben's greatest legacy is this: if someone could emerge from here with a message of unity and peace, then anything might be possible.

MEMORIAL TO APARTHEID

Long before Nelson Mandela was locked up here, Robben Island was a prison (used by the Dutch East India Company), and it continued to house prisoners right up until 1996 (six years after Mandela was released). Now a Unesco World Heritage Site, the island is preserved as a memorial to its role in the history of apartheid. You can only visit on a tour, which lasts around four hours including ferry rides, departing from the Nelson Mandela Gateway beside the Clock Tower at Cape Town's Waterfront. The standard tours, which have set departure and return times, include a walk through the old prison (with the obligatory peek into Mandela's cell), and a 45-minute bus ride around the island with commentary on places of note, including the lime quarry in which Mandela and many others carried out hard labour; the little house where Robert Sobukwe, leader of the Pan-Africanist Congress, was held in solitary confinement for six years; and the church used during the island's stint as a leper colony. There's also a stop at the Alpha 7 cafe for a superb view of the mainland and Table Mountain.

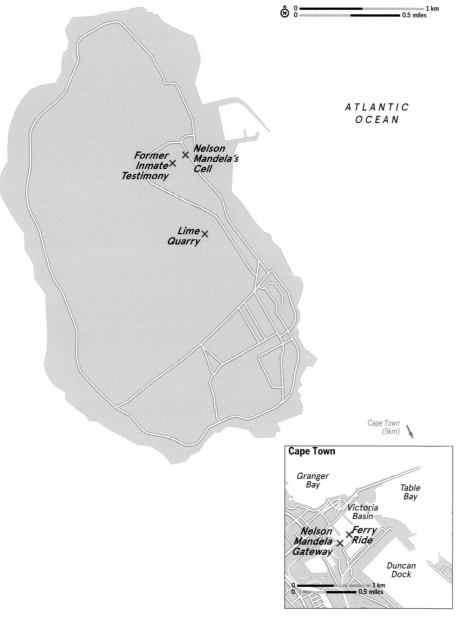

ATLANTIC
OCEAN

Former
Inmate ✕
Testimony

Nelson
✕ Mandela's
Cell

Lime ✕
Quarry

Cape Town
(5km)

Cape Town

Granger
Bay

Table
Bay

Victoria
Basin

Nelson
Mandela ✕
Gateway

✕ Ferry
Ride

Duncan
Dock

X MARKS THE SPOT

Nelson Mandela Gateway The small waterfront museum has displays on the struggle against apartheid; Jetty 1 was the departure point for Robben Island when it was still a prison.

Ferry Ride A video on Robben Island's history screens on board. Enjoy the video on the way out, the views on the trip back.

Mandela's Cell Seeing the incredibly cramped conditions where Mandela spent nearly three decades reduces many visitors to tears.

Lime Quarry If the sun's beating down when you visit, you'll wonder how any of the prisoners survived.

Former Inmate Testimony Former Robben inmates provide an unforgettable personal history.

1. Robben Island from above, looking back to Cape Town and Table Mountain

2. Nelson Mandela's cell

3. Robben Island's sun-scoured quarry, where prisoners carried out hard labour

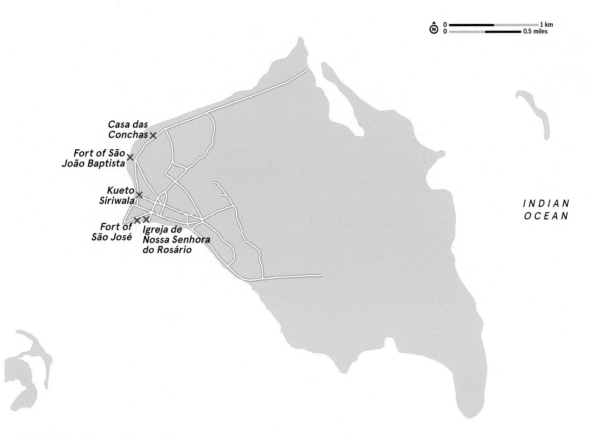

0   1 km
0   0.5 miles

Casa das
Conchas ✕

Fort of São ✕
João Baptista

Kueto ✕
Siriwala

Fort of ✕
São José   Igreja de
           Nossa Senhora
           do Rosário

INDIAN
OCEAN

1. Island life

2. Underwater Ibo

Ibo Island

COUNTRY MOZAMBIQUE
COORDINATES 12.337° S, 40.599° E • **AREA** 75 SQ KM (29 SQ MILES)

Time seems to stand still when visiting Ibo Island, which is like stepping back into a quieter, simpler past. It's part of Mozambique's Quirimbas Archipelago, and has been saved from overdevelopment by to the fact that it doesn't have many beaches. What it does have is a languid, subtropical charm that owes everything to its decaying African-Portuguese architecture, its proliferation of palm trees and to the Indian Ocean sunsets out over the mudflats. If you want to catch a glimpse of what Mozambique's coastline used to look like, Ibo Island is a grand old place to do so.

SENSE OF TIMELESSNESS

History is everywhere on Ibo Island, and resides not just in the sense of timelessness that is such a hallmark of life here. One of Mozambique's oldest settlements, Ibo's human story dates back to around 600 CE, a stirring tale of oceangoing spice vessels, Muslim trading posts and even a visit by Portuguese explorer Vasco da Gama. Echoes of history take on many forms here: the poignant silence of fortresses where enslaved people were held, or the trade winds that whisper through the palms and ease the dhows (traditional Indian Ocean wooden sailing ships) across the horizon.

Ibo is one of those places that has seen the rise and fall of great political and trading empires and survives as an outpost sinking quietly (and happily) into obscurity. Its small but surprisingly diverse tourist industry has plenty to offer. A walking tour of Ibo's stone-built town provides so many entry points into the island's history, but there's also birdwatching, kayaking, diving and snorkelling, the latter especially good in the coral gardens that lie close to the main lighthouse. The astonishing marine life here is one of the reasons why Ibo Island was made part of the 11-island Quirimbas National Park.

X MARKS THE SPOT

Casa das Conchas Ibo's House of Shells is among the island's loveliest structures; shop for handicrafts and enjoy the local coffee.

Fort of São João Baptista The Portuguese built this star-shaped fort in 1791 to house enslaved people; it now hosts silversmiths creating Swahili designs.

Fort of São José Ibo's oldest fort dates back to 1760 and offers a haunting window into the island's history.

Igreja de Nossa Senhora do Rosário This Portuguese-built Catholic church tells of different times on this overwhelmingly Muslim island.

Kueto Siriwala Running since 1773, this three-day cultural festival in June has dhow races, lots of music and endless fun.

Ilha de Moçambique

COUNTRY MOZAMBIQUE • **COORDINATES** 15.036° S, 40.732° E • **AREA** 0.96 SQ KM (0.37 SQ MILES)

Bathed in cooling trade winds and buffeted by the tides of history, Ilha de Moçambique is a classic northern Mozambique outpost of culture and somnambulant tropical beauty. Strewn across the island are signposts to an extraordinary past: a museum housed in a former governor's palace, imposing stone fortresses, churches, mosques and Hindu temples. It's the kind of place where you'll hear the cries of fishers selling their catch in the markets before you wander down to watch dhows (traditional wooden sailboats) from beneath a palm tree on white sands or from the shallows of a turquoise sea.

ARISING FROM THE SEA

Even more than the architecture and historical displays, it's the dhows that tell the story of Ilha de Moçambique: everything about this island arises from the sea. Thanks to its location along the major trading routes of the ancient world, and despite its diminutive size, Ilha de Moçambique has been an important centre for boatbuilding since the 15th century. Traders and emissaries from the storied ports of the Indian Ocean's centres of power – Madagascar, Persia, Arabia, Oman, Zanzibar and elsewhere – came to the island to do business. So important was the location that the island rose to significance despite having no fresh water; even today, the island's water is piped in from the mainland. Understanding its strategic value, the Portuguese, too, stopped here, including Vasco da Gama. They later made it the capital of Portuguese East Africa. At first glance, the island's centuries as a base of power can be difficult to discern. And yet, Ilha de Moçambique's architectural mosaic, its ringing of church bells and the muezzin's call to prayer, its hot curry of culinary influences from across the Portuguese- and Swahili-speaking world all speak to a place that has always been the Indian Ocean coast in microcosm.

1. Fort of São Sebastião

2. Igreja da Misericórdia

3. Dhow sailing around São Sebastião

0 | 500 m
0 | 0.25 miles

*Mossuril
Bay*

*Chapel of
Nossa Senhora
de Baluarte*
× *Fort of
São Sebastião*

× **Camões
Statue
& House**

*INDIAN OCEAN
(Mozambique
Channel)*

× **Church of
Santo António**

*Goa Island
(5.5km)*

São Lourenço
× **Island**

*Sena Island
(6km)*

X MARKS THE SPOT

Camões Statue & House The 16th-century Portuguese poet Luís de Camões watches over a small park and the house has a stunning facade.

Churches Of the impressive Portuguese-era churches, the Chapel of Nossa Senhora de Baluarte (1522) is the oldest European building in the Southern Hemisphere.

Cemetery Overlooking Makuti Town, the abandoned Church of Santo António has a cemetery with Christian, Muslim and Hindu graves.

Fort of São Sebastião Begun in 1558, this splendidly crumbling relic is Africa's oldest surviving fort south of the Sahara.

Outer Islands Other nearby islets include Goa (with a lovely beach); São Lourenço (with its island-sized fort); and rocky Sena (a gorgeous lagoon).

185

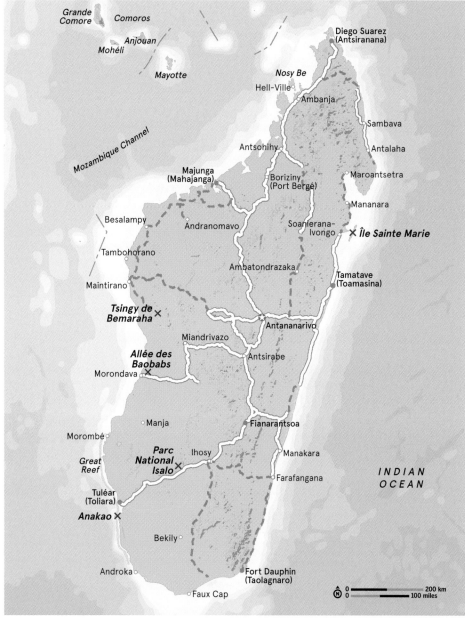

Grande
Comore   Comoros
      Anjouan
Mohéli
        Mayotte

Diego Suarez
(Antsiranana)

Nosy Be
Hell-Ville
      Ambanja

Sambava

Antsohihy   Antalaha

Mozambique Channel

Majunga
(Mahajanga)   Boriziny
                (Port Bergé)   Maroantsetra

Besalampy   Mananara

Andranomavo   Soanierana-
                   Ivongo   ✕ Île Sainte Marie
Tambohorano

Ambatondrazaka

Maintirano   Tamatave
                                (Toamasina)

Tsingy de   ✕
Bemaraha
                    Antananarivo
Miandrivazo

Allée des
Baobabs   Antsirabe
Morondava ✕

         Manja   Fianarantsoa
Morombé

Great   Parc
Reef   National   Ihosy
         Isalo ✕   Manakara

Tuléar   Farafangana   INDIAN
(Toliara)   OCEAN

Anakao ✕

         Bekily

Androka   Fort Dauphin
                  (Taolagnaro)
     Faux Cap

0 _____ 200 km
N 0 _____ 100 miles

X MARKS THE SPOT

Parc National Isalo One of Madagascar's epic desert landscapes, with canyons, ravines, gorges and savannah-like plains.

Île Sainte Marie Tropical Sainte Marie is quite simply heavenly, with whales and turtles, dreamy beaches, and idyllic Île aux Nattes.

Allée des Baobabs Few things say Madagascar more than this small baobab-lined stretch between Morondava and Belo-sur-Tsiribihina.

Tsingy de Bemaraha There is nothing else on Earth quite like the jagged, otherworldly limestone pinnacles of Unesco World Heritage–listed Parc National Bemaraha.

Anakao Madagascar boasts the world's fifth-largest coral reef, the Great Reef running from Morombé in the north to Itampolo in the south. Anakao is the perfect base.

Madagascar

COUNTRY MADAGASCAR • **COORDINATES** 18.766° S, 46.869° E • **AREA** 587,041 SQ KM (226,658 SQ MILES)

Often called the Eighth Continent, Madagascar is actually the world's fourth-largest island (after Greenland, New Guinea and Borneo). Separated from the African mainland for up to 165 million years, Madagascar is extraordinarily diverse, with plants and animals like no other collection of creatures on the planet.

As a travel destination, it's a fascinating pastiche of resort-style tourism, barely accessible wilderness and just about everything in between. Wild Madagascar is best known for its lemurs, baobab trees and, in northern and western Madagascar, the weird-and-wonderful limestone karst formations known as *tsingy*.

ENDEMIC & ENTERTAINING

Thanks to its millions of years of isolation, 70% of Madagascar's animals and 90% of the island's plants are endemic. The most remarkable of these are Madagascar's 111 lemur species. They're entertaining to watch (they are primates after all, and therefore distant cousins of ours). They're also found nowhere else on Earth. Lemurs are divided into five families: the beautifully marked sifakas and indris (of which only one species is extant), all known for their leaping abilities; a family of small, nocturnal mouse lemurs that includes the world's smallest primates; the 'true' lemurs, such as the ring-tailed and ruffed lemurs;

the sportive lemurs; and, most remarkable of all, the bizarre, nocturnal aye-aye, which extracts grubs from under bark with its long, bony middle finger. Madagascar's most famous carnivore is the puma-like, lemur-eating fossa.

When it comes to plants, Madagascar has a remarkable 15,000 species, including bizarre octopus trees, several species of baobab, nearly a thousand different kinds of orchids and more than 60 kinds of aloe, all spread across spiny deserts, rainforests and coastal mangroves. More than half of the 200-plus bird species which breed in Madagascar are found nowhere else on Earth.

1. Allée des Baobabs

2. Coquerel's sifaka, Palmarium Reserve

3. Tsingy de Bemaraha

Réunion

COUNTRY FRANCE • **COORDINATES** 21.115° S, 55.536° E • **AREA** 2512 SQ KM (970 SQ MILES)

Rising from the Indian Ocean like a basaltic shield cloaked in green, Réunion seems designed with adventure tourism in mind. Hiking in the emerald interior mountains is the top activity in this French *département* (overseas territory), but canyoning, mountain biking, paragliding, rafting, diving, whale-watching and horseriding are also possible in this volcanic wonderland.

Claimed by France in the 17th century, the uninhabited isle was initially used to exile mutineers. As Réunion became more developed, enslaved people were transported from Africa and Madagascar to work its coffee plantations. Revolts in the late 18th century saw a number of large numbers of *marrons* (the name given to enslaved people fleeing the plantations) take refuge in the interior, and today their Creole cultural heritage remains particularly strong in the remote villages of the hikers' paradise known as the Cirques.

Each region of Réunion has its own personality, from the bustling capital of St-Denis in the north to the low-key villages of the east, the bastion of Réunion's Tamil community. The south coast is known for its wild scenery, while the west coast with its idyllic lagoon can feel like a tropical French Riviera, complete with beach bars and plenty of French tourists from the mainland. With direct flights from Paris, it's easy to understand why.

NO SURFING

Situated on a 'shark highway' between Australia and Africa, Réunion has one of the world's highest shark-attack rates. In 2013, authorities reacted to a string of attacks by banning swimming and surfing outside Réunion's lagoon, devastating the island's main surf hub of St-Leu – though diehards still paddle out here. While there are no waves in the huge turquoise lagoon stretching from La Saline-les-Bains to L'Hermitage-les-Bains, this natural pool is a beautiful place to swim, snorkel, paddleboard and kayak. A fringing reef keeps most of the sharks out, though the odd one has been known to slip in.

St-Denis

Ste-Suzanne

La Possession

Le Port

St-André

St-Paul

Bras-Panon

✕ *Cirque de Mafate*

St-Benoît

St-Gilles-les-Bains

✕ *Hell-Bourg*

Ste-Anne

L'Hermitage-les-Bains

Ste-Rose

✕ *Plage La Saline*

Cilaos

Plaine-des-Palmistes

Réunion National Park

St-Leu

Piton St-Leu

Piton de la Fournaise ✕

Entre-Deux

St-Louis

Le Tampon

✕ *Cascade de la Grande Ravine*

Rivière des Remparts

INDIAN OCEAN

St-Pierre

Petite-Île

St-Philippe

St-Joseph

Vincendo

20 km
10 miles

© Eric Valenne geostory | Shutterstock

X MARKS THE SPOT

Piton de la Fournaise Hike around the rim of this active volcano, which typically erupts several times per year.

Cascade de la Grande Ravine On the Rivière Langevin in the south, this spectacular waterfall forms part of one of the world's most thrilling canyoning routes.

Cirque de Mafate Soak up geological grandeur and Creole culture on this multi-day hike in the interior.

Plage La Saline This more relaxed section of the long beach fringing the lagoon is pure heaven.

Hell-Bourg With streets lined by colourful Creole villas, this mountain village is easily the island's most atmospheric town.

❷

1. Piton de la Fournaise

2. Paragliding

Mauritius

COUNTRY MAURITIUS • **COORDINATES** 20.348° S, 57.552° E • **AREA** 2040 SQ KM (788 SQ MILES)

The Mauritian tourism authorities don't need to come up with a catchy slogan: Mark Twain did it for them back in the 19th century, when he wrote that 'Mauritius was made first, and then heaven. Heaven was copied after Mauritius.' Mauritius is, quite simply, a beautiful island nation deep in the Indian Ocean, with a green, mountainous interior surrounded by a thin ribbon of white sand and a turquoise lagoon. The island also has an intriguing cultural and culinary mix that add depth and substance to its undeniably good looks.

STRETCHES OF SAND

No matter where you are on the island, there's a pretty, lightly trammelled stretch of sand not far away. The beaches of Mauritius' eastern and southern coastlines tend to be quieter, but the legendary surf or diving culture of the west coast can be just as appealing. But there's a chilling history to go with the beauty around Unesco World Heritage–listed Le Morne, on the island's southwest coast.

Le Morne's is a harrowing story known by every Mauritian: in the early 19th century, enslaved people fleeing the plantations found refuge in Le Morne Peninsula, where they established settlements high on Le Morne Brabant – Mauritius' most abrupt and dramatic rock formation. Living in this remote spot, they were unaware that slavery had been abolished; when soldiers were sighted climbing Le Morne, they chose to jump to their deaths from the cliffs rather than leave in chains. The steep hike to the summit is the island's most poignant, offering time to reflect on the past; it also promises heady views and the chance to see Mauritius' national flower, the boucle d'oreille.

Le Morne Brabant provides a backdrop to luxury resorts and one of the Indian Ocean's most unusual surfing experiences: surfers who catch the perfect wave will, according to local legend, see a small hole (or 'eye') appear in Le Morne's rock face.

1. Terres de 7 Couleurs, Chamarel

2. Chamarel Waterfall

3. Boating the shallow waters of the Black River district

INDIAN
OCEAN

0 — 20 km
0 — 10 miles

Île aux Serpents
Nature Reserve

Rodrigues
(600km)

Île Plate
Nature Reserve

Île Ronde
Nature
Reserve

Îlot
Gabriel

Coin de Mire
(Nature Reserve)

Pereybère

Grand
Gaube

Grand
Baie

Goodlands

Trou aux
Biches

Poudre
d'Or

Triolet

*Château
Labourdonnais*

*Sir Seewoosagur
Ramgoolam
Botanical Gardens*

Rivière
du Rempart

Port
Louis

Poste de Flacq

Centre
de Flacq

Belle Mare

Albion

Eureka

Moka

Bambous

Rose
Hill

Quartier
Militaire

Trou d'Eau
Douce

Flic en
Flac

Quatre
Bornes

Phoenix

Bel Air

Île aux
Cerfs

Vacoas

Tamarin

Curepipe

*Lion
Mountain*

Grande
Rivière Noire

*Black River
Gorges
National Park*

Rose
Belle

Vieux
Grand Port

Île aux
Bénitiers

La Gaulette

Chamarel

Mahébourg

Île aux
Aigrettes

Baie
du Cap

Chemin
Grenier

Rivière des
Anguilles

Plaisance

Souillac

X MARKS THE SPOT

Chamarel Home to a rum distillery, an ebony forest, a stunning landmark of coloured sands, a fun museum and a growing culinary reputation.

Black River Gorges National Park Mauritius' mountainous interior is thickly forested, with stunning waterfalls and hiking trails.

Botanical Gardens & Mansions See giant lily pads and giant tortoises in Sir Seewoosagur Ramgoolam Botanical Gardens, and the elegant colonial-era mansions of Eureka or Château Labourdonnais.

Rodrigues Marooned 600km (373 miles) from the main island of Mauritius, Rodrigues is the island time forgot, a mini-Mauritius and bastion of traditional Creole culture.

Lion Mountain A lion-shaped mountain, fabulous hiking and a fascinating wildlife backstory.

INDIAN OCEAN

1. Coral-stone coastline

2. Turquoise ornate day gecko

Île aux Aigrettes

COUNTRY MAURITIUS

COORDINATES 20.420° S, 57.732° E • **AREA** 0.27 SQ KM (0.1 SQ MILES)

In the outer reaches of a lagoon, 800m (2297ft) offshore from the main island in the country's southeast, this diminutive 26-hectare (64-acre) island is like a Mauritian Noah's Ark. Watched over by the Mauritian Wildlife Foundation, Île aux Aigrettes has an ancient ebony forest and endangered wildlife species: this is what Mauritius must have looked like before the first settlers arrived in the 16th century. It's a short boat ride out to the island from close to Mahébourg, and the views along the way, across the lagoon towards the mainland's Lion Mountain, are some of the loveliest anywhere in Mauritius.

THE WAY OF THE DODO

One of the first sights to greet you on arrival at Île aux Aigrettes is a bronze statue of a dodo, and that's no accident. This giant relative of the pigeon was once widespread across Mauritius, but it was plump and tame and no match for the Dutch sailors who wiped out the bird within decades of their arrival; the last confirmed sighting was in 1660. Ever since, the dodo has become a symbol of extinction. In response, Mauritius decided to become famous for the birds it has saved. By clearing pests and non-native predators from Île aux Aigrettes and other selected sites, the local government, working with the Mauritian Wildlife Foundation, has been remarkably successful: one 2007 study found that Mauritius had pulled more bird species (five) back from the brink of extinction than any other country on Earth. That some of these can now be seen on the island is one of the greatest conservation success stories anywhere in the Indian Ocean. Visits to the island are easy to organise, yet carefully controlled. Keeping visitor numbers down means that guides can easily find some of the sought-after species that could have gone the way of the dodo.

X MARKS THE SPOT

Pink Pigeon In 1986 there were just 12 left; today there are nearly 500, some living on Île aux Aigrettes.

Mauritian Kestrel In 1974 this was the world's most endangered bird species, with just four birds. Now 350 survive.

Other Birds Île aux Aigrettes is a vital refuge for the olive white-eye, with half of the species' remaining birds. It also shelters the Mauritius fody.

Reptiles Look down from time to time to see beautiful turquoise-and-red ornate day geckos and Telfair's skink (a clawed lizard).

Giant Tortoises The last surviving Indian Ocean giant tortoise (the Aldabra giant tortoise from Seychelles) was reintroduced to Île aux Aigrettes in 2000.

Map

400 km
200 miles

AMIRANTES
GROUP

Inner Islands
See Main Map

OUTER ISLANDS

ALPHONSE
GROUP

ALDABRA
GROUP

FARQUHAR
GROUP

INDIAN
OCEAN

Aride
Island

Curieuse
Island

Petite
Soeur

Grande
Soeur

Anse Lazio ✕

Praslin

Anse
Volbert

Cousin
Island

Félicité
Island

Marianne

Grand
Anse

Baie
Ste Anne

La
Passe

La
Digue

✕ **Anse Cocos**

Cousine
Island

**Anse
Source
d'Argent** ✕

✕ **Anse
Marron**

INNER ISLANDS

North
Island

La Passe

Silhouette
Island

Las
Mamelles

Île aux
Récifs

**Anse
Maquereau**
✕

Îlot
Frégate

Frégate
Island

Beau
Vallon

Ste Anne
Island

Victoria ★

Cerf
Island

Mahé

INDIAN
OCEAN

20 km
10 miles

X MARKS THE SPOT

Anse Source d'Argent This La Digue slice of paradise has perfect sand, stone and water, and is the beach you're probably thinking of when you imagine Seychelles.

Anse Marron Another La Digue stunner, backed by granite boulders and palm trees.

Anse Cocos Part of La Digue's extraordinary collection of beaches, Anse Cocos is secluded and blissfully beautiful.

Anse Lazio At the northwestern tip of Praslin, this stunner has palm trees, powder-like sand, granite boulders for bookends and bath-warm waters.

Anse Maquereau On the remote and exclusive island of Frégate, Anse Maquereau is the ultimate deserted-tropical-island experience.

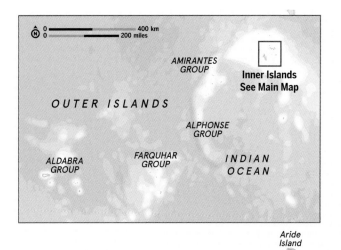

Seychelles

COUNTRY SEYCHELLES • **COORDINATES** 4.679° S, 55.492° E • **AREA** 458 SQ KM (179 SQ MILES)

There are few paradises quite so perfectly named as Seychelles: even the sound of its name suggests waves lapping gently on some deserted tropical shore. This 115-island archipelago is a stunning series of mountainous volcanic islands rising from the Indian Ocean off Africa's east coast. Apart from the main three islands – Mahé, Praslin and La Digue – most of the archipelago is uninhabited, save for exclusive island resorts in blissful isolation far out to sea. Seychelles is also home to what may be the world's smallest capital city, its smallest national park, and some of the most beautiful beaches on Earth.

ISLAND PARADISE

Mahé is the largest island in the archipelago and the gateway to Seychelles. Ringed by picturesque beaches, home to spice gardens and Seychelles' best restaurants, the island is the nation's cultural and political capital.

It also has a luxury marina and a steeply forested interior criss-crossed by the hiking trails of Morne Seychellois National Park.

Connected to Mahé by regular ferry, Praslin also has a dense forest at its core, and an impressive portfolio of beaches, while La Digue, watched over by a near-perfect volcanic cone, is quieter again and every bit as beautiful.

Beyond the main islands, Seychelles has some teardrop-sized islands offering varying degrees of isolation. Visible from Mahé, Silhouette is a beautiful pyramid of forest with luxury accommodation and the usual Seychelles mix of great snorkelling, hiking, and even an indulgent spa. Bird Island has astonishing colonies of seabirds and a fascinating ecological story. North Island is another ecological outpost of astonishing mid-ocean abundance, while Denis, Frégate and Félicité feel like lost worlds far from civilisation. Even further out to sea, the Aldabra Atoll has 150,000 giant tortoises and countless birds on one of the most remote pieces of land on the planet.

1. Granite rock formations on Anse Source d'Argent

2. George, the eldest giant tortoise on Cousin Island

3. Vallée de Mai, Praslin

X MARKS THE SPOT

Aga Khan Mosque One of Zanzibar's largest mosques, with pointed Arabesque windows, a large airy courtyard and a Gujarati-style carved door.

Darajani Market It's easy to imagine Zanzibar's spice-trading and fishing heyday in this aromatic market.

Forodhani Gardens These waterside gardens date back to 1936 and are a real hub of local community life.

House of Wonders This glorious 19th-century home rises in impressive tiers of slender steel pillars and balconies, and enormous carved wooden doors.

Old Dispensary With green latticework balconies and sculpted clock tower, this 19th-century, Indian-built gem is one of the most attractive landmarks on the waterfront.

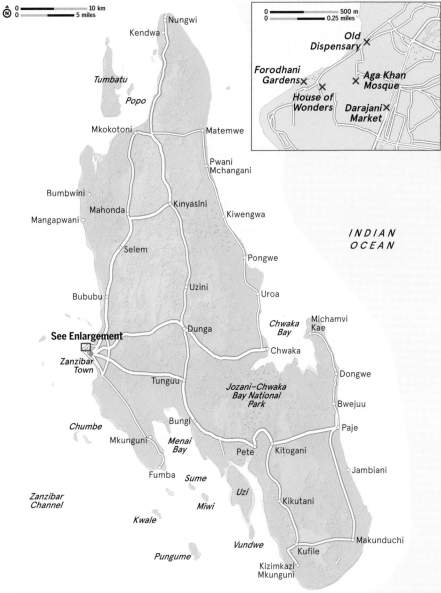

© Africarway | Getty Images. © ImageGap | Getty Images

Zanzibar

COUNTRY TANZANIA • **COORDINATES** 6.135° S, 39.362° E • **AREA** 2461 SQ KM (950 SQ MILES)

Bathed in spice-laden trade winds down through the centuries and beloved by travellers looking for a multi-layered Indian Ocean escape, Zanzibar is an East African destination utterly unlike anywhere else. The island's cultural and historical stories come to life in the exquisite architecture of Stone Town, in the enticing smells from spice warehouses along the waterfront on a steamy tropical afternoon, and in the call to prayer that animates the tangle of laneways unchanged in centuries. It's also an island of swaying palm trees, perfect sunsets and incredible fun, both on and under the water.

BUILDINGS TELL THEIR HISTORY

Shaped like a triangle, Stone Town is bounded on two sides by the sea, with most sights along the northern seafront or hidden away in the narrow streets between Creek Rd and the ocean. And as befits its prime position at the crossroads of civilisations, Stone Town's architecture is a fusion of Arabic, Indian, European and African influences.

As you wander the labyrinth, you'll quickly learn the historical influences that lie behind each building: Arab architects built multistorey homes that surrounded an inner courtyard, with ingenious designs that allowed cooling sea breezes to circulate naturally; wealthy Indian merchants commissioned ornate facades and buildings with shops at street level and living quarters on the upper floors. Most famously in Zanzibari architecture, the carved wooden door was a symbol of wealth and status, and was very often the first part of a house to be built; some of the doors are centuries old, with elaborate calligraphic passages in Arabic from the Quran. Others have semicircular tops and intricate floral decorations or aspirational designs: a fish expressed the owner's hope for many children, a date tree symbolised prosperity. The brass spikes were of Indian origin: according to tradition, the spikes protected doors from being battered down by elephants.

1. Darajani Market

2. Kiwengwa Beach

3. Zanzibari carved wooden door

❸

Socotra

COUNTRY YEMEN • **COORDINATES** 12.463° N, 53.823° E • **AREA** 3796 SQ KM (1466 SQ MILES)

Lying offshore from the Horn of Africa and the Arabian Peninsula, Socotra belongs politically to Yemen and is geographically a part of Africa. The island has been a Unesco World Heritage site since 2008, and its rugged, blistered interior shelters remarkable diversity: more than 700 of the island's species (including one-third of Socotra's plant species) are found nowhere else on Earth. Geographers consider Socotra to be one of the most isolated non-volcanic landforms on the planet, and its millions of years of isolation from other land masses is responsible for its famously biodiverse ecosystems.

ENDS OF THE EARTH

Part of the Gondwana supercontinent in ancient geological times, Socotra has always been a place of raw natural beauty and swirling legends. Everyone from Plato to Marco Polo ascribed magical powers to Socotra's inhabitants, while some believe it to have been the long-lost Garden of Eden. It is home to Socotra dragon trees and Sinbad the Sailor – he of *The Thousand and One Nights* fame – who lost his boat here to a gigantic bird while visiting the island on his fifth voyage.

Buffeted by wild weather and in keeping with its location at the geographical crossroads of historical trading empires, civilisations and religions, Socotra is quintessentially Arabian and African, and yet very much its own place, with a fiercely independent streak. Its geography, too, is unlike anywhere else, with a desert shoreline rising abruptly from the ocean's edge.

In the interior, otherworldly plant species cling to jagged rocky outcrops and barren moonscapes. Elsewhere, the land falls away to oasis-like deep canyons filled with palm forests. Barely 60,000 people now live on the main island, but away from the small settlements it can feel as if you've landed on a silent desert island somewhere close to the end of the Earth.

X MARKS THE SPOT

Socotra Dragon Tree (*Dracaena cinnabari*) A bizarre tree that looks like the cross between an umbrella and a candelabra, with red sap oozing from within.

Other Endemic Plants How about the cucumber tree (*Dendrosicyos socotranus*), the Socotran pomegranate (*Punica protopunica*), or the baobab-like Socotra desert rose (*Adenium socotranum*).

Reptiles Of Socotra's 31 reptile species, 29 are endemic, including the island's very own chameleon (*Chamaeleo monachus*).

Birds Socotra has 225 bird species, including six that are only found here: endemic varieties of sparrow, cisticola, starling, Socotra sunbird, warbler and bunting.

Roc This gigantic mythical bird of prey destroyed Sinbad the Sailor's boat – or so he said...

❶

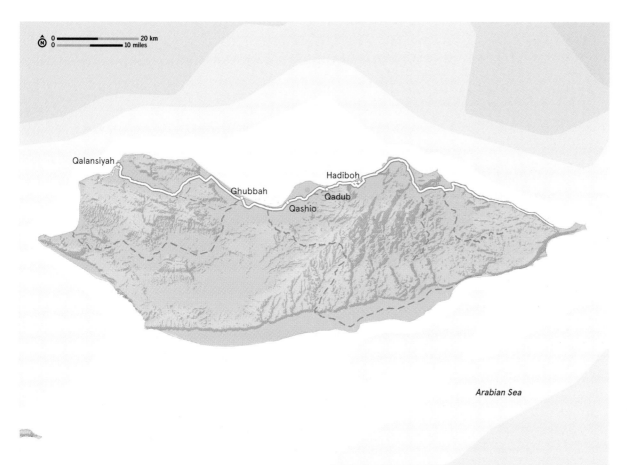

Qalansiyah

Ghubbah

Hadiboh

Qashio

Qadub

Arabian Sea

1. The Roc, a gigantic mythical bird of prey

2. Socotra dragon trees

São Tomé

Príncipe
(150km)

Morro
Peixe

Praia
Gamboa

Neves   Guadalupe

São Tomé

Pico de
São Tomé

Santana

Agua Izé

Ribeira
Afonso

Volta
a ilha

Sao João Angolares

Praia
Pesqueira

Malanza   Monte Mario

Gulf of
Guinea

Porto Alegre   Ponta Baleia

Praia
Café

Ilhéu
das Rolas

0   20 km
0   10 miles

Príncipe

Ilhéu
Bom Bom

Praia
Banana

Santo
Antonio

Baia das
Lagunhas

Gulf of
Guinea

Ilhéu
Caroço

0   10 km
0   5 miles

1. Cão Grande

2. Portuguese
architecture along the
streets of Santo António

1

São Tomé & Príncipe

COUNTRY SÃO TOMÉ & PRÍNCIPE
COORDINATES 0.186° N, 6.613° E • **AREA** 1001 SQ KM (386 SQ MILES)

Adrift in the Gulf of Guinea, this two-island nation is Africa's second-smallest, and one that blends natural wonders with a gripping history. São Tomé & Príncipe (STP) is a safe and welcoming ecotourism destination, as rich in jungles as it is beautiful. This is especially true on unspoiled Príncipe, which has a population of just 7000. A canopy of green broken by spires of primordial rock, Príncipe is magnificent and wild, offering fantastic beaches, jungle exploration, snorkelling, fishing and birdwatching. A centre of cacao production and with a promising economic future as an oil producer, it's an island nation on the cusp of great change.

COMEBACK OF THE RAINFOREST

São Tomé & Príncipe belong to a chain of volcanoes that begins in Cameroon and extends 1600km (994 miles) out into the Gulf of Guinea along a geographic fault line some 3000m (9843ft) deep. Príncipe is around 31 million years old, twice the age of São Tomé, and was once much larger, extending outward to encompass the small Tinhosa islands, now some 20km (12 miles) distant. Throughout STP erosion has left behind magnificent spires of phonolite, the hardened remains of ancient magma columns. On São Tomé the most striking of these is Cão Grande (Great Canine), the country's postcard view; Príncipe has the gloriously primeval-looking Baía das Agulhas (Bay of Spires).

Prior to the arrival of the Portuguese, in around 1470, both islands were covered in rainforest. During colonial rule, this primary forest was almost completely cut down, the exception being only the highest, most inaccessible peaks. With the decline of the *roças* (plantations) the jungle has made an extraordinary comeback. Today Príncipe has a secondary canopy covering almost the entire island. Thanks to its remoteness, STP has a high level of endemism in its flora and fauna. This includes 25 bird species (the highest concentration of endemic bird species in the world) and 120 plant species (including the world's smallest and largest begonias).

X MARKS THE SPOT

Baía das Agulhas Take a spectacular trip back in time via boat to see Príncipe's extraordinary volcanic skyline.

Praia Café Relax and enjoy a picnic on this stunning beach on Ilhéu das Rolas.

Praia Banana Admire the golden curves, swaying palms and turquoise waters of a paradise beach, and have them all to yourself.

Pico de São Tomé Climb the highest peak in the country for an unforgettable jungle adventure.

Volta a Ilha For the truly ambitious, this coastal hike is a two-day journey into wilderness.

ASIA

Bozcaada

COUNTRY TURKEY • **COORDINATES** 39.8205°N, 26.0357°E • **AREA** 38 SQ KM (14.6 SQ MILES)

A showcase of rustic Aegean style, Bozcaada (Tenedos in Greek) is a delightful Turkish island with an incredibly storied history, having been occupied by everyone from the Phoenicians to the Persians, Venetians and the Ottomans over the centuries. This small and windswept isle even scored a few Homeric shout-outs in *The Iliad*.

A (very) popular weekend and summer getaway for Turkish tourists, Bozcaada remains little-known internationally. But there is much to tempt the 35-minute ferry ride from Geyikli, south of Troy. Most of the action occurs in Merkez (Bozcaada Town), which has an atmospheric historic Greek quarter full of brightly painted houses converted into boutique hotels, B&Bs, bars and tavernas strung with fairy lights (most only open during the mid-June to mid-September high season). Beyond lie sandy beaches lapped by gin-clear turquoise water, while vineyards stretch across the gentle rolling hills that rise up behind the coast.

WINE ISLAND

Bozcaada has been one of Turkey's great winegrowing regions since ancient times, when enormous quantities of wine were used to fuel the debauchery at festivals for the wine god Dionysus. Nobody is quite why, but the island's *terroir* perfectly suits the growing of grapes. Among Bozcaada's best-known winemakers are Corvus, Talay, Amadeus and Yunatçılar, which markets its wines under the Çamlıbağ label.

The four major indigenous grape varietals are Vasilaki and Cavus for the production of white wine, Kuntra and Karalahana for red. Generally speaking, the Cabernet Sauvignon and Cabernet Shiraz wines produced here are the most impressive. Sample them at cellar doors and in the many Greek-style tavernas in Merkez, or join the festivities during the annual Bozcaada Wine Festival, held over the first weekend of September during the grape harvest.

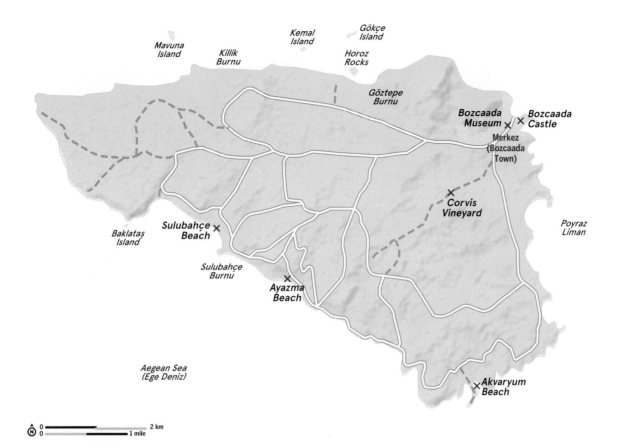

Mavuna Island

Kemal Island

Gökçe Island

Killik Burnu

Horoz Rocks

Göztepe Burnu

Bozcaada Museum × × Bozcaada Castle

Merkez (Bozcaada Town)

× Corvis Vineyard

Poyraz Liman

Baklataş Island

Sulubahçe Beach ×

Sulubahçe Burnu

× Ayazma Beach

Aegean Sea (Ege Deniz)

× Akvaryum Beach

0 ————— 2 km
0 ————— 1 mile

X MARKS THE SPOT

Beaches The southern side of the island is home to the best swimming beaches: Akvaryum (Aquarium), Ayazma and Sulubahçe.

Cuisine Local specialities include *kurabiye* (biscuits) made with *bademli* (almonds) and *sakızlı* (mastic); *oğlak kapama* (goat meat stewed with lettuce and fennel); and *domates reçeli* (tomato jam).

Bozcaada Castle Looming over Bozcaada Town's ferry terminal, this fortress is thought to date from Byzantine times.

Corvus Vineyards Taste award-winning drops at Bozcaada's best-known winery, on the road to Akvaryum Beach.

Bozcaada Museum In Bozcaada Town, this small museum and local-history research centre is a treasure trove of island curios.

❷

❸

1. Fishing boats

2. Bozcaada Castle

3. Autumn harvest, Bozcaada vineyard

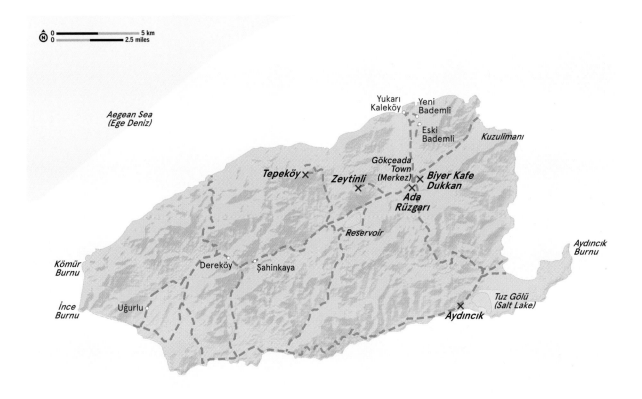

Aegean Sea
(Ege Deniz)

Yukarı Kaleköy
Yeni Bademli
Eski Bademli
Kuzulimanı

Tepeköy ✕
Zeytinli ✕
Gökçeada Town (Merkez) ✕
Biyer Kafe Dukkan ✕
Ada Rüzgarı ✕

Reservoir

Aydıncık Burnu

Kömür Burnu
Dereköy
Şahinkaya

İnce Burnu
Uğurlu

Tuz Gölü (Salt Lake)

Aydıncık ✕

X MARKS THE SPOT

Tepeköy Great for an island stay, this Greek village offers spectacular views over the countryside.

Aydıncık Gökçeada's best beach is adjacent to Tuz Gölü (Salt Lake), a favourite shelter for pink flamingos between November and March.

Biyer Kafe Dukkan Enjoy the island's best homestyle cooking at this Merkez restaurant. There's no fixed menu, but everything is delicious.

Zeytinli Another fine island base is this revitalised village, where you can sip Turkish-style coffee in traditional Greek cafes.

Ada Rüzgarı From olive oil to jams, Gökçeada is committed to producing organic foodstuffs, and this shop in Merkez is one of the best places to buy them.

1. Kitesurfers off the coast of Gökçeada

2. Pink flamingos

Gökçeada

COUNTRY TURKEY • **COORDINATES** 40.1940°N, 25.9047°E • **AREA** 279 SQ KM (108 SQ MILES)

Just 20km (12 miles) from the Gallipoli (Gelibolu) Peninsula, 'Heavenly Island' is a spectacular Aegean outpost, its population of around 9500 swelling in the summer months as domestic tourists are drawn by its unspoiled landscape, sandy beaches, charming villages and Greek-influenced culture. At other times of the year, Gökçeada is a tranquil, windswept place where visitors are rare and the surroundings are truly bucolic.

A ferry links the island with Kabatepe at the heart of the Gallipoli Peninsula, a journey of just 75 minutes – yet few foreign travellers make the trip beyond the Gallipoli battlefields. Those who do will find a small but alluring range of accommodation options and plenty of opportunities for swimming, windsurfing, trekking and cultural tourism.

GREEK EXODUS

Gökçeada was once a predominantly Greek island known as Imbros or İmroz. During WWI, it was an important base for the Gallipoli campaign; indeed, Allied commander General Ian Hamilton stationed himself at the village of Aydıncık (then Kefalos) on the island's southeastern coast. Along with its smaller island neighbour to the south, Bozcaada, Gökçeada was ceded to the new Turkish Republic in 1923 as part of the Treaty of Lausanne but was exempted from the population exchange, retaining a predominantly Greek population.

However in 1946, Turkish authorities installed the first wave of Turkish settlers from the Black Sea region, starting a clear but unstated process of 'Turkification' that reached its height in the 1960s and 1970s, when up to 6000 ethnic Turks from the mainland were relocated here. Greek schools were forcibly closed, many Greek churches were desecrated and 90% of the island's cultivatable land was appropriated from Greek residents, most of whom had no choice but to leave. In 1970, the island was renamed Gökçeada by the Turkish government. These days, there are approximately 200 Greek residents.

❷

Sri Lanka

COUNTRY SRI LANKA • **COORDINATES** 7.873° N, 80.771° E • **AREA** 65,610 SQ KM (25,332 SQ MILES)

In the 13th century, Venetian explorer Marco Polo opined that Sri Lanka was, 'for its size, better circumstanced than any island in the world', and it remains one of the world's most fascinating destinations. Influenced by its strategic position at the centre of trading routes, Sri Lankan cuisine features echoes of many cultures, while an exceptional cultural and architectural heritage includes the ancient cities of Anuradhapura and Polonnaruwa built by the first Sinhalese rulers, and the shaded streets and heritage Dutch mansions of Galle. And on such a compact island nation, the influence of the sea is always tangible: from the colourful fishing boats of Sri Lanka's southern coast to the Arugam Bay surfing scene.

BEYOND 'RICE & CURRY'

Has any other such interesting cuisine ever been so prosaically described? Restaurants and cafes throughout Sri Lanka offer 'rice and curry', but the reality when travelling in the country is much more exciting. Even breakfast can be a multi-dish extravaganza, with a variety of side dishes including chilli- and coconut-laced *pol sambol* partnering with egg hoppers (bowl-shaped pancakes), or delicate string hoppers (steamed noodles) served with grated coconut and a drizzle of unctuous sweet syrup from the kitul palm. Order the dish known as *lamprais* – the name derives from *lomprijst* (a packet of rice), a dish

enjoyed by the first Dutch settlers to Sri Lanka in the 17th century – and there's a whole world of flavours. All baked slowly together in a banana leaf, a trio of Indian-influenced curries are served with turmeric-infused rice and condiments tinged with Southeast Asian-style shrimp paste or spicy Malay sambal. Journey by train through the cooler forests and tea plantations of the Hill Country, and you'll be gently interrupted by snack vendors proffering roti flatbreads and samosas, both originally introduced to Sri Lanka by Arab traders. Throughout the country, you'll find tasty evidence of the waves of culinary influences that have washed over this teardrop-shaped island.

1. Hill Country tea plantation

2. *Bittara aappa*, the Sri Lankan egg hopper

3. Mannar Island beach

X MARKS THE SPOT

Sigiriya Ascend this terracotta-hued monolith of rock for views of ancient frescoes and stunning central Sri Lankan vistas from the sprawling summit.

Kandy Sri Lanka's second-largest city is a cool-climate Hill Country destination enlivened by compact Kandy Lake and the Temple of the Sacred Tooth.

Mirissa The waters off this southern Sri Lankan beach town are visited by both sperm whales and blue whales from December to April.

Adam's Peak Walking up Adam's Peak, known to Sri Lankans as Sri Pada (Sacred Footprint), usually begins around 2am to ensure reaching the summit around sunrise.

Galle Dutch-colonial architecture, including stellar accommodation in restored mansions, combines with a thriving arts and literary scene in this fort town.

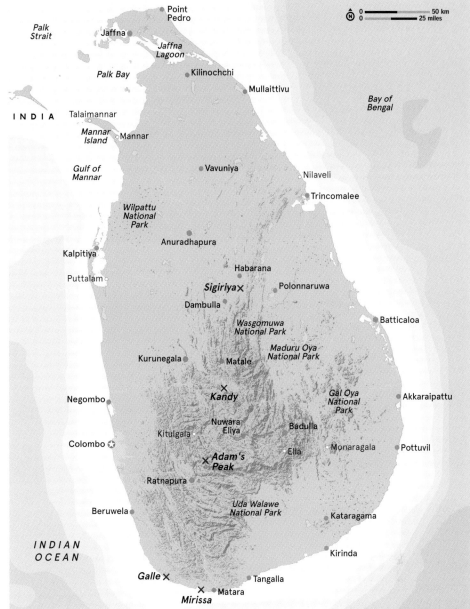

West
Beach ✕

✕ Oceanic

Southern
Lagoon

Bay of Bengal

✕ Cherradhip

0 ———— 1 km
0 ———— 0.5 miles
N

X MARKS THE SPOT

West Beach This scenic sweep of beach is the island's main attraction.

Diving & Snorkelling You can dive and snorkel between November and March with the dive group Oceanic, based on East Beach.

Fish New species are still being discovered in these waters, with three new specimens recorded in 2021.

Cherradhip Visiting the island's southern tip – also Bangladesh's southernmost point, which is cut off at high tide – is now banned for conservation reasons, but you can still admire it from the shore.

Coconuts St Martin's is also known as Narikel Jinjira (Coconut Island); pick up a nut from one of the beach vendors.

❶

❷

St Martin's Island

COUNTRY BANGLADESH
COORDINATES 20.6237°N, 92.3234°E • AREA 3 SQ KM (1.1 SQ MILES)

South from the coastal tourism centre of Cox's Bazar, postcard-worthy St Martin's Island is Bangladesh's only coral island, and when you step off the ferry, you'll discover that its palm-shaded beaches, fringed by crystal-clear water, actually match the hype. Only about 6km (3.7 miles) in length and rarely more than 1km (0.6 miles) wide, St Martin's is easy to navigate. Rickshaws are available, but you can also just walk around the island, from beach to beach.

Locals primarily work as fishers, but increasingly from the domestic tourism industry – pre-pandemic, St Martin's had become one of the nation's premier tourism destinations. There are a few hotels and hotels and restaurants in Narikeldia at the northeast tip of the island, where the ferry arrives. From here you'll pass through the small village of Uttarpara en route to West Beach, which is the nicest place to stay – for now, at least.

CHASING CORAL

Home to an impressive diversity of marine life, including 234 fish species and globally threatened marine mammal, turtle and cetacean species, the coral reefs and associated habitats of St Martin's Island aren't only ecologically important. They also contribute US$33.6 million per year to the local economy via tourism, fishing, seaweed farming and other activities.

However, with unregulated tourism development (including the harvesting of coral to sell to tourists) increasingly putting stress on these fragile habitats, researchers have warned that the island's coral – and as a result, its economy – is under threat. Oceanographers have called for the island to be declared a marine protected area in order to help safeguard both. But as Bangladesh's government continues to drag its feet in mandating and policing protections, it's anyone's guess how long St Martin's will survive – as a tourism destination, a critical habitat or a viable place to live.

1. West Beach

2. Exposed coral, Cherradhip

3. St Martin's Island fishing boats

Andaman & Nicobar Islands

COUNTRY INDIA • **COORDINATES** 11.7401° N, 92.6586° E • **AREA** 8249 SQ KM (3185 SQ MILES)

Some of the world's most remote islands lie flung out in the Andaman Sea, several hundred kilometres off the coasts of Thailand, Indonesia and Myanmar (Burma). The twist is that, since the 1950s, they have been part of India – though they have been inhabited by groups of indigenous tribal communities for thousands of years. Resting almost 1400km (870 miles) east of mainland India, the 572 Andaman and Nicobar Islands appear in a blur of pearly white beaches, age-old forests, mangrove-fringed shallows and rustling coconut palms. Only a handful of them are open to travellers (the Nicobars are completely off-limits) and, once you've flown into the capital Port Blair, transport is by trundling ferry, bus or jeep-taxi.

THE ISLANDS' INDIGENOUS POPULATIONS

In 2010, a Great Andamanese elder by the name of Boa Sr, thought to be around 85, passed away in Port Blair, taking with her the 65,000-year-old Bo tribal language – she had become its last remaining speaker. Boa Sr reportedly survived the 2004 Indian Ocean tsunami by climbing up a tree, and in her final months had no one to talk to in her native language, though she also spoke an Andamanese dialect of Hindi. Her mother Boro had died the previous year, the final speaker of another ancient language, Khora.

Long before British colonisers swooped in from the mid-19th century onwards, for millennia the Andaman and Nicobar Islands were the home of 10 indigenous tribal communities, including the Jarawa, Onge, Sentinelese, Andamanese, Shompen and Nicobarese. New arrivals (which went on to include Indian and other Asian settlers) brought with them deadly diseases and violent attacks, leading to several indigenous groups being completely wiped out in a matter of decades. Today, most of the islands' indigenous populations live in off-limits tribal reserve areas; forest clearance, road construction, contact with settlers, tourism development, alcoholism and countless other factors pose an ever-growing threat to their survival.

Map

0 50 km
0 25 miles

Landfall Island

Narcondam Island

Shyamnagar

West Coral Reef

Aerial Bay · Diglipur

North Andaman

Ramnagar

Interview Island

✕ **Mayabunder**

Bay of Bengal

Tugapur

Anderson Island

Middle Andaman

Rangat · Amkunj

Middle Coral Reef

Barren Island

South Coral Reef

Kadamtala · *Henry Lawrence Island*

Baratang Island

John Lawrence Island

Port Meadows

✕ **Swaraj Dweep**

Havelock Island

✕ **Shaheed Dweep**

South Andaman

Neil Island

Bamboo Flat

✕ **Port Blair**

Wandoor · Sippighat

North Sentinel Island

· Chidiya Tapu

Rutland Island

Andaman Sea

Little Andaman ✕

· Hut Bay

↓ Nicobar Islands (250km)

X MARKS THE SPOT

Swaraj Dweep (Havelock Island) With its salt-white beaches, teal shallows, bamboo bungalows and fabulous diving, this beachy pearl is the Andamans' most popular destination.

Shaheed Dweep (Neil Island) A small sandy sweep of an island where you might spot rare dugongs offshore.

Port Blair The lively provincial capital (and transport hub) of the Andamans, with curious historical sights and teeming markets.

Mayabunder A handful of community tourism projects unveil traditional island life, with local villagers opening their homes to visitors in the little-visited northern half of the Andamans.

Little Andaman A whispered-about star of India's surf world; part of the island is an off-limits reserve for the indigenous Onge population.

1. Kids playing in the water on Swaraj Dweep (Havelock Island)

2. Giant sea fan

3. The resplendent Nicobar pigeon

Ao Phang-Nga

COUNTRY THAILAND
COORDINATES 8.2446° N, 98.5635° E • **AREA** 400 SQ KM (154 SQ MILES)

Paddling through emerald-green waters on a swaying kayak, gazing out on sky-reaching karst outcrops, you eventually emerge in a hushed *hôrng* (interior lagoon), with only the gentle rolling waves for company. This is the irresistible beauty of Ao Phang-Nga, the sprawling, twinkling bay wedged between Phuket and Krabi on Thailand's Andaman coast, where sheer limestone cliffs disappear into the jade-hued sea and cackling crab-eating macaques clamber through eerily quiet mangroves. A protected national park since 1981, its expanses are home to over 40 limestone islands, a series of tidal channels and Thailand's largest mangrove forests, creating an unrivalled coastal wildlife habitat. On a crack-of-dawn adventure here, you're galaxies away from Phuket's bustle.

MANGROVES, WILDLIFE & MASS TOURISM

Towering limestone karsts, shimmering tidal channels, shady mangrove forests – Ao Phang-Nga's spectacular landscape gives rise to a unique coastal ecosystem with a wonderfully rich parade of local wildlife. Roaming mammal characters here include crab-eating macaques, fruit bats, white-handed gibbons and dusky langurs, and reptiles range from Malayan pit vipers to Bengal monitor lizards, two-banded monitor lizards and flying lizards. The meandering mangroves play a key role in protecting corals by filtering out sediments and salt, and also provide an important feeding and breeding space for a wide range of fish and crab species. All kinds of land and seabirds swing by too, such as kingfishers, swallows, bee eaters, Brahminy kites, egrets, herons and edible-nest swiftlets.

Sadly, like much of Thailand's coastline, in recent years the bay has come under enormous threat from mass tourism, including visitors feeding fish and boats anchoring on delicate coral reefs. Anyone considering exploring Ao Phang-Nga should look for community-based initiatives that channel resources back into the local population, and responsible tour operators fuelled by respect for the natural environment, such as long-established John Gray's Seacanoe (johngray-seacanoe.com).

1. Ko Panyi floating fishing village

2. Passing through limestone formations on Ao Phang Nga

3. Aerial view of Ao Phang-Nga National Park

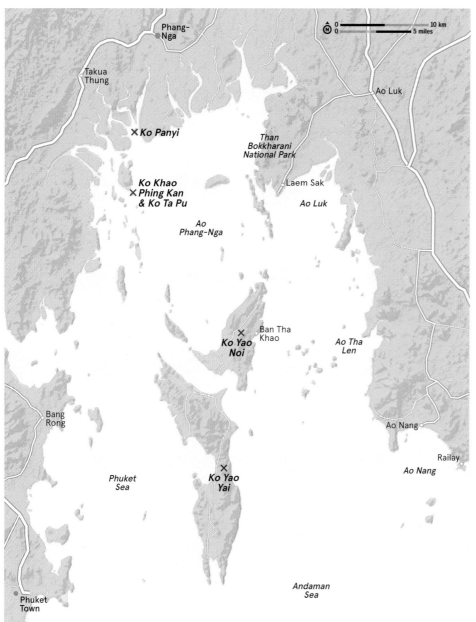

Phang-Nga

Takua Thung

× *Ko Panyi*

Than Bokkharani National Park

Ao Luk

Ko Khao
× *Phing Kan & Ko Ta Pu*

Laem Sak

Ao Luk

Ao Phang-Nga

Ban Tha Khao

× *Ko Yao Noi*

Ao Tha Len

Bang Rong

Ao Nang

Railay

× *Ko Yao Yai*

Ao Nang

Phuket Sea

Andaman Sea

Phuket Town

0   10 km
0   5 miles

X MARKS THE SPOT

Ko Panyi This karst-cliff islet is home to a Muslim fishing village (where visitors can stay overnight), with bamboo-and-wood stilt houses and a floating football pitch.

Ko Yao Noi Spectacular views of Ao Phang-Nga await on a low-key island in the middle of the bay, known for its sustainable and family-owned tourism initiatives.

Ko Khao Phing Kan & Ko Ta Pu These hugely popular twin karst islands were made famous as a location set for the James Bond film *The Man with the Golden Gun*.

Ko Yao Yai The lush, go-slow island of Ko Yao Yai remains a less-developed pocket of southern Thailand in the heart of Phang-Nga Bay.

2

3

0 | 5 km
0 | 2.5 miles

Ban Hua Hin

Ban Khlong Mak

Ban Lang Sot

Ban Sala Dan

Ko Lanta Noi

Ban Lu Yong

Ko Talabeng

Ko Klang

Ban Phra Ae

Ban Thung Yi Pheng

Ko Kam

Ban Phu Klom

Ko Lanta Yai

Ban Je Li

Ban Khlong Khong

Ko Bu Bu

Ban Khlong Tob

Ban Khlong Nin

✕ *Ban Si Raya*

Ko Por

Andaman Sea

Ban Hua Laem

Ban Khlong Hin

Ao Kantiang

Ban Sangka-U

Ko Kluang

Ko Lek

Ao Mai Phai ✕

✕ *Mu Ko Lanta National Park*

Laem Tanod

Ko Haa (22km);
Hin Daeng (40km);
Hin Muang (42km) ↓

X MARKS THE SPOT

Ban Si Raya Ancient teak stilt homes, waterside fresh-fish restaurants, vibrantly painted wooden shophouses – Lanta Old Town simmers with local history.

Mu Ko Lanta National Park Since 1990, this marine park has protected the southern tip of Ko Lanta along with a clutch of surrounding islands.

Hin Daeng & Hin Muang Among Thailand's most beloved dive sites, with likely sightings of whale sharks, manta rays and more.

Ko Haa One of the national park's standout spots for its limestone karsts and fantastic cave diving.

Ao Mai Phai Ko Lanta's secluded far southwestern beach is a back-to-nature delight, framed by lush forests.

~~~~~~~~~~~~

1. Firelight entertainment

2. Boats approach Ko Lanta

Ko Lanta

COUNTRY THAILAND • **COORDINATES** 7.6244° N, 99.0792° E • **AREA** 81 SQ KM (31 SQ MILES)

The origins of Ko Lanta's curious name are lost to history, though there are endless theories. Slung off southern Thailand's Andaman coast, south from Krabi, this is a go-slow jewel of an island awash with coconut palms, honey-gold sands, bamboo-built beach bars and whispering mangroves, where the culturally mixed local population takes in Thai-Muslims, Thai-Chinese and *chow lair* (sea gypsy) communities. Even getting here is a hardy adventure involving at least three different types of transport: there's no road connection to mainland Thailand, despite ambitious plans to build a 2km-long (1.2-mile)bridge. Then there's the famously terrific diving – whale sharks, manta rays, leopard sharks and other creatures lurk beneath the surface, among rainbow-coloured corals and dramatic drop-offs. And while a sprinkling of design-conscious lodgings might now mingle with the cheerful seaside huts, Lanta still moves to its own mellow beachy beat.

KO LANTA'S BACKSTORY

Around 500 years ago, a community of nomadic *chow lair* landed on the island today called Ko Lanta, and began settling along its eastern shore. Fast-forward a few centuries and they were joined by groups of Malay Muslims and, later on, by enterprising Chinese merchants. Ko Lanta's east-coast settlement, Ban Si Raya (now known simply as Lanta Old Town), grew into an important international trading outpost in the 20th century, dealing in local tin and other southern-

Thailand riches as a stopover between various key Asian ports, including Phuket and Penang; you'll still spot many original traditional Thai-Chinese homes here. The town eventually lost its 'capital' status to Ban Sala Dan, in northern Ko Lanta.

Meanwhile, tourism began to trickle in with the arrival of a few northern European backpackers in the 1980s, but it wasn't until 2016 that a road bridge swooped in, linking Ko Lanta Yai with Ko Lanta Noi to the north.

0 ——— 2 km
0 ——— 1 mile
N

Mosquito
Island ✕

Bamboo
Island ✕

Andaman
Sea

Ao Lo
Lana
Hat Nui ✕
Ko Nai   ✕ Ao Lo Bakao
Hat Noppharat
Tharañmu -
Ko Phi Phi National Park
Ao Lo
Dalam   Phi-Phi
Ton Sai   ✕ Viewpoint
Village
Ao Lo
Ko Nok   Ao Ton   Mu Di
Sai
Ao Wang
Long

✕ Ao Pileh
Ko Phi-Phi
Leh

X MARKS THE SPOT

Ao Pileh Emerald waters glitter
between the soaring limestone cliffs
of this beautiful natural lagoon on Ko
Phi-Phi Leh's eastern coast.

Ao Lo Bakao A blissful blonde strand
clings to Ko Phi-Phi Don's northeast
shore, fringed by coconut palms,
forested outcrops and a few upscale
resorts.

Phi-Phi Viewpoint Several hundred
steep steps twist and turn their
way up to a beloved, view-blessed
lookout.

Bamboo & Mosquito Islands Boat out
to these two offshore islets, whose
pale-gold beaches are washed by
sapphire waves.

Hat Nui A tiny, remote karst-framed
cove with good snorkelling on the
northwest side of Ko Phi-Phi Don.

Ko Phi-Phi Islands

COUNTRY THAILAND
COORDINATES 7.7407° N, 98.7784° E • **AREA** 12 SQ KM (4.6 SQ MILES)

In a far-flung patch of southern Thailand's Hat Noppharat Tharanmu Ko Phi Phi National Park, richly forested karst cliffs cascade into natural aquamarine lagoons and salt-white beaches stretch beneath bobbing palms. With their irresistible natural beauty and outstanding diving, it's no surprise that the twin Ko Phi-Phi islands have grown into one of Southeast Asia's most sought-after destinations. Yet despite sitting within a protected national park, the islands' enormous overtourism concerns have been hitting headlines for years, centred on once-heavenly Maya Bay. Now, in attempts to carve out a more sustainable path and combat overtourism, strict regulations include fines for anchoring on coral reefs, caps on visitor numbers and tightly controlled access to all the most popular spots. Visitors will want to carefully consider their potential impact on this fragile space and engage with it in a responsible, in-depth way; this includes choosing sustainably focused accommodation, avoiding single-use plastics, supporting genuinely local businesses and joining positive-impact activities (from cooking courses to expert-led hikes and beach clean-ups).

MAYA BAY: PARADISE LOST?

Accessible only via day trips by boat, the pearlescent, cliff-edged cove on the southwest coast of Ko Phi-Phi Leh was made world-famous by the 2000 Leonardo DiCaprio film *The Beach*, based on Alex Garland's novel of the same name. Maya Bay's popularity skyrocketed and, by 2018, over 5000 visitors a day were packing on to the 250m-long (820ft), 15m-wide (49ft) sandy strand, wreaking havoc on the fragile natural environment, particularly the underwater corals (an estimated 60% of coral here is thought to have been lost in a single decade). Amid local outrage about overtourism, in mid-2018 Thai authorities closed the bay completely to help it recover. This initial four-month closure turned into over three years entirely off-limits, spurred on by the Covid-19 pandemic's effects on tourism. Newly planted corals thrived, blacktip sharks returned, leatherback turtles and whale sharks were spotted offshore. And when Maya Bay finally reopened in early 2022, it was with fierce restrictions, including strict time limits, visitor caps and a ban on boats entering the cove itself. Only time will tell if this is enough to turn the tide for Thailand's most beloved pocket of paradise.

1. Ao Ton Sai and Ao Lo Dalam bays from Phi-Phi Viewpoint

2. Long-tail boat in Loh Samah Bay

Trang Islands

COUNTRY THAILAND
COORDINATES 9.9028° N, 103.9931° E • **AREA** 70 SQ KM (27 SQ MILES)

A sun-battered long-tail boat putters across emerald waves, its rainbow-coloured ribbons dancing in the breeze. Suddenly, a slender limestone karst looms directly ahead, then you spy a sliver of pale-blonde, tropical-forest-fringed sand glinting in the hazy distance. This dazzling natural beauty engulfs the go-slow Trang Islands, a little-touristed, hammock-happy archipelago strung off the coast of Trang Province in far southern Thailand. From uninhabited Ko Ngai, beach-bejewelled Ko Kradan and backpacker-vibe Ko Muk to mangrove-wrapped Ko Libong and distant Ko Sukorn, the five main Trangs remain largely off Thailand's well-trodden tourism path. There are a few mellow resorts and guesthouses for kicking back in, before plunging into the Andaman Sea on a dive trip, hiking through rubber forests to a sunset lookout or devouring a bowl of sizzling massaman curry on a blissfully undeveloped beach.

KO LIBONG'S THREATENED DUGONGS

In 2019, an orphaned eight-month-old dugong, named by rescuers as Marium, was found stranded along Krabi's coastline, and instantly captured Thailand's heart. Under 24-hour veterinary care, she was relocated to unhurried Ko Libong, Trang's largest island and the key stronghold for Thailand's shrinking dugong population. The waters off Ko Libong, richly carpeted with seagrass, are home to around 70% of Thailand's estimated 250 dugongs, which are close vegetarian marine cousins of the manatee and also related to elephants. Sadly, Marium didn't survive (several pieces of plastic were found in her stomach), but her story has put a spotlight on the plight of these majestic 'sea cows' under ever-growing threat from fishing nets, plastic pollution and habitat loss. For travellers keen to support local conservation efforts, Ko Libong's smattering of resorts can arrange dugong-spotting boat trips, and dugong-watching towers have been set up along the coast here.

Sikao
Ton Chot
X Trang
Pak Meng
Khlong Trang
Hat Chao Mai National Park
Ko Ngai
X
Ko Cheuk
Kantang
Ko Waen
Ko Muk
X
Tham Morakot (Emerald Cave)
Ban Nam Rap
Na Kluea
Yan Ta Khao
X *Ko Kradan*
Ban Na
Ko Libong
Sam Yaek
Ban Ta Seh
Palian
Ban Laem
Yong Sata
Andaman Sea
Ko Lao Liang
X
Ko Sukorn
Ko Phetra

0 — 10 km
0 — 5 miles
N

X MARKS THE SPOT

Ko Ngai The lush northernmost of the Trangs, bordered by a salt-white beach, teal waves and a sprinkling of thatched-roof resorts.

Tham Morakot (Emerald Cave) Swim through a limestone sea tunnel to Ko Muk's eerily beautiful cave beach, rumoured to be stuffed with pirate treasure.

Ko Kradan Protected by Hat Chao Mai National Park, Ko Kradan sparkles with cream-hued beaches, dense forest and blazing sunsets.

Trang The mainland's low-key springboard city for these delicious isles is also a culinary jewel of southern Thailand.

Ko Sukorn This sleepy rural island delights with its glistening rice paddies, stilt homes and gentle pace.

2

〜〜〜〜〜

1. Trang Island beach

2. Dugong

Selat Melaka
(Strait of Melaka)

Batu
Ferringhi

Pulau
Tikus

Teluk
Bahang

Tanjung
Bungah

Tanjung
Tokong

Selat Utara
(North Channel)

Penang
National
Park

Pulau
Tikus

Pantai
Acheh

George
Town

Butterworth

Sungai
Pinang

Air Itam

Balik
Pulau

Pekan
Genting

Relau

Pulau
Jerejak

Pulau
Betong

Kampung
Pulau
Betong

Bayan
Lepas

Selat Selatan
(South Channel)

Gertak
Sanggul

Teluk
Kumbar

Kampung
Sungai Batu

Batu
Maung

Pulau
Rimau

Pulau
Kendi

0   5 km
0   2.5 miles

X MARKS THE SPOT

Street Art George Town is among Asia's top cities for street art; check streetartpenang.com for a current map of the pieces.

Blue Mansion Built in the 1880s, this magnificent George Town mansion was rescued from ruin in the 1990s. Tour it or stay overnight.

Penang National Park Feel a world away from bustling George Town as you hike to hidden beaches through virgin rainforest.

Temples Exploring the many places of worship is among the joys of George Town, from dragon-pillared Chinese temples to grand English-style Palladian churches.

Fun Fact Penang is the only state in Malaysia to have consistently elected ethnic Chinese chief ministers since independence.

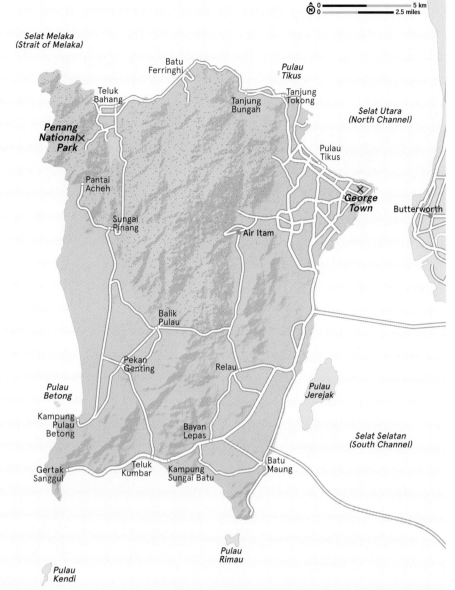

Penang

COUNTRY MALAYSIA • **COORDINATES** 5.4164°N, 100.3327°E • **AREA** 1048 SQ KM (405 SQ MILES)

If there's a more thrilling cocktail of Eastern cultures than in the island of Penang, we'll eat our hats. Connected to Malaysia's northwestern coast by bridge, this energetic outpost, once a British colony, was the crucible where the nation's fusion of cultures was forged, and the so-called Pearl of the Orient brings together the best of Malay, Chinese, Indian and British-colonial culture in one delicious and easily accessible – if a little sweaty – package.

At Penang's heart is diverse, cosmopolitan George Town, the main city, where the streets are paved not with gold, but with thousands of street-food stalls, and trishaws decked with plastic flowers amble past neat rows of Chinese shophouses and jewel-box clan houses perfumed by fragrant incense smoke. If you can tear yourself away, you'll find that the rest of the island is dotted with palm-fringed beaches and fishing villages, mountainous nature reserves and lush farms growing nutmeg and durian.

GET STUFFED IN GEORGE TOWN

The hawker stalls of George Town are renowned for their quality and value. *Char kway teow* (flat rice noodles flash-fried with egg, cockles, shrimp and chilli paste), oyster omelettes and peanut-slathered satay sticks whipped up on street corners rank among Malaysia's best street food.

Ask locals where their favourite hawker stalls are, and they'll generally mention mention the throng at Lorong Baru (New Lane). Located about 1km (0.6 miles) west of the city centre, this night-time street extravaganza is a great spot for *ikan bakar* (grilled seafood), *asam* and Penang laksa, fried oysters, *apong* (coconut pancakes), *Hokkien mee* (noodles in prawn broth) and *papiah* (spring rolls). But there are plenty of other fantastic hawkers to discover in George Town and beyond. There are some great restaurants in the city, too, including excellent long-standing Chinese eatery Teksen (try the double-roasted pork with chilli *padi*) and historic Hameediyah, serving up South Indian favourites since 1907.

1. George Town snack vendor

2. Lanterns

3. Bird's-eye view of George Town

Malaysian Borneo

COUNTRY MALAYSIA • COORDINATES 4.210° N, 101.975° E • AREA 198,801 SQ KM (76,757 SQ MILES)

Framing the compact oil-rich Sultanate of Brunei, Malaysian Borneo is made up of the Malaysian states of Sarawak and Sabah, bookending the northern coast of the world's third-largest island. Beyond the bigger cities of Kuching, Miri and Kota Kinabalu, visitors can expect diverse and rugged landscapes, with travel to some regions best achieved on speedboats coursing through a jungle-clad inland network of coffee-coloured waters. From above, flying from Miri to the trekking hub of Bario in Sarawak's remote Kelabit Highlands, there's stark evidence of the negative impact of palm-oil plantations on the tropical rainforest, but national parks and other protected areas are a fighting a rearguard action to protect – and hopefully ensure the future of – Borneo's most beloved primates.

VIEWING SEMI-WILD ORANGUTANS

Due to population encroachment and ongoing deforestation, it's now estimated there are only around 100,000 Borneo orangutans living in the wild, including south across the border in Indonesia's Kalimantan province. Joining a hiking expedition in Sarawak's Batang Ai National Park is usually not possible for time-strapped travellers to Malaysian Borneo, but in both Sarawak and Sabah, there are other destinations where viewing orangutans is more accessible. On the outskirts of Kuching, the Semenggoh Wildlife Centre fringes a stand of protected rainforest. Semi-wild orangutans feed off the reserve's fruit trees, but outside of the

'fruiting season' – usually December to January – they're regular visitors to one of the centre's twice-daily feeding sessions. There's no compulsion for the great apes to show up, but a few usually swing by for Semenggoh's treetop buffet of coconuts, bananas and mangoes.

Near Sabah's eastern coastal city of Sandakan, the Sepilok Orangutan Rehabilitation Centre covers 40 sq km (15.4 sq miles) of the Kabili-Sepilok Forest Reserve, and like Semenggoh, the centre's orangutans are fed at a feeding platform twice a day. At an adjacent outdoor nursery, orphaned youngsters between six and nine years old are often playing in fan-cooled stalls.

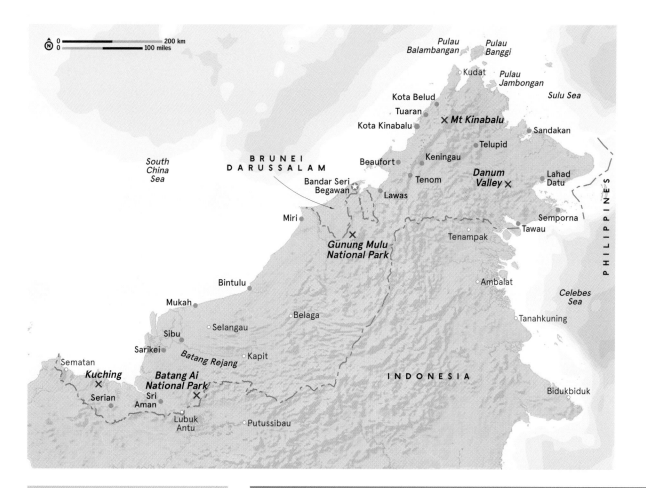

X MARKS THE SPOT

Kuching Indigenous Dayak flavours and Chinese and Malay culinary influences overlap in one of Southeast Asia's best destinations for travelling foodies.

Batang Ai National Park Journey by longboat to this Sarawak national park for the opportunity to see orangutans in the wild while negotiating the Red Ape Trail.

Gunung Mulu National Park Unesco World Heritage highlights include one of the planet's biggest caves and the thrilling three-day jungle trek to the Pinnacles.

Mt Kinabalu Ascending Borneo's highest mountain (4095m/13,435ft) reveals unique ecosystems, thousands of endemic plant species and sky-high views of Sabah.

Danum Valley Pygmy elephants, orangutans and shape-shifting flocks of colourful birds make Danum's primeval jungle a Sabah wildlife hotspot.

1. Orangutans at Semenggoh Wildlife Centre

2. Stilt hut near Semporna

3. Rafflesia, the world's largest flower

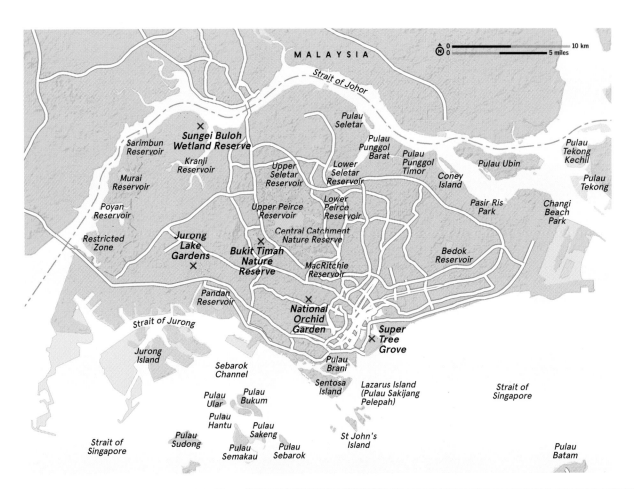

MALAYSIA

Strait of Johor

Sarimbun Reservoir

× Sungei Buloh Wetland Reserve

Kranji Reservoir

Murai Reservoir

Poyan Reservoir

Restricted Zone

Upper Seletar Reservoir

Lower Seletar Reservoir

Pulau Seletar

Pulau Punggol Barat

Pulau Punggol Timor

Pulau Ubin

Coney Island

Pulau Tekong Kechil

Pulau Tekong

Upper Peirce Reservoir

Lower Peirce Reservoir

Central Catchment Nature Reserve

Jurong Lake Gardens ×

× Bukit Timah Nature Reserve

MacRitchie Reservoir

Pasir Ris Park

Bedok Reservoir

Changi Beach Park

Pandan Reservoir

Strait of Jurong

× National Orchid Garden

Super × Tree Grove

Jurong Island

Sebarok Channel

Pulau Brani

Sentosa Island

Pulau Ular

Pulau Bukum

Pulau Hantu

Pulau Sakeng

Lazarus Island (Pulau Sakijang Pelepah)

Strait of Singapore

Pulau Sudong

St John's Island

Strait of Singapore

Pulau Semakau

Pulau Sebarok

Pulau Batam

10 km
5 miles

X MARKS THE SPOT

Super Tree Grove Sci-fi artificial 'trees' that generate solar power, collect rainwater and, after dark, put on a colourful light show.

National Orchid Garden The world's largest orchid garden, with over a thousand species of orchids on display, including some hybrids you can't see anywhere else in the world.

Jurong Lake Gardens Singapore's newest national garden blends nature and play, with streams and trampolines shaped like lily pads.

Bukit Timah Nature Reserve Old-growth tropical rainforest, home to an incredible diversity of plant and animal life (including lots of cheeky monkeys).

Sungei Buloh Wetland Reserve The place to spy egrets, spotted eagles and milky storks among mangroves and mudflats.

1. A view-rich dip at the Marina Bay Sands hotel

2. Lau Pa Sat hawker centre

3. Super Tree Grove

Singapore

COUNTRY SINGAPORE • **COORDINATES** 1.3521° N, 103.8198° E • **AREA** 728 SQ KM (281 SQ MILES)

Singapore looks like a vision from the future: the island nation is both one of the most densely populated places on Earth and shockingly green, with soaring glass office towers as well as ambitious developments like Gardens by the Bay, with its solar-punk Super Trees. It is a multicultural metropolis with four official languages (English, Mandarin Chinese, Malay and Tamil) and Southeast Asia's largest economy - and it's also home to one of the most exciting culinary scenes in the region, whether you're filling up on inexpensive hawker fare or indulging in Michelin-starred fine dining. Just slightly larger than New York City, Singapore is located across the Johor Strait – a narrow channel crossable by road – from peninsular Malaysia in the South China Sea. To the east, across the Malacca Strait, is the Indonesian island of Sumatra; to the south is the Singapore Strait and the Riau-Lingga Archipelago, also part of Indonesia.

'A CITY IN A GARDEN'

While Singapore's transformation from developing country to 'A City in a Garden' seemed like an overnight sensation, it was, in fact, half a century in the making. As early as the 1970s – just a few years after the establishment of Singapore as an independent nation – the country began implementing tree-planting schemes and green-orientated building codes.

Fast forward to the present and this home to nearly 6 million people is getting close to 50% green space. It's a fantastical place of rooftop gardens atop skyscrapers, lush green walls with cascading tropical foliage and

thoroughfares that pass under canopies of native trees. All of this helps to combat carbon emissions and the urban heat – crucial for a country that sits just about on the equator. Meanwhile, many of the parks and gardens are connected via elevated promenades that make walking and cycling around the island a pleasurable breeze.

Singapore is keenly aware of its vulnerability to climate change, and has even greener plans in the works, with the hopes of achieving net zero emissions around the middle of the century.

Sumatra

COUNTRY INDONESIA
COORDINATES 0.589° S, 101.343° E • AREA 473,481 SQ KM (182,812 SQ MILES)

Straddling the equator, sprawling Sumatra is the sixth-largest island in the world, a wild landscape that's occasionally disrupted by the natural energy of eruptions and earthquakes. Beyond the headlines, a huge population exceeding 58 million live in a land of lakes, forests and volcanoes, keeping alive and celebrating their unique Batak, Acehnese and Minangkabau cultures. Through resource exploration and the replacement of jungle by palm-oil plantations, the pressures of 21st-century development are impacting on Sumatran wilderness and wildlife, but key national parks and protected reserves continue to preserve habitats for some of Southeast Asia's most iconic species.

SUMATRA'S UNIQUE CUISINE

Reduced to a sticky, coconut-milk-infused and spicy curry paste, the traditional Sumatran dish of *rendang* – usually made with beef or buffalo - is known around the world, but it's just one of the highlights of the Sumatran cuisine known as *nasi Padang*. Very popular around the southwestern city of Padang, and also throughout the entire Indonesian archipelago, *nasi Padang* eateries are the ultimate in relaxed grazing. As many as 20 small plates of pre-prepared dishes are laid out before diners, and after surveying which ones look most delicious, customers are only charged for the ones they eat.

There's almost always no written menu, but dishes are guaranteed to be fresh and imbued with a significant hit of chilli. Beyond the ubiquitous *rendang*, other popular offerings include *telur balado* (spicy sambal-laced eggs) and *sotong hitam* (squid cooked with lemongrass, tamarind juice and squid ink). An overflowing plate of freshly-sauteed *kangkung* (water spinach) is usually served as a side dish, along with a big bowl of rice. Recommended form is to use your fingers to mix the rice in with the sides, and then dig in. Yes, it can be messy, even for Padang locals, but the reward is some of Asia's most fragrant and interesting food.

X MARKS THE SPOT

Danau Toba Chill out in the company of the easygoing Batak people on a lazy-days island sojourn on Lake Toba's Pulau Samosir.

Kernici Seblat National Park Covering almost 14,000 sq km (5405 sq miles), Sumatra's biggest national park is one of the last wild havens of the endangered harimau (Sumatran tiger).

Pulau Weh Adrift off Sumatra's northern tip, the crystalline waters surrounding this compact volcanic island are a coral-enlivened wonderland for snorkellers and divers.

Harau Valley Journey by motorbike-taxi to this sleepy rice-paddy-fringed valley for friendly homestays, wet-season waterfalls and some of Sumatra's best rock-climbing.

Bukit Lawang Rustic resorts along the Bohorok River are a convenient base for visiting the semi-habituated orangutans at the Bukit Lawang rehabilitation centre.

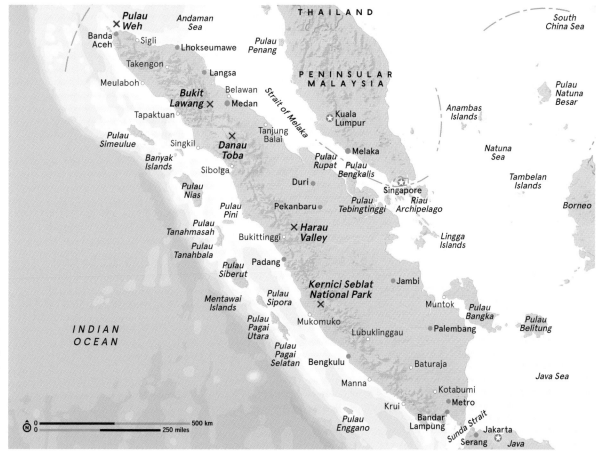

1. Surfer at Teluk Lagundri, at the southern end of Pulau Nias

2. Tea plantations overlooked by the peaks of Kernici Seblat National Park

Malapascua Island

COUNTRY PHILIPPINES
COORDINATES 11.3358°N, 124.1156°E • **AREA** 2 SQ KM (0.7 SQ MILES)

Off the north coast of Cebu, this tiny tropical island is famous for its world-class diving. But even if you've no interest in marine life, Malapascua makes a brilliant beach destination, with more than a dozen pretty beaches and bays to discover. Curving around the southeastern corner of the island, beautiful Bounty Beach is lined with hotels and bars that buzz at sunset.

Behind the beachfront hotels, shanty settlements are the legacy of Typhoon Yolanda, which tore off every roof on the island in 2013. Nearly a decade later, in December 2021, Malapasuca was lucky to escape a direct hit from Typhoon Odette, which decimated southern Cebu. As the only way to get here is by van or bus from Cebu City to the northern village of Maya (followed by a 45-minute ferry ride), visits to Malapascua play a role in the region's typhoon recovery.

THRESHER SHARK HAVEN

Many visitors come here with a singular goal: to scuba dive with thresher sharks. Known for their exceptionally long tails, which they use to 'swat' prey, threshers congregate at Monad Shoal, a nearby seamount, in the early morning to get their beauty scrub courtesy of cleaner fish that peck off parasites. This is one of the only places in the world where elusive threshers can be seen on a near-daily basis, and the chances of spotting them are pretty good – about 75%, but be warned

that there can be hundreds of divers here at weekends.

But this isn't the only local dive site. Macrophotographers will love Gato Island, a marine sanctuary and sea-snake breeding ground (February to September). A passenger ferry that tragically sank during a typhoon in 1988, the MV *Dona Marilyn* ferry has been repurposed as a dive site, covered in soft corals that attract abundant marine life. Lapus Island is another good dive location, just off Malapascua's northwestern tip.

X MARKS THE SPOT

Coastal Walk A good four-hour walk will take you around the entire coast, with plenty of photo opportunities along the way.

Unexpected Treat Among Malapascua's decent dining options is an excellent Italian restaurant, Angelina.

Local Snorkelling Good snorkelling spots include Dakit-Dakit Island, a short boat ride off Bounty Beach, and the Coral Garden off the east side of the island.

Island-Hopping Day trips run to Carnassa and Calangaman Islands, which have great beaches and snorkelling.

Lighthouse Enjoy striking views over the island from this lighthouse accessed via a steep path from the edge of Guimbitayan village. There's a fun beach bar nearby.

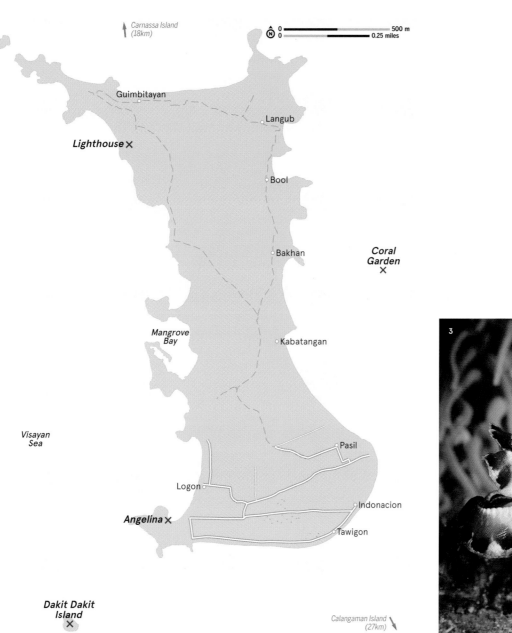

Carnassa Island
(18km)

0   500 m
0   0.25 miles

Guimbitayan

Langub

Lighthouse ✕

Bool

*Coral
Garden*
✕

Bakhan

Mangrove
Bay

Kabatangan

Visayan
Sea

Pasil

Logon

Indonacion

Angelina ✕

Tawigon

Dakit Dakit
Island
✕

Calangaman Island
(27km)

1. Thresher shark

2. Bounty Beach

3. Colourful cuttlefish

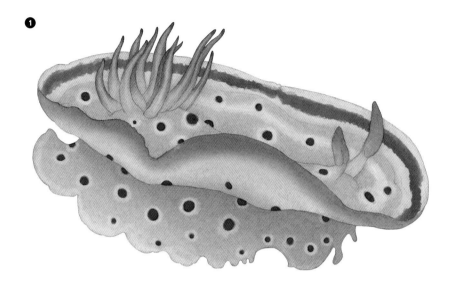

Komodo Island

COUNTRY INDONESIA

COORDINATES 8.5850° S, 119.4411° E • **AREA** 390 SQ KM (150 SQ MILES)

Komodo has a dramatic landscape of rugged, sun-parched hills rising sharply from sugary beaches and azure waters. The island is part of the Lesser Sunda Islands, which also includes Bali and Lombok, and is located on the Sape Strait between the larger islands of Flores and Sumbawa. Deep trenches between some of the islands have historically restricted the movement of flora and fauna, resulting in localised biomes. In addition to Komodo's most famous inhabitant, the Komodo dragon, the island is also home to Timor deer and the critically endangered yellow-crested cockatoo. Komodo also sits on the Sunda Arc, one of the most volcanically active parts of the world.

KOMODO DRAGON

A member of the monitor lizard family, the Komodo dragon *(Varanus komodoensis)* is the world's largest lizard, known to grow upwards of 3m (9.8ft) long and weigh over 100kg (220lb). With armoured scales, serrated teeth and a long, fork-shaped tongue they are the closest thing to a real-life dragon on Earth today. Island inhabitants call them *ora*. They are also fearsome apex predators, fast and with a venomous bite capable of taking down a grown human. And like the raptors in *Jurassic Park*, Komodo dragon females can reproduce asexually. Despite all this, these mighty lizards are endangered, numbering

now in the low thousands and found only on the islands of Komodo, Flores, Rinca, Gili Motang and Gili Dasami; rising sea levels threaten to wipe them out completely in the next century. In 1980, Indonesia established Komodo National Park, which also includes the islands of Rinca and Padar, to protect the animals' habitat; in 2019 the government decided to limit the number of tourists who visit each year.

Scientists believe that Komodo dragons are likely related to an even larger lizard, called Megalania – a now extinct species of megafauna that lived in Australia tens of thousands of years ago.

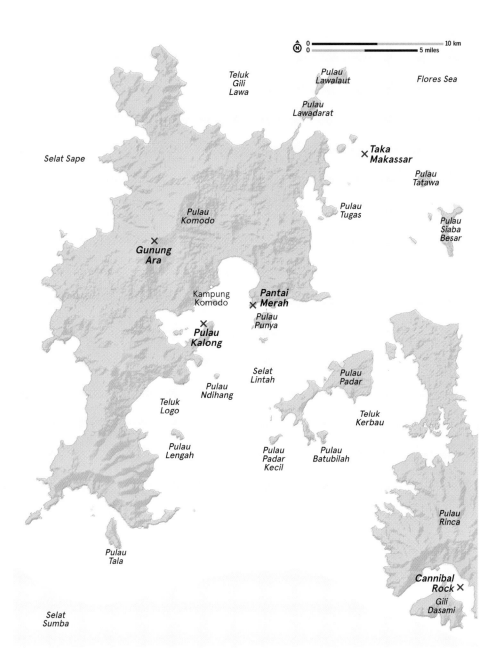

Teluk Gili Lawa

Pulau Lawalaut

Flores Sea

Selat Sape

Pulau Lawadarat

✕ *Taka Makassar*

Pulau Tatawa

Pulau Komodo

Pulau Tugas

Pulau Siaba Besar

✕ *Gunung Ara*

Kampung Komodo

Pantai Merah ✕

Pulau Punya

✕ *Pulau Kalong*

Selat Lintah

Pulau Ndihang

Pulau Padar

Teluk Logo

Teluk Kerbau

Pulau Lengah

Pulau Padar Kecil

Pulau Batubilah

Pulau Rinca

Pulau Tala

Selat Sumba

Cannibal Rock ✕

Gili Dasami

X MARKS THE SPOT

Pantai Merah 'Pink Beach' is one of the world's few shores with naturally blush-coloured sand (thanks to minute coral particles).

Taka Makassar Crescent-shaped sandbar – surrounded by glassy emerald waters and coral reefs – that only appears during low tide.

Pulau Kalong This teeny-tiny offshore islet is known as 'Bat Island' for the great flocks of fruit bats that can be seen in the skies here at twilight.

Cannibal Rock Small seamount covered in coral and home to a rainbow array of nudibranchs, frogfish and pygmy seahorses.

Gunung Ara Komodo's highest peak, at 538m (1765ft), with sweeping views over the island and cockatoos to boot.

1. Nudibranch

2. Pulau Padar

3. Komodo dragon

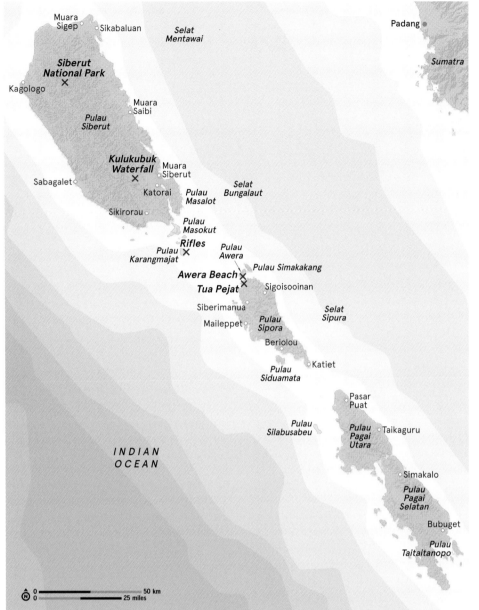

X MARKS THE SPOT

Siberut National Park Covering the northern half of Siberut, with primary rainforest and mangrove swamps, plus over a hundred varieties of colourful birds.

Rifles Ranked among the best surf breaks in the world, this is an epic right that comes in long and fast, barrelling from start to finish.

Awera Beach Sand like powder, water like liquid glass and a fring of shade-granting coconut palms.

Kulukubuk Waterfall Two-tiered, 70m-long (230ft) cascade pouring down to a natural bathing pool encircled by dense foliage.

Tua Pejat The capital of the Mentawai Islands Regency, on Pulau Sipora (the most developed of the islands), and home to approximately 5000 people.

Mentawai Islands

COUNTRY INDONESIA • **COORDINATES** 1.4260° S, 98.9245° E • **AREA** 6034 SQ KM (2330 SQ MILES)

Much of the Mentawai Islands is covered in primary tropical rainforest, where flowering keruing and shorea trees form a canopy some 40m-high (131ft) and monkeys swing from limb to limb. This chain of four major islands (and dozens of smaller, mostly uninhabited ones) runs alongside the west coast of Sumatra, Indonesia's largest island; west of the islands, there is nothing significant but the Indian Ocean, not until the Maldives nearly 3000km (1864 miles) away. The islands, which sit on top of the Sunda megathrust – one of the most seismically active regions of the world – likely broke away from Sumatra around half a million years ago. This has resulted in the evolution of a number of endemic species such as the Mentawai gibbon, whose females are known for their otherworldly, mellifluous calls. The islands also have the highest concentration of consistently excellent waves in all of Indonesia, if not the world, with massive swells and powerful reef breaks. These same rough seas also served to keep the Mentawai Islands largely isolated until the 19th century.

THE PEOPLE OF MENTAWAI

The indigenous people of the Mentawai Islands, who number in the tens of thousands, traditionally led a semi-nomadic lifestyle, hunting and gathering in the rainforest and cultivating crops like taro. Throughout the 20th century their independence and way of life has been threatened by missionaries, assimilation policies and commercial logging. Those that continue to practise the old ways now live mostly in the south of the largest island, Siberut, where they reside in communal longhouses, called *uma*, made of woven bamboo and grasses. Their relationship to their environment is complex and synergistic, organised around a belief system that sees trees, rivers and rocks (among other things) as kindred spirits. Most famously, they are known to tattoo their bodies with intricate, abstract patterns – though today there are only a few hundred islanders, mostly elderly, who still have these tribal markings.

1. Pulau Karangmajat

2. Mentawai surfers

3. Poisoning arrowheads for hunting

235

PACIFIC OCEAN

Pulau Wayag

Pulau Kawe

Pulau Gebe

Kabare

Pulau Waigeo

Waisilip

Warsanidin ✕ Kali Biru

Pulau Gag

Pulau Gami

Waisai

Gam Bay ✕

Pianynemo ✕

Pulau Mansuar

✕ Cape Kri

Pulau Kri

Halmahera Sea

Fam Islands

Dampier Strait

Makebon

Pulau Batanta

Sagewin Strait

Sorong

Boo Islands

Pulau Kofiau

Samale

Pulau Salawati

Klasuat

Wejim

Teminabuan

Waigama

Pulau Misool

Seram Sea

Harapan Java

Lilinta

Misool Eco ✕ Resort

1. Raja Ampat's dazzling coastline

2. Diving the superlative coral reef

Raja Ampat Islands

COUNTRY INDONESIA
COORDINATES 1.0915° S, 130.8779° E • **AREA** 8034 SQ KM (3102 SQ MILES)

The symbol of the Raja Ampat Islands is the red bird of paradise
(Paradisaea rubra), an endemic species with trailing crimson feathers
that's found only in the lowland rainforests of Waigeo and Batanta
islands. These same forests are also home to Wilson's bird of paradise
– which looks like a bird masquerading as a butterfly – as well as
carnivorous pitcher plants, bioluminescent mushrooms and numerous
orchid species. And that's just a snapshot of what sits above sea level.
The 'Four Kings' – Waigeo, Misool, Salawati and Batanta – are the largest
of the 1500-odd islands, islets and shoals that make up the Raja Ampat
Islands. Marked by karst formations, they sit just west of West Papua's
Bird's Head Peninsula. The islands' residents are the descendents
of ancient settlers from the island of New Guinea and of seafaring
Austronesian peoples.

BIRD'S HEAD SEASCAPE
The Bird's Head Seascape is said to be
the most biodiverse marine site in the
world. Part of the 'Coral Triangle', it
includes the waters around the Raja
Ampat Islands as well as Cenderawasih
Bay (Bird of Paradise Bay) and Triton
Bay, both off the coast of Bird's Head
Peninsula. Among the fringing reefs,
lagoons, mangrove forests and seagrass
beds are dugongs, 'walking sharks',
saltwater crocodiles, giant clams, over
600 kinds of coral – 75% of all known
species – and more than 1800 different
reef fish. It's also the most popular
nesting spot for leatherback turtles in
the Pacific. In 2004, a global consortium
of NGOs and local community alliances
joined together to work to protect this
underwater Eden whilst also charting a
path that addresses both the short- and
long-term needs of those who live on
its shores. Since 2013, all of the waters
of Raja Ampat have been designated a
shark and ray sanctuary, the first of its
kind in the region.

X MARKS THE SPOT
Piaynemo The view from here, of
numerous karst atolls dotting teal
waters, is the most photographed
spot in the Raja Ampat Islands.

Gam Bay Blooms of moon jellyfish can
be seen floating in the waters off the
coast of Gam Island after dark.

Kali Biru The naturally 'Blue River',
teal like the nearby ocean but set
amidst verdant rainforest, is a popular
swimming hole.

Cape Kri Dive site with the greatest
variety of visible coral and fish
discovered so far in the world, off the
coast of tiny Kri Island.

Misool Eco Resort Landmark
eco-lodge and community-based
conservation centre on a private
island southwest of Misool.

X MARKS THE SPOT

Pulau Bunaken Snorkel or dive along unbelievably rich coral drop-offs in North Sulawesi's top tourist destination, which remains refreshingly low-key.

Tana Toraja This compelling corner of South Sulawesi is known for the ritual and tradition of its elaborate funeral ceremonies.

Lore Lindu National Park Stare into the stony faces of ancient megaliths of unknown origin, and look out for rare wildlife.

Togean Islands Find barefoot bliss and superb diving in these off-grid, paradisaical Central Sulawesi islands.

Tangkoko-Batuangas Dua Saudara Nature Reserve Spot big-eyed tarsiers, black macaques and a bevy of birds in this accessible North Sulawesi wilderness area.

Sulawesi

COUNTRY INDONESIA • **COORDINATES** 1.847°S, 120.527°E • **AREA** 189,216 SQ KM (73,057 SQ MILES)

Roughly in the centre of the Indonesian archipelago, Sulawesi is the nation's third-largest island – so big it's divided into six provinces. Yet aside from keen divers and discerning culture-seeking tourists, international travellers have been slow to discover that between Sulawesi's incredible ecosystems and diverse social fabric, this splay-limbed island is an awe-inspiring destination that deserves a higher ranking on must-visit lists.

Fringed by teeming waters and coral reefs that promise some of the world's best diving, Sulawesi's interior is mountainous and cloaked in dense jungle. Here rare species such as adorable tarsiers and flamboyant maleo birds survive, as do proud cultures, long isolated from the onslaughts of modernity by impenetrable topography. Meet Toraja highlanders, with their elaborate funeral ceremonies and beautiful architecture; the Minahasan people of the north are known for their spicy dishes, while the lowland and coastal Bugis are Indonesia's most (in)famous seafarers.

THE WALLACE LINE

Detailed surveys of Sulawesi and neighbouring Borneo in the 1850s by English naturalist Alfred Russel Wallace resulted in some inspired correspondence with Charles Darwin. His letters to Darwin, detailing evidence of his theory that the Indonesian archipelago was inhabited by one distinct fauna in the east and one in the west, prompted Darwin to publish similar observations from his own travels. The subsequent debate on species distribution and evolution transformed modern thought.

Wallace refined his theory in 1859, drawing a boundary between the two regions of fauna. The Wallace Line, as it became known, divided Sulawesi and Lombok to the east, and Borneo and Bali to the west. He believed that islands to the west of the line had once been part of Asia, and those to the east had been linked to a Pacific–Australian continent. Sulawesi's wildlife was so unusual that Wallace suspected it was once part of both, which geologists have since proven to be correct.

1. Morning view in Makassar, South Sulawesi

2. Knobbed hornbill

3. Toraja houses in the village of Palawa

Hong Kong Island

COUNTRY HONG KONG SPECIAL ADMINISTRATIVE
REGION OF THE PEOPLE'S REPUBLIC OF CHINA
COORDINATES 22.2588° N, 114.1911° E
AREA 79 SQ KM (30 SQ MILES)

Hong Kong – pronounced *heung gong* in Cantonese – means 'fragrant harbour', a relic from when, centuries ago, incense was traded at what is now Aberdeen, on the southwest coast of Hong Kong Island. Back then Hong Kong was little more than a series of sleepy villages at the southeastern fringe of the vast Chinese empire. Following the first Opium War, China officially ceded control of Hong Kong Island to the British in 1842, ushering in in a period of colonial control which would last until the return of the territories to China in 1997. During this time, Hong Kong, and particularly Hong Kong Island's Central district, developed into one of the world's most important financial hubs, with a forest of glittering skyscrapers. Hong Kong Island is the second-largest of the 200-plus islands that, along with Kowloon and the New Territories, make up Hong Kong. It sits across Victoria Harbour from Kowloon at the mouth of the Pearl River Delta.

HONG KONG TRAIL

Among all the dizzying lights and crowds of districts like Central, it's easy to forget that much of Hong Kong Island is actually green space. The Hong Kong Trail stretches for 50km (31 miles) and traverses all five of Hong Kong Island's country parks. It wends from Victoria Peak to Big Wave Bay, over hills and valleys forested with pines and acacia trees and home to a plethora of colourful butterflies, frogs and birds. Though it can be done in one very intense day, the trail is broken up into eight sections, the most spectacular of which is the final one, known as Dragon's Back. This follows an undulating ridge – picture the spines of a dragon's back – and has spectacular views over the lapis-blue water of the South China Sea and some of Hong Kong's smaller islands.

X MARKS THE SPOT

Victoria Peak The highest point on the island at 552m (1811ft) with dramatic views over Hong Kong's iconic skyline.

Man Mo Temple This landmark 19th-century temple, right in the middle of Central, is dedicated to the God of Literature (Man) and the God of War (Mo).

Hong Kong Park This signature urban park has a spectacular aviary as well as historical buildings – all surrounded by lush green.

Aberdeen Promenade The spot for views over Aberdeen Harbour at the southern end of Hong Kong Island – come early to see fishing boats pull up.

St Stephen's Beach A quiet, sandy cove near the very southern tip of Hong Kong Island, where a finger of land trails out into the South China Sea.

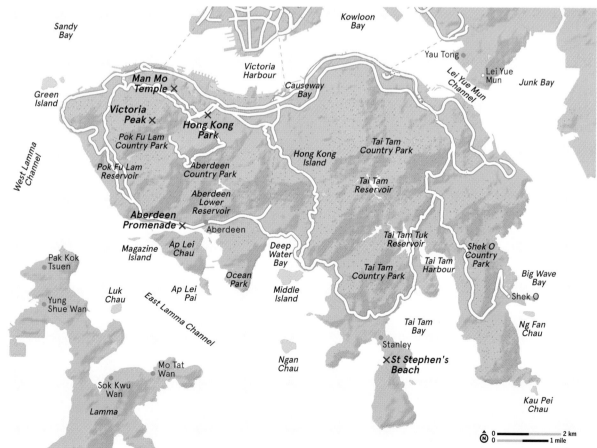

Sandy
Bay

Kowloon
Bay

Victoria
Harbour

Yau Tong

Green
Island

Man Mo
Temple ✕

Causeway
Bay

Lei Yue
Mun

Junk Bay

West Lamma Channel

Victoria
Peak ✕

Hong Kong
Park

Lei Yue Mun Channel

Pok Fu Lam
Country Park

Hong Kong
Island

Tai Tam
Country Park

Pok Fu Lam
Reservoir

Aberdeen
Country Park

Tai Tam
Reservoir

Aberdeen
Lower
Reservoir

Aberdeen
Promenade ✕

Aberdeen

Tai Tam Tuk
Reservoir

Shek O
Country
Park

Pak Kok
Tsuen

Magazine
Island

Ap Lei
Chau

Deep
Water
Bay

Tai Tam
Harbour

Big Wave
Bay

Yung
Shue Wan

Luk
Chau

Ap Lei
Pai

Ocean
Park

Middle
Island

Tai Tam
Country Park

Shek O

East Lamma Channel

Mo Tat
Wan

Ng Fan
Chau

Sok Kwu
Wan

Ngan
Chau

Tai Tam
Bay

Stanley

✕St Stephen's
Beach

Lamma

Kau Pei
Chau

N 0   2 km
   0   1 mile

© Adrienne Pitts | Lonely Planet

1. Cantonese barbecue restaurant

2. The view to Hong Kong Island from Victoria Harbour's ferry dock

X MARKS THE SPOT

Jibei Sand Tail A glorious spit of sand stretching into azure waters off the coast of Jibei, one of Penghu's more popular outer islands.

Tongliang Banyan Tree This magnificent tree on Baisha Main Island, believed to be 300 years old, has a canopy that covers an area of more than 660 sq metres (7104 sq ft).

Zhongshe Penghu's best-preserved traditional village, with Fujian-style homes made from coral stone, on Wang'an Island.

Tongpan Island This small island boasts some of the most impressive basalt column cliffs – reaching 7m (23ft) high – in all of Penghu.

Suogang Pagodas Twin seven-tiered pagodas made from basalt stones and intended, in the Taoist tradition, to ward off evil spirits.

0 ——— 10 km
0 ——— 5 miles

Jibei Island
Jibei Village
Kupo Island
✕ **Jibei Sand Tail**
Tiechen Island
Tongliang Banyan Tree
Pehu Island
Chihkan
Niao Island
Xiaomen Island
✕ BAISHA TOWNSHIP
Qitou
Yuanpei Island
XIYU TOWNSHIP
Tatsang Island
Tingkou Island
Xiyu Island
Penghu Bay
HUXI TOWNSHIP
Guoyeh
Nei'an
Penghu Island
Makung
Suogang Pagodas ✕
Tongpan Island ✕
Shanshui
Hujing Island

Taiwan Strait

Jiangjun Island
Zhongshe ✕
Jiangjun
Wang'an Island

Xiyuping Island
Dongyuping Island
Xiji Island
Dongji Island
Chimei Island
Nanhu

Penghu Islands

COUNTRY TAIWAN

COORDINATES 23.5833° N, 119.5833° E • **AREA** 141 SQ KM (54 SQ MILES)

The Penghu Islands have some of the world's most otherworldly geological formations, including staggering basalt columns and dramatic sea cliffs. This archipelago of over 60 small islands – more when the tide is low – in the Taiwan Strait was formed by a succession of prehistoric volcanic eruptions that pushed layers of rock to the surface. All that rock, however, makes for poor farming, meaning centuries of island inhabitants, mostly descended from mainland Chinese, have been left to eke out a difficult life based around fishing. So associated with fishing are the islands that the Portuguese, when they arrived in the 16th century, called them Ilhas dos Pescadores (Fishers Islands).

PENGHU TIANHOU TEMPLE

Penghu Tianhou Temple is dedicated to Mazu, a Chinese sea goddess and protector of sailors, fishermen and travellers. Of the thousand-odd Mazu temples in Taiwan – which has the largest concentration of any country – this one, in Penghu's only city, Magong, is considered the oldest. It was established in the 16th century (and possibly earlier), and the city of Magong grew up around it. Mazu is a popular deity in coastal communities and also among the Chinese diaspora: it was common for new immigrants to erect a temple to her in gratitude for a safe arrival. The goddess is often depicted in red robes and shining jewels – the better to lead seafarers out of storms. Unusually, it's thought that she is based on an actual person, a 10th-century fisherman's daughter from Fujian named Lin Mo. Penghu Tianhou Temple is constructed from local coral stone; it has a dramatic swallowtail roof and camphorwood lintels with elaborate, meticulous carvings that rival any of Penghu's natural wonders. For the Lantern Festival, held each year on the 15th day of the first lunar month, turtle-shaped cakes are given out at the temple – in honour of another famous symbol of Penghu, the sea turtle.

1. One-Heart Stacked Stones (Eye of Tiger Fish Trap) bathed in the turquoise sea water

2. Tongpan Island basalt column

3. Mazu temple

Jeju-do

COUNTRY SOUTH KOREA

COORDINATES 33.4890° N, 126.4983° E • **AREA** 1826 SQ KM (705 SQ MILES)

Jeju-do, the largest island in South Korea, is presided over by Halla-san, the country's tallest mountain at 1950m (6398ft) and the only shield volcano in Asia. The island's volcanic origins are still evident today, in a number of impressive lava formations. At lower altitudes, Jeju-do has a humid subtropical climate, which has made it one of South Korea's most popular tourist destinations; millions visit every year, and the island has earned the nickname 'Honeymoon Island'. Jeju-do was an independent kingdom known as Tamna (Island Country) until the 10th century, when it became a protectorate of the Korean kingdom of Silla. Today it retains a modicum of autonomy as South Korea's only self-governing province.

HAENYEO

According to a popular saying, Jeju-do has three abundances, known collectively as the *samda*: stone (another volcanic legacy); wind, which regularly lashes the island; and women, as too often men were lost at sea. The latter is floated as one of the reasons why it is Jeju-do's women who specialise in shellfish diving. (Japan is the only other country with a significant culture of female divers.) It is certainly not easy work: the *haenyeo* (sea women), as they are called, spend hours in the water, holding their breath for up to three minutes and freediving as deep as 30m (98ft) to harvest abalone, sea urchins, oysters and other shellfish. Nowadays they wear modern wetsuits, weight belts and masks, but they used to go in wearing cotton clothes. When they emerge from the water they let out an eerie, piercing whistle, which functions to clear carbon dioxide from their bodies. In some communities, the *haenyeo* became the main family breadwinners, resulting in a reversal, to varying degrees, of traditional, patriarchal gender roles. Though their numbers are declining, they remain an enduring symbol of Jeju-do.

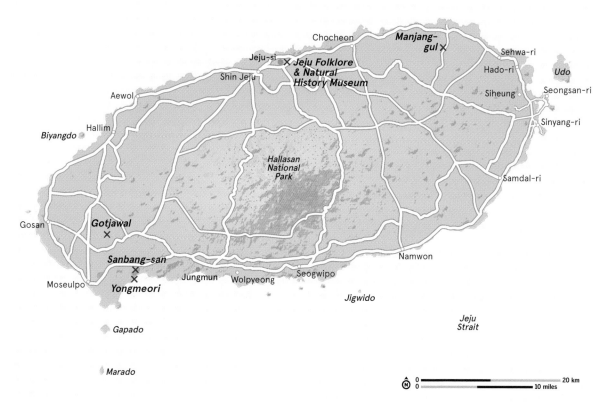

X MARKS THE SPOT

Gotjawal A forest on the rocky slopes of Halla-san that, due to its difficult terrain, remains fairly untouched by human settlement.

Manjang-gul The world's longest lava tube, at 13.4km (8.3 miles) in length, and filled with neat lava formations (and lots of bats).

Sanbang-san Formed by an ancient volcanic eruption, this lava dome looms large over Jeju-do's southwest coast and offers spectacular ocean views.

Yongmeori Stacks of sandstone accumulated over millions of years that form, with a little imagination, a dragon's head facing the sea.

Jeju Folklore & Natural History Museum Exhibitions on Jeju-do's fascinating geology plus artefacts from traditional life, including those relating to *haenyeo*.

~~~~~~~~

1. Jeju-do's famed *haenyeo* divers

2. Jusangjeolli Cliff

3. Bonsai tree, Hallim Park

Hokkaidō

COUNTRY JAPAN • COORDINATES 43.2203° N, 142.8635° E • AREA 83,424 SQ KM (32,210 SQ MILES)

Hokkaidō is Japan's northernmost major island and also its second-largest, occupying one-fifth of the country's land mass but home to fewer than 5% of its total population. Hokkaidō is the Japan of wide-open spaces, of big mountains and even bigger skies. To the east and south is the Pacific Ocean; to the west, the Sea of Japan; and to the north, the icy waters of the Sea of Okhotsk. In the centre is Japan's largest national park, Daisetsuzan – which means 'Great Snowy Mountains' – a largely untouched wilderness. In the language of Hokkaidō's indigenous people, the Ainu, Daisetsuzan is known as *kamuy mintar*, which means 'the playground of the gods'. The Ainu have called the island home for centuries, long before Japanese settlers began arriving in earnest in the 19th century; Hokkaidō was officially annexed by Japan in 1869.

YEZO BROWN BEAR

Hokkaidō's fauna differs dramatically from that of the rest of Japan to the south of the Tsugaru Strait, having more in common with the island of Sakhalin to the north. This zoogeographical boundary is called the Blakiston Line for Thomas Blakiston, the Brit who first noted it in the 19th century. The most iconic species native to Hokkaidō is the Yezo brown bear, also known as the Ussuri brown bear and, in Japanese, *higuma*; it's Japan's largest land mammal – with males easily topping 200kg (440lb) – and much bigger than the Asiatic black bears found elsewhere in Japan. Yezo brown bears have long been worshipped by the Ainu, who consider the bear to be a god – one that provided gifts of meat and fur after their spirits departed.

Today the bear population numbers in the thousands, with the majority concentrated within Shiretoko National Park in the remote northeast.

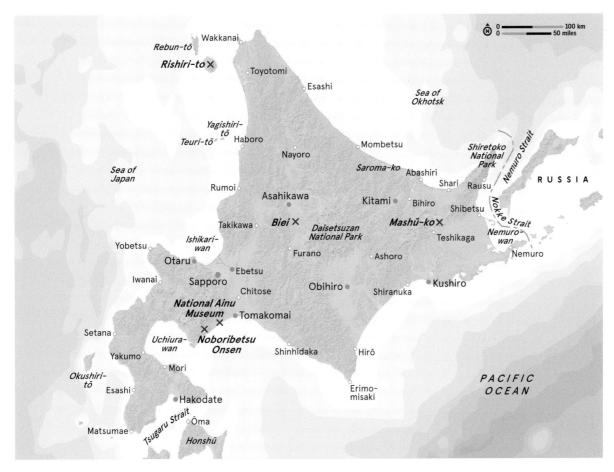

X MARKS THE SPOT

Mashū-ko Startlingly blue caldera lake, among the deepest in Japan and among the clearest in the world.

Rishiri-tō Small island off the northwest coast of Hokkaidō, where skiing and surfing are possible on the same trip.

Noboribetsu Onsen Famous hot-spring town, known as 'hell valley', where naturally heated waters flow down from sulphuric pools.

National Ainu Museum Japan's newest and northernmost national museum, dedicated to the history and culture of the island's indigenous people.

Biei Classic rural Hokkaidō town with flower fields, B&Bs, cycling routes and farm-to-table restaurants.

1. Noboribetsu Onsen

2. Shikisai Hill, Biei

3. Red-crowned cranes

Naoshima

COUNTRY JAPAN • **COORDINATES** 34.4574° N, 133.9866° E • **AREA** 14 SQ KM (5.4 SQ MILES)

Naoshima is one of roughly 3000 small islands in Japan's Seto Inland Sea, a region known for its mild climate and gentle beauty, praised in literature dating back to the country's earliest recorded works. Picture tranquil blue waters, windswept coasts dotted with pine trees and fishing boats strung with colourful pendants. For centuries, the inhabitants of Naoshima survived on fishing and trading (and sometimes piracy). In the early 20th century, a copper smelter arrived, bringing stability and prosperity but also industrial waste, pollution and environmental degradation. Fast-forward a century, however, and Naoshima is now held up as a great success story, having undergone a radical transformation into an international destination for contemporary art.

THE SETOUCHI TRIENNALE

The first Setouchi Triennale was held in 2010, the culmination of over two decades of work to restore Naoshima and its surrounding islands. Held every three years, the event features over a hundred installations from Japanese artists (like Yayoi Kusama and Hiroshi Sugimoto) and international ones (like James Turrell and Pipilotti Rist). Some works are displayed in the contemporary art museums that have been erected on Naoshima in recent years, including the stunning Chichū Art Museum designed by Tadao Ando, one of Japan's most influential modern architects. Other works make use of existing structures on Naoshima as well as its natural environment, drawing attention to and reframing the natural beauty of this small rural island in the Seto Inland Sea. There are permanent attractions, too: in Honmura, Naoshima's largest village, the Art House Project has transformed several traditional homes – constructed of dark timber with sloping slate roofs – into site-specific art installations. As visitors make their way from site to site they also encounter everyday life on the island. Once sceptical, Naoshima islanders have largely embraced the project, opening inns and cafes and even helping to set up artworks.

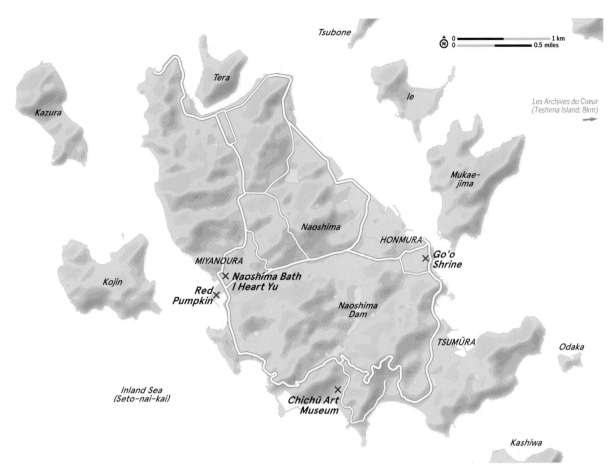

Les Archives du Coeur
(Teshima Island; 8km)

X MARKS THE SPOT

Red Pumpkin A giant red-and-black polka dot gourd sculpture by artist Yayoi Kusama, set on the end of a pier and now a symbol of Naoshima.

Chichū Art Museum Subterranean museum lit with skylights that illuminate – differently at different times of the day – several paintings from Claude Monet's *Water Lilies* series.

Go'o Shrine A crumbling, centuries-old Shintō shrine given new life by contemporary artist Hiroshi Sugimoto.

Naoshima Bath I Love Yu Public bathhouse reimagined by artist Shinro Ohtake, full of colourful and somewhat kooky installations.

Les Archives du Coeur At this installation of human heartbeats recorded by French artist Christian Boltanski, you can add your own heartbeat to the collection.

~~~~~~~~~~

1. Shinro Ohtake's Naoshima Bath building

2. Naoshima's coast

3. Shinro Ohtake's *Shipyard Works 'Stern with Hole'*

Ogasawara Archipelago

COUNTRY JAPAN • **COORDINATES** 26.9642° N, 142.1063° E • **AREA** 79 SQ KM (30 SQ MILES)

Also known as the Bonin Islands, the Ogasawara Islands are Japan at its most remote, located roughly 1000km (621 miles) south of Tokyo and reachable only via a 24-hour ferry ride from the capital. The island group, which is part of Micronesia, consists of over 30 subtropical islands, but only two are inhabited: Chichi-jima (Father Island), the largest and most populated, home to roughly 2000 people; and Haha-jima (Mother Island), where just under 500 people live. For centuries, from the 1500s onwards, the islands served as a pit stop for international whaling ships; Japan officially claimed them in 1875. The Ogasawara Islands were part of the Pacific Theatre during WWII, and as a result were occupied by the US Navy until 1968 – meaning a whole generation of islanders grew up speaking English. This, along with their cosmopolitan heritage – which includes European, Micronesian and Polynesian ancestry – sets the islanders apart from most mainland Japanese.

JAPAN'S GALÁPAGOS

The Ogasawara Islands, located where the Pacific and Philippine sea plates meet, were formed some 48 million years ago. These remote islands have never been joined to any other land mass, and the many endemic species here have earned them the nickname 'Japan's Galápagos'. Scientists have counted over 400 species of endemic plants here, plus more than a hundred varieties of land snails, most of which exist nowhere else. These are joined by a plethora of native birds – including the Bonin white-eye, a small yellow and olive-green songbird – as well as insects, fungi and, in the surrounding reefs and waters, an abundance of fish, turtles, cetaceans and even giant squids. Conservation efforts are focused on protecting native species from invasive ones that were introduced with human settlement, and on restoring the natural scrub and subtropical rainforests, harmed by grazing, that make up the habitat for so many endemic species.

1. *Munin himetsubaki*, an evergreen Ogasawara endemic

2. Bonin Honeyeater

3. Ogasawara coast

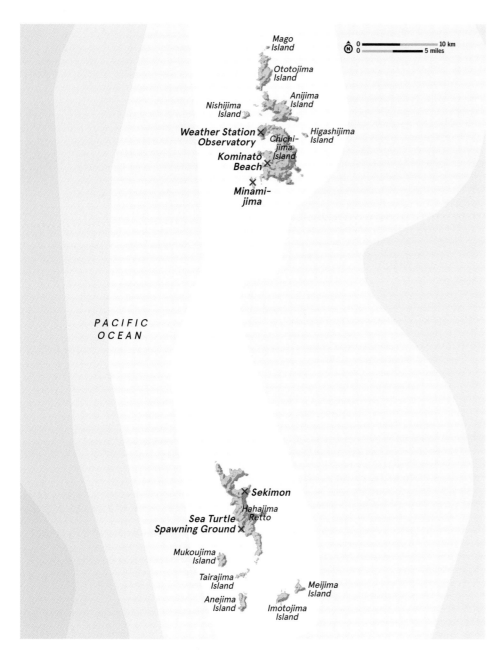

Mago
Island

Ototojima
Island

Anijima
Island

Nishijima
Island

Weather Station ✕
Observatory   *Chichi-*
                  jima
Kominato   *Island*
Beach ✕

Higashijima
Island

✕
Minami-
jima

PACIFIC
OCEAN

✕ **Sekimon**

Hahajima
Retto

Sea Turtle
Spawning Ground ✕

Mukoujima
Island

Tairajima
Island

Anejima
Island

Imotojima
Island

Meijima
Island

0   10 km
0   5 miles

X MARKS THE SPOT

Minami-jima The only uninhabited island that can be visited as a day trip, known for its untouched landscape of white-sand beaches and unique rock formations.

Sekimon Pristine protected rainforest on Haha-jima, home to rare endemic species – including its namesake sekimon (*Claoxylon centinarium*) – and only accessible with a guide.

Weather Station Observatory Chichi-jima lookout point for stunning sunsets and humpback whale spotting.

Sea Turtle Spawning Ground Sandy sanctuary on Haha-jima where tiny sea-turtle hatchlings make their heroic trek to the water.

Kominato Beach One of Chichi-jima's finest stretches of white sand, a sweeping arc fronted by lapping emerald seas.

251

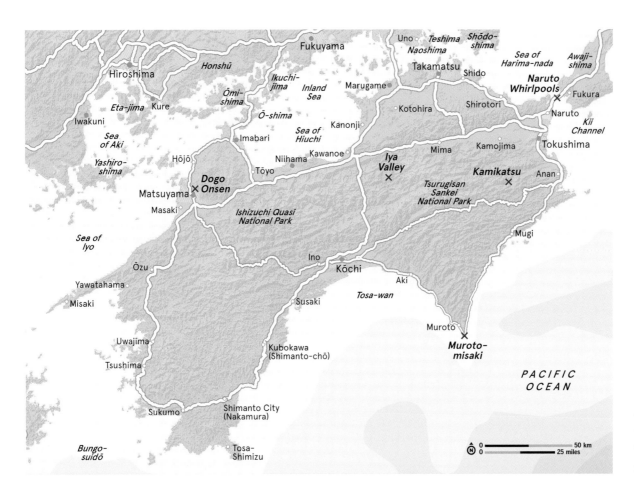

Hiroshima
Fukuyama
Honshū
Ikuchi-jima
Ōmi-shima
Inland Sea
Uno *Teshima*
Naoshima
Shōdo-shima
Takamatsu
Shido
Sea of Harima-nada
Awaji-shima
Kure
Eta-jima
Iwakuni
Sea of Aki
Matsuyama
Ō-shima
Imabari
Kanonji
Marugame
Kotohira
Shirotori
Naruto Whirlpools
Naruto
Fukura
Kii Channel
Sea of Hiuchi
Kawanoe
Niihama
Mima
Kamojima
Tokushima
Yashiro-shima
Hōjō
Tōyo
Dogo Onsen
Masaki
Iya Valley
Kamikatsu
Anan
Tsurugisan Sankei National Park
Ishizuchi Quasi National Park
Sea of Iyo
Ōzu
Ino
Kōchi
Aki
Mugi
Yawatahama
Misaki
Susaki
Tosa-wan
Uwajima
Kubokawa (Shimanto-chō)
Muroto
Muroto-misaki
Tsushima
PACIFIC OCEAN
Sukumo
Shimanto City (Nakamura)
Bungo-suidō
Tosa-Shimizu

0   50 km
0   25 miles

1. Naruto Whirlpools under Onaruto Bridge

2. Cherry in bloom

Shikoku

COUNTRY JAPAN

COORDINATES 33.7432° N, 133.6375° E • **AREA** 18,802 SQ KM (7259 SQ MILES)

Shikoku is the smallest of Japan's four major islands, a vaguely bat-shaped landmass with twin capes jutting into the Pacific Ocean to the south. Most of the population live in the cities in the north, where bridges hopscotch across the islands of the Seto Inland Sea to the Japanese main island of Honshū. The south, meanwhile, is sparsely populated, with undulating forested peaks and valleys spotted with rural hamlets and citrus groves. Though long considered isolated and remote – those bridges didn't arrive until the 1980s – Shikoku has nonetheless played a role in every era of Japanese history, often positioned as a foil to the development and cosmopolitanism seen in the likes of Tokyo and Kyoto. Though population on the island has been declining since the 1950s – it's currently home to some 3.6 million people – it continues to draw those looking to live an off-grid or back-to-nature lifestyle.

THE 88-TEMPLE PILGRIMAGE

Kūkai, known posthumously as Kōbō Daishi, was a Buddhist ascetic who found enlightenment meditating at Muroto-misaki, a cape in southern Shikoku, around the turn of the 9th century. With time, he would become enshrined as one of the greatest religious figures in Japanese history. He is also the inspiration behind the island's 88-Temple Pilgrimage, called the Ohenro, a walking meditation that takes a circular route around the island – covering some 1200km (746 miles) – with stops at 88 temples associated with Kūkai. The pilgrimage is believed to have existed since the 12th century, and is still practised today – although an increasing percentage of the 60,000 to 80,000 people who complete at least part of it each year do so via bus tour rather than on foot. Pilgrims, who often dress in white and wear conical sedge hats, undertake the journey for various reasons, including atonement, supplication for health, happiness and preparation for the next life.

X MARKS THE SPOT

Iya Valley Forested peaks, riverside hot springs and plunging gorges traversed by vine bridges in the heart of Shikoku.

Kamikatsu Small rural village in the mountains and the first community in Japan to pursue a zero-waste policy.

Dōgo Onsen An ancient hot springs referenced in Japanese myth and literature, with a 19th-century bathhouse said to have inspired the Studio Ghibli animated classic *Spirited Away*.

Muroto-misaki Forlorn, rocky headland – considered, poetically, as a doorway to the land of the dead – where Kōbō Daishi achieved enlightenment.

Naruto Whirlpools Japan's most impressive whirlpools, where the Pacific Ocean and the Seto Inland Sea meet at the narrow Naruto Strait.

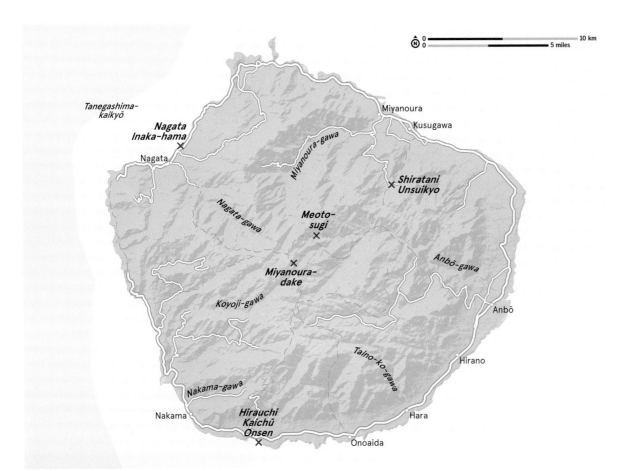

Tanegashima-
kaikyō

Nagata
Inaka-hama
×

Nagata

Miyanoura

Kusugawa

Miyanoura-gawa

*Shiratani
Unsuikyo*
×

*Meoto-
sugi*
×

Nagata-gawa

*Miyanoura-
dake*
×

Anbō-gawa

Koyoji-gawa

Anbō

Taino-ko-gawa

Hirano

Nakama-gawa

Nakama

*Hirauchi
Kaichū
Onsen*
×

Hara

Onoaida

0   10 km
0   5 miles

1. Hiking in the forest
near Shiratani Unsuikyo

2. Aerial view of
Yakushima island

3. Yakushima spotted
sika deer

Yakushima

COUNTRY JAPAN

COORDINATES 30.3446° N, 130.5127° E • AREA 505 SQ KM (195 SQ MILES)

Yakushima is Japan's fairy-tale island, mist-cloaked land of ancient trees and lush carpets of soft green moss that famously inspired the visuals for the iconic Studio Ghibli animated film *Princess Mononoke*. The interior features granite peaks that rise to nearly 2000m (6562ft) – rare on an island of this size – and fall off sharply to the coast. This extreme elevation change means that Yakushima has both subarctic and subtropical climates, snowy peaks and coral reefs. Much of the island, which receives upwards of 8m (26ft) of rain annually, is covered in temperate rainforest. Yakushima is part of the Ōsumi Islands, which in turn form the northernmost part of the Ryūkyū Archipelago – a 1100km-long (683-mile) chain of islands that stretches from Kyūshū (the southernmost of Japan's four major islands) all the way to Taiwan.

YAKUSUGI

Yakushima has incredible biodiversity, but one species in particular has come to define the island – the Japanese cedar *(Cryptomeria japonica)*, called *sugi* in Japanese. Japanese cedars are found elsewhere, too, but those on Yakushima have notably longer lifespans, living upwards of a thousand years as opposed to approximately 500 years on the mainland. This is due to the island's unique geology and climate: the rocky soil means the trees grow slower while copious rainfall and humidity

encourages resin production, which keeps trees from rotting. Those that pass the 1000-year mark are called *yakusugi*, at which point they appear deeply weathered by the elements, with thick, gnarled trunks and an undeniable gravitas. Several of the island's *yakusugi* have names, including the oldest, which is known as Jōmon Sugi after Japan's prehistoric Jōmon period. Its exact age is unknown; it's at least 2000 years old, but could very well be over 5000 years old, making it among the world's oldest trees.

X MARKS THE SPOT

Shiratani Unsuikyo One of the island's most magical spots, a ravine lush with verdant mosses and ferns.

Miyanoura-dake Yakushima's highest peak (and the tallest mountain in Kyūshū) at 1935m (6348ft), reachable via trails that pass through primeval forests.

Hirauchi Kaichū Onsen Natural hot-spring pools on Yakushima's rocky southern coast that only appear during low tide.

Nagata Inaka-hama This stretch of golden sand is Japan's largest breeding ground for sea turtles; it's also the spot to see sunsets over neighbouring Kuchinoerabu Island.

Meoto-sugi Two *yakusugi* joined by a branch, looking like a couple holding hands – hence the nickname 'Husband and Wife Cedar' (*meoto-sugi* in Japanese).

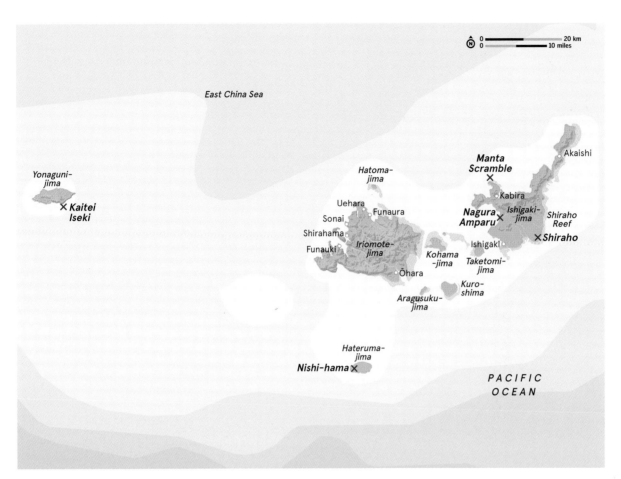

East China Sea

0 ——— 20 km
0 ——— 10 miles

Yonaguni-
jima

× Kaitei
Iseki

Hatoma-
jima

Manta
Scramble
×

Akaishi

Uehara
Funaura

Sonai

Shirahama

Funauki

Iriomote-
jima

Kabira

Nagura
Amparu ×

Ishigaki-
jima

Shiraho
Reef

Ishigakl

× Shiraho

Ōhara

Kohama
-jima

Taketomi-
jima

Aragusuku-
jima

Kuro-
shima

Hateruma-
jima

Nishi-hama ×

PACIFIC
OCEAN

1. Kabira Bay beach,
Ishigaki-jima

2. Water buffalo ferry
passengers to the
botanic garden of Yubu
Island

3. Sanshin

Yaeyama Islands

COUNTRY JAPAN

COORDINATES 24.406° N, 124.175° E • **AREA** 591 SQ KM (228 SQ MILES)

The Yaeyama are the southernmost islands of the Ryūkyū Archipelago, roughly 300km (186 miles) east of Taiwan and nearly 2000km (1243 miles) from Tokyo. There are 12 inhabited islands, which include both Japan's southernmost point (Hateruma-jima) – just shy of the Tropic of Cancer – and its westernmost point (Yonaguni-jima). For centuries, until 1879, the Yaeyama Islands belonged not to Japan but to the independent Ryūkyū Empire, which spread over present-day Okinawa. The Ryūkyū Empire, though influenced by trade partners in Japan, China and Southeast Asia, had a distinct culture that included its own languages, of which Yaeyama is one example. Much of this culture has been lost to time and assimilation policies; however, the islanders have retained their appreciation for, among other things, plaintive, twangy folk music played on the *sanshin* (a banjo-like instrument) and *awamori*, a fiery spirit distilled from long-grain rice.

TAKETOMI ISLAND

Each of the Yaeyama Islands have their own charms: Iriomote-jima has mangrove swamps and a primeval forest; Yonaguni-jima has Japan's best diving, with the chance to encounter hammerhead sharks. And tiny Taketomi-jima, which covers just over 5 sq km (2 sq miles), is something like a living museum of Ryūkyū culture. By local ordinance, only traditional structures – single-storey, with terracotta roofs decorated with *shisha* (half-dog, half-lion guardian creatures) statues and surrounded by stone walls – can be built on the island. Cars are not permitted on Taketomi roads, which are made of crushed coral; instead water buffalo pull wooden carts around the island. There are no chain stores, not even mini marts; there is, however, an abundance of hibiscus in almost every colour of the rainbow. Recently Taketomi has had to reckon with overtourism, as upwards of half a million people visit each year – a huge number considering the island is home to just over 300 people.

X MARKS THE SPOT

Kaitei Iseki Either an unusual rock formation off the coast of Yonaguni-jima, or remnants of a lost civilisation now at the bottom of the sea.

Shiraho The waters off the coast of this Ishigaki-jima village are home to the largest colony of blue coral in the northern hemisphere.

Nishi-hama Claimed by many to be Okinawa's most beautiful beach, with shifting shades of blue and green fronted by fine white sand, on Hateruma-jima.

Nagura Amparu Protected tidal flat at the mouth of Iriomote-jima river Nagara-gawa, with Japan's largest mangrove forest.

Manta Scramble Coral- and anemone-encrusted Ishigaki-jima dive spot that draws plentiful fish and those most graceful creatures of the sea, manta rays.

OCEANIA

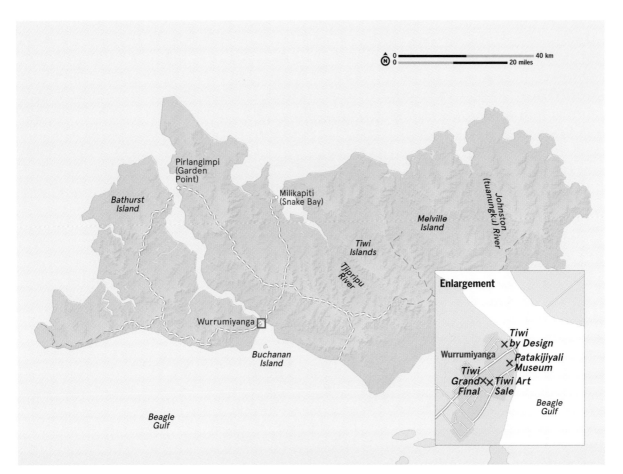

Enlargement

Tiwi
by Design
Wurrumiyanga Patakijiyali
Museum
Tiwi
Grand Tiwi Art
Final Sale
Beagle
Gulf

Pirlangimpi
(Garden
Point)

Milikapiti
(Snake Bay)

Bathurst
Island

Melville
Island

Johnston
(tuanungkJ) River

Tiwi
Islands

Tiotripu
River

Wurrumiyanga

Buchanan
Island

Beagle
Gulf

0 .... 40 km
0 .... 20 miles

1. Bathurst mangroves

2. Tiwi Islands artist
painting a shell

3. Ochre on the fire

Tiwi Islands

COUNTRY AUSTRALIA • **COORDINATES** 11.6969°S, 130.8779°E • **AREA** 8320 SQ KM (3212 SQ MILES)

Once the travel domain of keen anglers, the sultry Tiwi Islands – Bathurst and Melville – have become one of the cultural highlights of the Northern Territory's Top End. Around 80% of the islands' population identify as Tiwi, and this remote Aboriginal group has a strong and distinct culture. Tiwi artists are renowned for their vibrant printed designs, and Tiwi language, ceremony and sexual politics are also unique to that of mainland Aboriginal groups. The main settlement on the islands, 80km (50 miles) north of Darwin, is Wurrumiyanga in the southeast of Bathurst Island, which was founded in 1911 as a Catholic mission. A permit from the Tiwi Land Council is required to visit the Tiwis independently, but you don't need one to join an arts-focused day tour from Darwin. Several secluded, fishing-based lodges offer multi-day packages.

LET'S HEAR IT FOR THE SISTERGIRLS

Home to Australia's largest per capita transgender population, where around 50 of approximately 2500 residents reportedly identify as trans, the Tiwi Islands are the heart of Australia's Sistergirl community. Sistergirl (or Brotherboy) is a respectful term for an Indigenous transgender person, but this respect has been hard won in the Tiwis and beyond. Following a string of Tiwi Sistergirl suicides in the early 2000s, a community meeting was held where Sistergirls approached Tiwi Elders for permission to perform traditional women's dances. Elders agreed; the meeting served as a turning point in the Sistergirls' fight for acceptance within their community where, as in most Aboriginal communities, issues are divided into 'men's' and 'women's' business.

In 2017, a group of 30 Tiwi Sistergirls made their debut at the Sydney Gay & Lesbian Mardi Gras. Among them was drag performer Foxxy Empire, aka Jason de Santis, who made an appearance as Foxxy in Aussie rom-com *Top End Wedding* (2019), starring Tiwi actress Miranda Tapsell.

X MARKS THE SPOT

Tiwi by Design This day trip from Darwin immerses you in the daily operations of Tiwi Design, one of three Tiwi art centres.

Patakijiyali Museum Learn about Tiwi spirituality, the Catholic Mission, the islands' role in WWII and more at this Bathurst Island museum.

Tiwi Grand Final Held in March, this sporting spectacular displays the Tiwis' passion for Australian Rules football.

Tiwi Art Sale Coinciding with the Grand Final is this fantastic opportunity to purchase local art.

Ceremonies Pukumani (burial ceremonies) and Kurlama (a celebration of life held towards the end of the wet season) are the most important ceremonies in Tiwi culture.

❸

Christmas Island

COUNTRY AUSTRALIA
COORDINATES 10.4475° S, 105.6904° E • AREA 135 SQ KM (52 SQ MILES)

Closer to Java than mainland Western Australia, this wild and remote Australian external territory has made headlines for its controversial detention centre in recent years. Yet the unique topography, wildlife and culture of Christmas Island continue to make it one of Australia's most intriguing travel destinations.

Administratively part of Singapore until Britain transferred its sovereignty to Australia in 1958, Christmas Island's human mix of Chinese, Malay and European-Australian is reflected in its food, languages and customs. Most of the island's 600-odd annual visitors, however, come to see its famous red crabs, millions of which march to the ocean each summer to breed in what British naturalist Sir David Attenborough has described as one of his greatest TV moments.

Crabs of all kinds can be seen year-round, and the island's soaring limestone cliffs attract a superb array of rare seabirds. Centuries of isolation have also seen Christmas Island's tropical reefs birth hybrid fish species that can be spotted on a dive or snorkel.

With the island now shifting its focus to ecotourism as its phosphate mining industry winds down, future visitors can look forward to new hiking and mountain-biking trails in Christmas Island National Park, which covers more than half of the island.

X MARKS THE SPOT

Hugh's Dale Waterfall A boardwalk leads to this glorious waterfall in Christmas Island National Park, the damp environment making it a prime crab hangout.

The Blowholes An elevated walkway provides a front-row seat to the dramatic 'whoosh' of seawater blasted up through limestone caves.

The Grotto Scenic rock pool, just 5km (3 miles) east of the visitor centre in the main village of Flying Fish Cove.

Dolly Beach Camp at this remote beach deep in the national park, reached via a gnarly 4WD trail.

South Point In the island's south, visit a mining settlement abandoned in the 1970s, as well as one of the island's largest Taoist temples.

LAST LIZARDS

Introduced species have wreaked havoc on Christmas Island's endemic wildlife since its first settlers arrived in the late 19th century, leading to a string of extinctions. Feral cats have now been almost completely eradicated on the island, with conservation efforts now largely focused on rehabilitating the Christmas Island blue-tailed skink and the Lister's gecko. Thought to be extinct in the wild, these two critically endangered endemic lizard species can be viewed at the Pink House Research Centre's Lizard Lounge, which opens to visitors on Wednesdays. On the free one-hour tour, you'll also learn about the biological control for the introduced yellow crazy ants, which prey on the Christmas Island red crab.

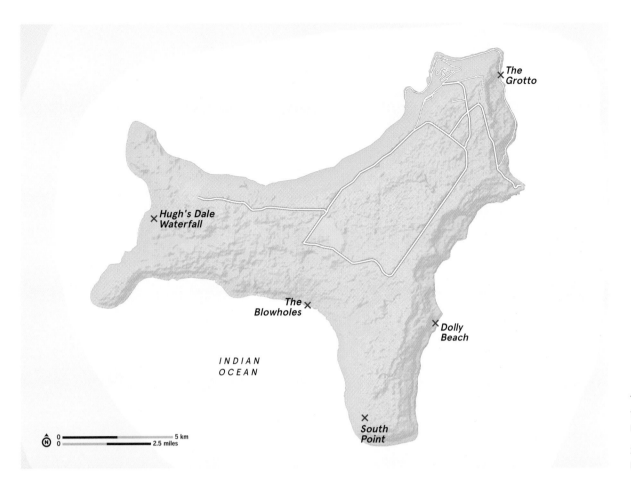

INDIAN
OCEAN

The
Grotto

Hugh's Dale
Waterfall

The
Blowholes

Dolly
Beach

South
Point

0   5 km
0   2.5 miles

1. Blowholes, Christmas
Island National Park

2. A bevy of Christmas
Island red crabs

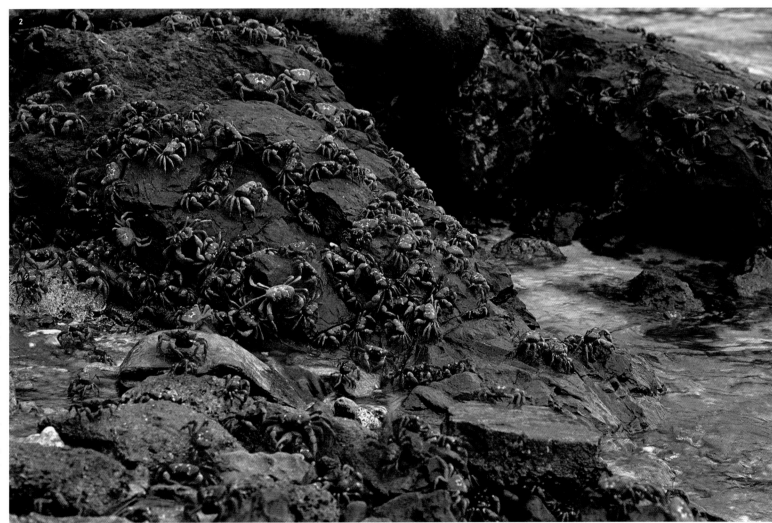

Rottnest Island/ Wadjemup

COUNTRY AUSTRALIA

COORDINATES 32.0064° S, 115.5073° E • **AREA** 19 SQ KM (7.3 SQ MILES)

Rottnest Island/Wadjemup has always been an important place for the Whadjuk Noongar people of southwest Western Australia, whose oral history documents their ancestors walking to the low-lying limestone island to perform traditional activities before sea levels rose at the end of the last Ice Age. More recently, 'Rotto' has become a top tourism draw, famed for its beaches and equally photogenic quokkas – tiny wallabies mistaken for giant rats by the Dutch navigator who gave the island its European name (which means 'Rats Nest') in 1696.

An easy day trip from Perth, the protected reserve is best explored by bike. There are also plenty of walking trails and a hop-on, hop-off bus, which stops within easy reach of lookout points, lighthouses and other attractions. The clear turquoise waters that lap the island's powder-white beaches also proffer great snorkelling.

If one day on the island isn't enough, Rotto's handful of accommodation options were recently joined by eco-glamping outfit Discovery Rottnest Island and the luxe Samphire Rottnest hotel.

HEALING ROTTO

Rottnest Island's natural beauty belies its dark history, notably its tenure as an Aboriginal prison from 1838 until 1904, then as a forced labour camp until 1931.

Nearly 400 of the 4000 Aboriginal men and boys incarcerated on Rotto never made it off the island. Buried in unmarked graves, the deaths of these Elders, warriors and lawmen from across Western Australia were literally covered up for decades, until a string of bone discoveries finally led the island to face its truth.

Rotto's healing took an important step forward in 2020 upon the announcement of a project to convert the Wadjemup Aboriginal Burial Ground, a mass burial site near the township's Quod (former prison), into a memorial. To learn more about Rotto's rich Aboriginal history and culture, book a Noongar-guided walking tour with Go Cultural.

X MARKS THE SPOT

The Basin Unleash your kids at Rotto's top family swim spot – a sheltered, sandy-floored natural pool just a short cycle from the township.

Snorkel Trails Read up on local marine life while navigating the snorkel trails at Parker Point and nearby Little Salmon Bay.

Wadjemup Museum Learn about the island's natural and human history in an old hay-store building built by Aboriginal prisoners.

Vlamingh Lookout Just south of Garden Lake, off Digby Dr, this vantage point offers panoramic views of the island.

Wadjemup Lighthouse Take a guided tour of Western Australia's first stone lighthouse, built in 1849.

INDIAN
OCEAN

Armstrong
Rock

The
Basin ✕

Rottnest
Museum

Lake
Baghdad

Lake
Negri

Garden ✕
Lake

Lake
Herschel

Vlamingh
Lookout ✕

Pink
Lake

Thomson
Bay

Stark
Bay

Serpentine
Lake

Government
House Lake

Wadjemup
Lighthouse ✕

Wallace
Island

Narrow
Neck

Green
Island

Salmon
Bay

Porpoise
Bay

Dyer
Island

Cathedral
Rocks

West
End

Snorkel Trails ✕

Little
Salmon
Bay ✕ Snorkel
Trails

1. The super-cute
quokka

2. Longreach Bay

Kangaroo Island

COUNTRY AUSTRALIA

COORDINATES 35.7752° S, 137.2142° E • **AREA** 4405 SQ KM (1701 SQ MILES)

Rising from the ashes after having been ravaged by fire in the Black Summer bushfires of 2019-20, when nearly half of the island burned, Kangaroo Island (or KI, as locals call it) remains a world-class wildlife and wilderness destination. The island, off the southern coast of South Australia, is home to iconic and charismatic native Australian animals on both land and sea. Add to that a delightfully slow pace of life – it's the kind of place where children ride bikes to school and farmers advertise for wives on noticeboards – and a small but well-regarded winegrowing reputation, and it's hard not to fall in love with KI.

SANCTUARY FROM EXTINCTION

On the western end of Kangaroo Island, Flinders Chase National Park is best known for its wild coastline, mallee scrub and sugar-gum forests; look for prime examples of the latter around Rocky River and the Ravine des Casoars, close to Cape Borda. And, of course, there's KI's world-famous wildlife. Kangaroos, wallabies, bandicoots and possums come out at night, while koalas and platypuses were introduced to Flinders Chase in the 1920s when it was feared they would become extinct on the mainland. Echidnas forage in the undergrowth, where you might also come across goannas and tiger snakes. Of the island's 267 bird species, several are rare or endangered. One notable species – the dwarf emu – has gone the way of the dodo; glossy black cockatoos may soon follow in its footsteps due to habitat depletion. Offshore, dolphins and southern right whales are often seen cavorting, and there are colonies of little penguins, New Zealand fur seals and Australian sea lions here too. Exploring the island on foot is an excellent way to go, but diving, snorkelling, fishing, swimming, surfing and cycling are also all possible here.

0 ___ 20 km
0 ___ 10 miles

Middle
River

Stokes
Bay

Emu
Bay

Cape
Jervis

Cygnet
River

Kingscote
Brownlow

Penneshaw

**Kangaroo Island
Farmers Market**

**Dudley Wines
Cellar Door**

Parndana

American
River

Baudin
Beach

**Flinders Chase
National Park**

*Rocky
River*

Snake
Lagoon

**Kangaroo Island
Wilderness Trail**

Karatta

Vivonne
Bay

*Seal Bay
Conservation
Park*

*GREAT
AUSTRALIAN
BIGHT*

X MARKS THE SPOT

Seal Bay Conservation Park
Listen to seals snort and
snore at this south-coast
wildlife haven.

**Kangaroo Island Wilderness
Trail** Hike through 61km (38
miles) of KI's wildest wilds over
five days.

Wineries Sip island wines with
an ocean view at Dudley Wines
near Penneshaw.

Flinders Chase National Park
Check out weirdly wonderful
rock formations, remote
lighthouses and meandering
bushwalks.

**Kangaroo Island Farmers
Market** Shop for the best
island produce – cheese,
honey, meats, breads,
beer, wine and spirits – at
Penneshaw's monthly food
market.

1. Aerial view of Snelling
Beach and Middle River

2. Remarkable Rocks

3. Australian sea lions
tussling on the beach

Bass Strait

Emita · *Flinders Island*

Whitemark · Lackrana · Lady Barron

Cape Barren Island

Stanley
Marrawah · Smithton · *Rocky Cape National Park*
Arthur River · Wynyard · Burnie
Ulverstone · Devonport
Savage River National Park · Latrobe
Arthur-Pieman Conservation Area
Waratah
Savage River
Corinna · *Cradle Valley*
Rosebery · **Cradle ✕ Mountain**
Zeehan · *Cradle Mountain–Lake St Clair National Park*
Queenstown
Strahan · Derwent Bridge
Franklin-Gordon Wild Rivers National Park
Mount Field National Park
SOUTHERN OCEAN · Strathgordon
Huonville · Kingston
Snug
Southwest National Park · Geeveston · Port Arthur
Melaleuca
Hartz Mountains National Park · Dover · *Bruny Island*
Ile Du Golfe · *South Bruny National Park*

George Town · Bridport
Scottsdale
Mt William National Park
Larapuna (Bay of Fires) ✕
St Helens · Binalong Bay
Launceston
Evandale
Longford
Central Plateau Conservation Area
Douglas-Apsley National Park
Campbell Town · Bicheno
Ross
Swansea · Coles Bay
Oatlands
Freycinet ✕ National Park
Triabunna
Maria Island · *Maria Island National Park*
Brighton
MONA ✕ Hobart
✕ Port Arthur Historic Site
Tasman Peninsula
Tasman Island

St Marys

X MARKS THE SPOT

MONA Hobart's Museum of Old and New Art (MONA) is world-class, in turn subversive, confronting and downright weird.

Port Arthur Quiet Port Arthur Historic Site is a compelling, disquieting mix of gorgeous coastal scenery and a sombre past.

Cradle Mountain Tasmania's most recognisable – and spectacular – mountain peak, with fabulous wildlife-watching across the surrounding national park.

Freycinet National Park Freycinet has transparent waters, white beaches and pink-granite headlands, as well as Tasmania's most photographed beach: Wineglass Bay.

Larapuna (Bay of Fires) With azure ocean, eucalypt forests and granite outcrops, the Larapuna (Bay of Fires) could be Tasmania's most scenic slice of coastline.

1. Dolerite rock stacks at the Tasman Peninsula's southern end

2. Museum of Old and New Art (MONA)

Tasmania

COUNTRY AUSTRALIA • **COORDINATES** 42.0409° S, 146.8087° E • **AREA** 68,401 SQ KM (26,410 SQ MILES)

Australia's largest island, Tasmania has vast tracts of wilderness, an intriguing human history that stretches back millennia and a modern reputation for artistic and culinary excellence. Much of the island's west is uninhabited and covered by forests, and some of its west-coast beaches have recorded the cleanest air on the planet – the winds that pummel the southern and western shore circle the Earth unimpeded by human beings and untouched by their pollution. Tasmania has been separated from the Australian mainland for at least 12,000 years and its very own wildlife story is one of Australia's most unusual, from the fearsome Tasmanian devil to the mystery of the thylacine.

CARVING OUT AN ECOLOGICAL NICHE

Adrift some 240km (149 miles) south of Victoria, across tumultuous Bass Strait, Tasmania is Australia's only island state. To the east is the Tasman Sea, separating Australia and New Zealand; to the south and west the Southern Ocean rolls nonstop to Antarctica. Even if you include the surface area of its offshore islands, Tasmania is Australia's smallest state. But though it may be small by Australian standards, Tasmania is still larger than Sri Lanka, and is the size of a small European country – it's bigger than Switzerland or Belgium, and only slightly smaller than Ireland. There's also plenty of room for the island's unique flora and fauna to carve out its own ecological niche.

Many of the distinctive mammals of mainland Australia – the marsupials and monotremes (such as the platypus or echidna) isolated for at least 45 million years – are also found in Tasmania, and the island has dozens of mammal species (but no koalas, and few kangaroos). Apart from the endemic Tasmanian devil, there are eastern quolls, eastern barred bandicoots, bettongs, pademelons, wallabies, echidnas, wombats and more. At last count, 383 bird species had been recorded in Tasmania, including 12 endemics such as the forty-spotted pardalote, black currawong, Tasmanian thornbill, green rosella and the Tasmanian native hen.

Bruny Island

COUNTRY AUSTRALIA • **COORDINATES** 43.3937° S, 147.2679° E • **AREA** 362 SQ KM (140 SQ MILES)

Located off the southeastern coastline of Tasmania, Bruny Island is actually a brace of islands linked by a narrow 5km (3-mile) isthmus of sand dubbed the Neck. To the north, the terrain is more sparse and dry, while southern Bruny, especially the sea cliffs and towering coastal landscape of South Bruny National Park, is often enlivened by wind, rain and ocean swells sweeping in from the Tasman Sea. For visitors from the Tasmanian capital of Hobart, the island's appeal is centred on an interesting food and wine scene, and the opportunity to see the diverse populations of birdlife and marine mammals that call Bruny home.

BRUNY ISLAND ON A PLATE

It's a drive of less than two hours from Hobart south to Bruny, and beyond the island's stunning southern coastline and fascinating natural history, it's also a popular weekend destination for travelling food, wine and beer fans from Tasmania's biggest city. Cool-climate varietals including Chardonnay, Riesling, Sauvignon Blanc and Pinot Noir are the award-winning focus at Bruny Island Premium Wines, and Australia's southernmost vineyard also produces excellent cider, using apples from the world-renowned Huon Valley orchards just across the D'Entrecasteaux Channel. An essential destination for beer fans is the Bruny Island Beer Co, where

farmhouse brews are teamed with artisan cheeses made at the adjacent Bruny Island Dairy Co. A popular pairing is the Cloudy Bay IPA, made entirely with Tasmanian hops and barley, and the sharp tang of the aged Northern Italian–style C2 cheese. From November to April, 'pick your own' strawberries, blackberries and boysenberries attract families to the Bruny Island Berry Farm, and this juicy summertime bounty is harnessed for ice cream, pancakes and scones with jam islandwide. Summer is also a popular time to visit Bruny for briny-fresh oysters, served with Tabasco sauce and a splash of lemon juice at the Get Shucked Oyster Farm.

1. Shucked oysters

2. The Neck

3. Cheese and bread platter, Bruny Island Dairy Co

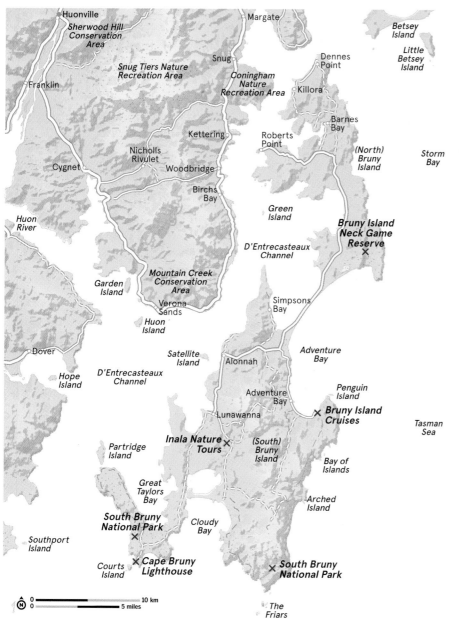

X MARKS THE SPOT

Bruny Island Neck Game Reserve
Negotiate convenient boardwalks to viewing platforms showcasing the island's marine birdlife. Short-tailed shearwaters and fairy penguins are often seen around dusk.

South Bruny National Park Coastal trails include the stroll to the historic Cape Bruny Lighthouse, and the challenging 12km (7.4-mile) hike to spectacular East Cloudy Head.

Cape Bruny Lighthouse Built in 1836, Australia's second-oldest lighthouse punctuates a windswept peninsula on Bruny's southwestern tip.

Bruny Island Cruises Tasmania's most exciting maritime experiences take in Bruny's spectacular southeastern coastline. Look forward to spotting marine mammals including dolphins, whales and seals.

Inala Nature Tours Head out with a natural botany and zoology expert on walking or 4WD tours uncovering Bruny's diverse flora and fauna.

Macquarie Island

COUNTRY AUSTRALIA · **COORDINATES** 54.6208° S, 158.8556° E · **AREA** 128 SQ KM (49 SQ MILES)

One of the Earth's more remote islands, Macquarie is roughly halfway between Tasmania and Antarctica. Its leading attractions are its epic colonies of 100,000 seals (mainly elephant seals) and four million penguins, including about 850,000 breeding pairs of royals (which only raise young here and on the nearby Bishops and Clerks islands). That these huge colonies survive is remarkable: sealing (for skins) and penguin-hunting (for oil) historically wrought havoc upon seal and bird populations: after the discovery of then-uninhabited Macquarie in the early 19th century, the wildlife was pretty much wiped out by the dawn of the 20th century. Apart from the hunting, whalers and sealers upset the ecosystem by bringing horses, donkeys, dogs, cats, mice, rats, rabbits, goats, pigs, cattle, ducks, chickens and sheep to Macquarie. Rats, mice and rabbits remain numerous and problematic, but penguin and seal numbers rebounded following legal protections in the 1980s and beyond.

SEISMIC ACTIVITY; STABLE WEATHER

The island is the only place in the world where rocks from the Earth's mantle, 6km (4 miles) below the ocean floor, are exposed above sea level by the gradual but continuing upthrust of the plate. Macquarie was granted Unesco World Heritage status in 1997, primarily because of this geological uniqueness. With all of this seismic activity, large earthquakes occur often. Macquarie's rocks are buffeted by the wild Southern Ocean weather (strong westerlies blow nearly every day), and yet the climate is one of the most stable on Earth: mean annual temperatures range from 3.3°C (38°F) to 7.2°C (45°F), there is no permanent snow or ice cover, and yearly rainfall (91cm/36in) is spread out over more than 300 days in a variety of forms: snow, rain, hail, sleet, mist and fog – sometimes all in the same day. Macquarie has no trees – none! – on the island, with tussock grass, two species of 'megaherb', and yellow-flowering Macquarie Island cabbage being the only vegetation.

1. Royal penguins, Sandy Bay

2. Australian Antarctic Research Base, Macquarie Island Station

3. Royal penguin

0 5 km
N 0 2.5 miles

Buckles
Bay

Island
Lake

Bauer
Bay

Tulloch
Lake

Prion
Lake

Major
Lake

Lake
Tiobunga

Waterfall
Lake

X MARKS THE SPOT

Discovery The first recorded sighting of Macquarie was on 11 July 1810 by the sealing brig *Perseverance*.

Slaughter The *Perseverance* crew killed 80,000 seals on their first visit.

Name The crew of the *Perseverance* named the island after Lachlan Macquarie, governor of New South Wales (of which Tasmania was then a part).

Explorers Douglas Mawson, Robert Scott, Ernest Shackleton and other Antarctic explorers all stopped here on their long journeys south.

Population Macquarie has a human population of between 20 and 40 people; the Australian Antarctic Division has a permanent base on the island.

2

0 ————————— 5 km
0 ————————— 2.5 miles

Telefon
Bay

× Pendulum
  Cove

× Port
  Foster

Fumarole
Bay

Bransfield
Strait

× Baily
  Head

Crater
Lake

Whalers ×
Bay

× Neptune's
  Bellows

Lavebrua
Island

Bransfield
Strait

X MARKS THE SPOT

Port Foster The sheltered waters encircled by Deception Island are almost completely enclosed by the remains of a sunken volcanic caldera.

Neptune's Bellows Named after the Roman god of the sea, the entrance to Port Foster is only 560m (1837ft) wide, and often very windy.

Whalers Bay At the eastern end of Port Foster lir bleached whale bones and the abandoned detritus of early 20th-century whaling activity.

Baily Head With a vast breeding colony of chinstrap penguins, this rocky headland has been declared an Important Bird Area (IBA) by BirdLife International.

Pendulum Cove Around low tide, it's sometimes possible to bathe in the hot springs bubbling up from this beach's black volcanic sand.

1. Chinstraps navigate the 'penguin highway'

2. Deception Island whaling station

Deception Island

COUNTRY ADMINISTERED UNDER THE ANTARCTIC TREATY SYSTEM
COORDINATES 62.9409° S, 60.5554° W • **AREA** 72 SQ KM (28 SQ MILES)

Part of the South Shetland Islands, and just 100km (62 miles) from the frozen expanses of Antarctica, Deception Island is the exposed crater of a still-active shield volcano 30km (19 miles) in diameter. During summer, scientists from Argentina and Spain conduct research on the island, and more than 15,000 passengers on expedition cruise ships also visit from November to March, drawn by Deception's stark volcanic landscapes, a fascinating history involving whaling and sealing, and some of the southern continent's best natural history and wildlife experiences.

VISITING DECEPTION ISLAND

Cruise ships first visited Deception Island in 1966, and today it's one of the most popular destinations for birdwatching and wildlife encounters in the Antarctic. Marine mammals include Weddell seals, Antarctic fur seals and larger southern elephant seals, all of which 'haul out' to relax and recharge on the rocky bays and sandy coves around Port Foster. Seabirds including south polar skuas, Cape petrels and Antarctic terns soar on southern breezes above the cliffs framing Deception's central safe haven, and passengers on visiting expedition ships are able to hike amidst the avian throng. A popular trail is from Whalers Bay to a 425m-high (1394ft) lookout high above Neptune's

Bellows for views of the jagged rocky outcrops known as the 'Sewing Machine Needles'.

The world's largest colony of chinstrap penguins, numbering more than 400,000 birds, also live on the exterior of the island's volcanic caldera, and while most sea-facing parts of Deception Island are off-limits to visitors, passengers on visiting ships – if the surf and swell are not too rough – can ride in inflatable Zodiacs for landings on Baily Head's black-sand beach. Antarctic fur seals are also regular visitors to the area, but Baily Head's southern continent stars of the show are definitely the 100,000 breeding pairs of chinstrap penguins.

Norfolk Island

COUNTRY AUSTRALIA
COORDINATES 29.0408°S, 167.9547°E • **AREA** 35 SQ KM (13.5 SQ MILES)

Twice used as a notorious penal colony before being settled, in 1856, by the descendants of Tahitians and HMS *Bounty* mutineers escaping an overcrowded Pitcairn Island, Norfolk Island may use New South Wales postcodes, but it isn't technically part of a mainland state or territory. This offers the first hint of the island's uniqueness.

Located roughly halfway between Australia and New Zealand, this intriguing island has a beautifully preserved convict-built heritage precinct to explore in south-coast Kingston; scenic bushwalking trails to tackle in Norfolk Island National Park to the north; and even a second official language – Norfuk – to wrap your tongue around.

Despite its dark history, today's Norfolk Island is a friendly place where wandering cattle have right of way, everyone knows everyone, and the distance that fresh food travels to your plate is measured in metres, not miles. The island even has its own craft brewery.

HELL IN THE PACIFIC

In 1788, only weeks after the First Fleet reached Port Jackson to settle Sydney, convicts were shipped to Norfolk Island to develop the remote island and prevent its seizure by another European power. With rough seas and the absence of good landing sites making it difficult to supply and sustain the colony, it was abandoned in 1814, with the convicts shipped down to Van Diemen's Land (Tasmania).

Just over a decade later, in 1825, the British government prescribed a new use for the island: a place of banishment for problem convicts. It was during this period that the penal colony became known as 'hell in the Pacific' after being declared 'a place of the extremest punishment short of death'. The ruins of an early pentagonal prison, a lime pit (into which convict murder victims were sometimes thrown) and a convict cemetery stand testament to the convicts' suffering.

SOUTH PACIFIC
OCEAN

X MARKS THE SPOT

Kingston The Unesco-listed site is crammed with historic buildings, four of which house museums.

Foundation Day Visit on 6 March to catch the island's main festival, including a re-enactment of the boats arriving at Emily Bay.

Captain Cook Monument Enjoy superb views along the cliffs of Norfolk Island National Park from this lookout marking the spot of Cook's 1788 landing.

Birdwatching Norfolk Island is an important nesting ground for a variety of seabirds. Plus, look out for the endangered Norfolk Island green parrot.

Philip Island Part of Norfolk Island National Park, this small uninhabited island is worth a day trip for its unusual geology.

1. View of Slaughter Bay and Kingston from Elizabeth Lookout

2. Norfolk pine cones

3. Blue morpho butterfly

SOUTH PACIFIC OCEAN

Malabar Hill

North Beach

Ned's Beach

Tasman Sea

Mt Gower

0 ___ 2 km
0 ___ 1 miles
N

X MARKS THE SPOT

Mt Gower Scale Lord Howe's highest peak (875m/2871ft) in the company of a guide.

Ball's Pyramid Board a boat to reach this spectacular volcanic crag, popular for birdwatching and diving.

North Beach Hike or kayak to this beautiful crescent-shaped beach, from where a trail leads to the even more secluded Old Gulch cove.

Malabar Hill Soak up one of the best views of Lord Howe from this stunning lookout reached by an uphill slog from Ned's Beach.

Ned's Beach Enjoy some of the island's best snorkelling at this pretty beach.

1. Paddleboarding with a Mt Gower view

2. Lord Howe Island stick insects

3. Mt Gower and Mt Lidgbird

Lord Howe Island

COUNTRY AUSTRALIA

COORDINATES 31.5553° S, 159.0821° E • **AREA** 14.5 SQ KM (5.5 SQ MILES)

Rising dramatically from the Pacific some 700km (435 miles) northeast of Sydney, Lord Howe's World Heritage–listed beauty and its forward-thinking approach to sustainable tourism have thrust this small, remote island into the international spotlight.

Formed by volcanic activity around seven million years ago, Lord Howe's 'youth' and isolation lends it a unique ecology, with approximately 50% of the flora and fauna endemic to an island that's home to just 300-odd residents, many descended from 19th-century settlers.

From hiking lush rainforest walking trails – including the epic trek to the summit of Mt Gower at the island's southern tip – to snorkelling and diving amongst teeming coral reefs, there are plenty of ways to immerse yourself in the natural wilderness of Lord Howe, which makes a gentle arc around a protected turquoise lagoon. And with daily visitors capped at 400, you'll often feel like you have the idyllic isle, which forms part of New South Wales, all to yourself.

Public barbecues dotted around Lord Howe encourage DIY alfresco dining, and with a new microbrewery opened in 2021, you can now top off a day of exploring by sampling a local beer straight from the source.

ECOLOGICAL RENAISSANCE

Fifteen years in the planning, an extensive rodent eradication program enacted in 2019 has seen Lord Howe's introduced rats and mice all but wiped out. In the short time since, native birds, insects and plants threatened by rodents have reportedly recovered at a rapid rate. Never-before-seen fruits and flowers now blossom from native plants, and snails have made a comeback to the island's misty cloud forests. But the most remarkable recovery is that of the endemic Lord Howe Island woodhen. Collected from the island and placed in specially created enclosures during the eradication program, the island's 220-strong woodhen population has now more than tripled.

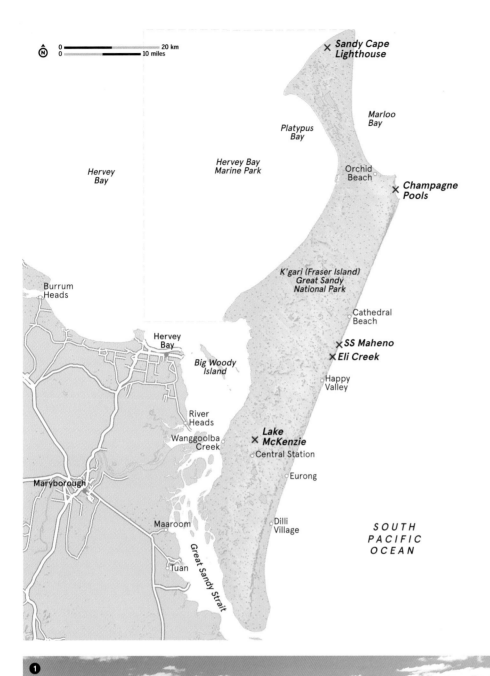

0 ____ 20 km
0 ____ 10 miles

Sandy Cape Lighthouse

Marloo Bay

Platypus Bay

Hervey Bay Marine Park

Hervey Bay

Orchid Beach

Champagne Pools

K'gari (Fraser Island) Great Sandy National Park

Burrum Heads

Cathedral Beach

Hervey Bay

Big Woody Island

SS Maheno
Eli Creek

River Heads

Happy Valley

Wanggoolba Creek

Lake McKenzie

Central Station

Maryborough

Eurong

Maaroom

Dilli Village

SOUTH PACIFIC OCEAN

Tuan

Great Sandy Strait

X MARKS THE SPOT

Lake McKenzie Powder-white sands meet the turquoise shallows of this azure freshwater lake, K'gari's most famous swimming spot.

Eli Creek Stroll along the waterside boardwalk then float back down this shallow freshwater creek.

SS *Maheno* The rusting wreck of this ocean liner, which ran aground in 1935, is a photographer's dream at any time of the day.

Sandy Cape Lighthouse Learn about the island's WWII history and maritime incidents on the Sandy Cape Lighthouse Walk (4.8km/3 miles return) at the island's northern tip.

Champagne Pools Just north of Indian Head, these natural rock pools 'fizz' when seawater spills into them.

1. Champagne Pools

2. The banksia's brush-like flower

3. Off-roading on K'gari/Fraser Island

K'gari/Fraser Island

COUNTRY AUSTRALIA

COORDINATES 25.2398°S, 153.1325°E • **AREA** 1655 SQ KM (639 SQ MILES)

Stretching alongside the southern Queensland coast for 123km (76 miles) , World Heritage-listed K'gari/Fraser Island is the world's largest sand island – and one of Australia's greatest adventures. Join an organised tour or tackle the island's 4WD-only trails in your own vehicle in search of wild, empty beaches, idyllic freshwater lakes, otherworldly geological formations, historic relics, native wildlife – including K'gari's notorious dingoes – and more.

There are guesthouses and two resorts on the island, but bush and beach camping is a highlight of the off-grid K'gari experience, along with lazy days by the lakes, wild walks and simply being immersed in nature.

NATURAL & CULTURAL WONDER

K'gari isn't just a big sand island, but an incredibly unique one, offering what Unesco describes as an 'outstanding example of ongoing biological, hydrological and geomorphological processes'. Here majestic remnants of tall rainforest grow on the longest and most complete age sequence of coastal dune systems on the planet. Did we mention K'gari is also home to half of the world's perched freshwater dune lakes?

What the Unesco listing doesn't recognise, however, is the island's deep and ongoing significance to the Butchulla people of the Fraser Coast, whose connection to K'gari (which means 'paradise' in

their language) is thought to date back up to 50,000 years. While historical Aboriginal artefacts on the island such as middens and scar trees aren't easy to spot, visitors will discover information panels revealing fascinating insights into the history and culture of the Butchulla, who maintained a complex system of lore that ensured a bountiful supply of resources throughout the year. Sharing is a way of life in Butchulla culture, a tradition that continues today through tourism, with visitors welcomed onto their Traditional Country with one caveat: that guests show care and respect for this special place, just as Butchulla people have for tens of thousands of years.

Horn Island/ Ngurupai

COUNTRY AUSTRALIA • **COORDINATES** 10.6116° S, 142.2869° E • **AREA** 53 SQ KM (20 SQ MILES)

Most travellers to the Torres Strait Islands don't get much further than Thursday Island, the administrative centre of this remote archipelago at Australia's northern tip. But this is a shame, for its larger and more sparsely populated neighbour Horn Island plays host to some of Australia's most fascinating – yet little-known – WWII heritage.

The Kaurareg people – Traditional Custodians of the Torres Strait's Inner Islands group – know Horn Island as Ngurupai. A flourishing pearling industry operated here in the early 20th century before most residents evacuated to Thursday Island at the onset of WWII, when Horn Island/ Ngurupai was used as an airbase. Torres Strait Islanders trickled back after the war, settling in the present-day Horn Island/Ngurupai village of Wasaga. With its rocky beaches patrolled by saltwater crocodiles, there's not much to do on the rugged island beyond seeking out its wartime heritage. But that's reason enough to come.

THE FORGOTTEN ARMY

Horn Island/Ngurupai was the second most attacked region of Australia after Darwin during WWII, when it was defended by the Torres Strait Light Infantry Battalion, the only all-Indigenous battalion in the Australian Army's history. More than a hundred military personnel (and nearly as many civilians) died during the campaign, after which their stories were all but forgotten – until Vanessa Seekee arrived on the island as a young teacher to find it littered with rusting war relics.

Seekee has since received an Order of Australia Medal in recognition of her dedication to preserve Horn Island/Ngurupai's wartime history in collaboration with veterans and Traditional Custodians – most notably at the Torres Strait Heritage Museum & Art Gallery she has curated since 1997; as well as via the WW2 Conservation Project she co-founded with husband Liberty, which works to restore wartime sites from plane wrecks to anti-aircraft batteries. The couple share their deep knowledge on their Horn Island WW2 Tour.

Keriri
Island

Thursday
Island

King Point
× Reserve

Public
Wharf
×

Wasaga × Torres Strait
Heritage Museum
& Art Gallery

× Slit
Trench

× Cable
Beach

Torres
Strait

Prince
of Wales
Island

N
0   4 km
0   2 miles

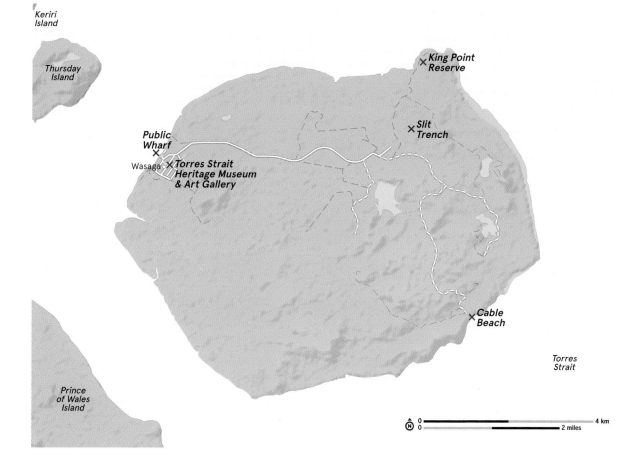

X MARKS THE SPOT

Wasaga Split into three sections focusing on the island's WWII history, its pearling days and Torres Strait art, Wasaga's rustic Torres Strait Heritage Museum & Art Gallery is a must-see.

Slit Trench Find this restored air-raid bunker just outside the airport's eastern boundary fence.

King Point Reserve Enjoy a seaside picnic, then check out the restored WWII anti-aircraft battery.

Public Wharf One of the best ways to meet Horn Island's locals is to join them on the public wharf for a spot of fishing.

Cable Beach Gaze across to the tip of mainland Australia from this remote south-coast beach.

1. Pearls

2. All the blues in the channel between Horn and Thursday islands

3. Fishing off the jetty

Stewart Island/ Rakiura

COUNTRY NEW ZEALAND • **COORDINATES** 47.0103° S, 167.8272° E • **AREA** 1746 SQ KM (674 SQ MILES)

Providing a southern anchor to New Zealand, Stewart Island is known in Māori as Rakiura – 'Glowing Skies' – in reference to the shimmering auora australis (Southern Lights) phenomenon that is often sighted during the cooler and longer nights of a Southern Hemisphere winter. A small population of around 400 ensures Rakiura's night skies remain largely pristine, and the island was awarded Dark Sky Sanctuary accreditation by the International Dark Sky Association in 2019. Beyond a concise and resourceful population living mainly around the Half Moon Bay settlement of Oban, both Stewart Island/Rakiura and neighbouring Ulva Island teem with native New Zealand birdlife; many species are sighted by outdoor adventurers.

BIRDLIFE ON NEW ZEALAND'S 'THIRD ISLAND'

With an absence of larger predators including ferrets, stoats and weasels, and expansive swathes of protected native forest, Stewart Island/ Rakiura has one of New Zealand's most diverse bird populations. Forests are soundtracked by the calls of kākāriki (parakeets) and kōtātā (fernbirds), while the quiet streets of compact Oban are enlivened by mellifluous tūī songbirds, and bold and inquisitive kākā (New Zealand parrots). Hikers on the Rakiura Track and the Northwest Circuit regularly see ground-dwelling weka, and even experience occasional surprise visits from kiwi.

Across on the nearby bird sanctuary of Ulva Island, declared rat-free in 1997, there's usually a symphony of overlapping bird calls, and it's one of the only places in New Zealand to see the endangered tīeke (South Island saddleback). Around the islands' shorelines and above Strewart/Rakiura's often rough waters, ocean-going mollymawks and petrels soar on Southern Ocean breezes, while dotterels and shags are smaller avian residents that don't venture as far out to sea. There's even a colony of kororā (little blue penguins) that make a regular evening appearance near Half Moon Bay's main wharf.

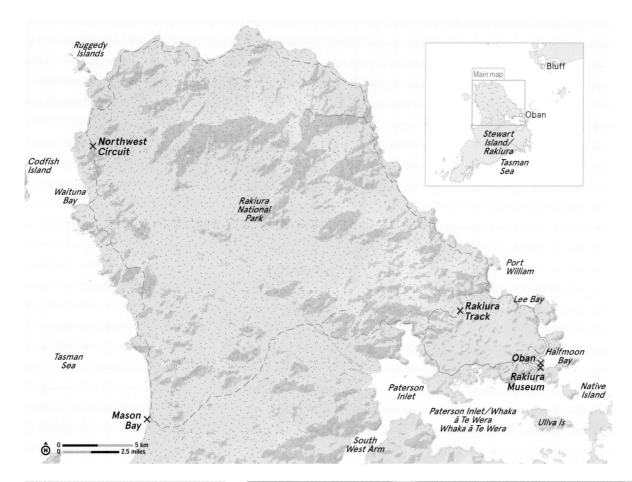

X MARKS THE SPOT

Rakiura Track One of New Zealand's Great Walks, this 32km (20-mile) loop includes beautiful beaches and echoes of the island's Māori and colonial history.

Mason Bay Join a sunset boat trip to see New Zealand's shy national bird, the kiwi, snuffling about on this remote beach.

Rakiura Museum Known as Te Puka O Te Waka, 'the anchor of the canoe', this excellent historical and cultural museum opened in late 2020.

Oban Blue-cod fish and chips and the world's southernmost pub quiz are essential highlights of Stewart Island/Rakiura's sleepy main village (population 387).

Northwest Circuit This intrepid 125km (78-mile) trail is the ultimate outdoor adventure, a demanding 10-day coastal epic traversing Rakiura National Park.

1. Rakiura Museum, Oban

2. Lush Stewart Island/Rakiura coastline

3. The often elusive kiwi

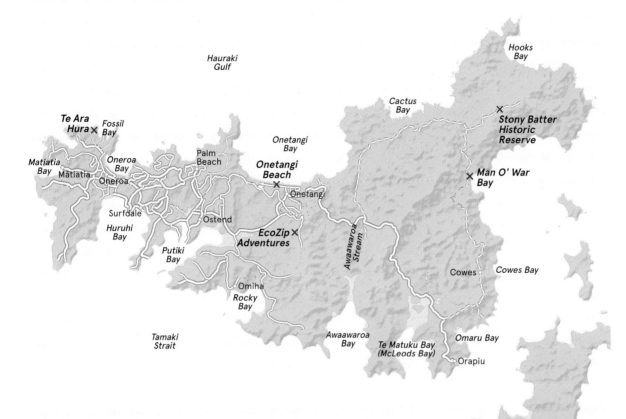

0   5 km
0   2.5 miles

Hauraki Gulf

Hooks Bay

Cactus Bay

Te Ara Hura ✕ Fossil Bay

Stony Batter Historic Reserve ✕

Matiatia Bay   *Oneroa Bay*   Palm Beach   *Onetangi Bay*

Mātiatia   Oneroa

Onetangi Beach ✕   Onetangi

✕ Man O' War Bay

Surfdale

Huruhi Bay   Ostend

EcoZip ✕ *Adventures*

Awaawaroa Stream

Putiki Bay   Cowes   *Cowes Bay*

Omiha Rocky Bay

Tamaki Strait   *Awaawaroa Bay*   *Te Matuku Bay (McLeods Bay)*   *Omaru Bay*   Orapiu

X MARKS THE SPOT

Man O' War Bay Negotiate unsealed roads to this compact tree-fringed bay for an afternoon of wine-tasting, swimming and perhaps a game of beach cricket.

Stony Batter Historic Reserve Part of Auckland's WWII defence planning, this underground labyrinth of tunnels and gun emplacements is showcased on one-hour guided tours.

Onetangi Experience Waiheke's best beach by steering a boogie board through gentle surf, or enjoying local seafood at the cool and casual Ki Māha.

EcoZip Adventures Take in views of island vineyards, downtown Auckland and the Hauraki Gulf on EcoZip's exciting trio of ziplines.

Te Ara Hura Best explored as a multi-day adventure, this 100km (62-mile) network of trails takes in coastline, forests and vineyards.

1. Mudbrick Vineyard and Restaurant, Oneroa

2. Stony Batter Historic Reserve

Waiheke Island

COUNTRY NEW ZEALAND
COORDINATES 36.8000° S, 175.1010° E • **AREA** 92 SQ KM (35 SQ MILES)

'Slow down, you're here.' Waiheke's most famous road sign exhorts arrivals to the island to take things easy, and following a ferry trip from Auckland across the Hauraki Gulf, most people have already switched into relaxed mode when they disembark. Once on Waiheke, an easygoing vineyard lunch is always a popular option, allowing diners to experience the island's southern-Pacific-meets-southern-Europe ambience. For more active travellers, kayaking, clifftop walking and ziplining are all opportunities to earn the right for a second Waiheke-brewed craft beer or local artisan gin at the end of the day. For history buffs, exploring subterranean memories of Auckland's WWII defence network is a fascinating alternative.

GOURMET WAIHEKE ISLAND

Blessed by a warm and dry Mediterranean-style microclimate, Waiheke is one of Auckland's most important winemaking regions, and the island's excellent vineyard restaurants and diverse food scene regularly attract visitors from the city. Premium quality red wine varietals including Bordeaux-style Cabernet Sauvignon, Merlot and Cabernet Franc kickstarted the Waiheke wine scene in the late 1970s, but in more recent decades, both Chardonnay and Viognier have become popular on the island.

Vineyard restaurants also channel a relaxed Southern Hemisphere version of Mediterranean Europe: Poderi Crisci's quiet valley location is a popular destination for legendary Italian-themed 'long lunches'; while Casita Miro team tapas with Albariño wine in a garden restaurant inspired by Spanish design masters Joan Miró and Antoni Gaudí. The grand entrance to Tantalus Estate may evoke Tuscany, but there's actually a singularly focused emphasis on New Zealand ingredients in its elegant dining room.

The freshest of local seafood is best enjoyed at two restaurants along Onetangi Beach, with both Three Seven Two and Ki Māha serving up oysters harvested from the cool southern Pacific waters of Waiheke's nutrient-rich Te Matuku Marine Reserve.

Great Barrier Island

COUNTRY NEW ZEALAND • **COORDINATES** 36.2027° S, 175.4118° E • **AREA** 285 SQ KM (110 SQ MILES)

Known to New Zealand's Māori people as Aotea – the name translates approximately to 'White Cloud' – Great Barrier Island sits at the eastern edge of Auckland's Hauraki Gulf. Ironically, it's actually part of the Auckland Central electorate, but the island's rugged landscape of forested mountains and remote coves is very different to the downtown urban buzz of the Central Business District. For several decades, Great Barrier Island has attracted alternative lifestylers, and their green and sustainable ethos is now influencing local businesses. Beer and gin are crafted entirely here off the national electricity grid, solar-powered e-bikes are a popular way for visitors to get around, and community-run gardens provide the island's select number of cafes and restaurants with fresh herbs and vegetables.

AOTEA'S DARK SKY SANCTUARY

It's a 30-minute flight from Auckland to Great Barrier Island, and this relative isolation means that this is a special place to observe the night skies of the Southern Hemisphere. There's no mains electricity or street lights here (all businesses and residents use solar power and batteries) and light pollution is minimal as the 88km (55-mile) separation from Auckland – a city of some 1.5 million people – means there's virtually no ambient light transferred across the southern Pacific.

Great Barrier Island was designated a Dark Sky Sanctuary by the International Dark Sky Association in 2017, and because almost 60% of the land here has protected conservation status, it's expected to maintain this designation. You can best appreciate the wonders of the night skies by way of the guided stargazing sessions offered by Good Heavens (goodheavens.co.nz): powerful telescopes are set up amid the sand dunes fringing Medlands Beach, with expert guides pointing out celestial attractions like Jupiter, Saturn and swirling Magellanic Clouds.

1. As well as its Dark Skies, the island offers brilliant surf breaks

2. Great Barrier Island's green hinterland

3. Surging seas around Great Barrier Island

X MARKS THE SPOT

Windy Canyon An easy 15-minute walk from Great Barrier's unsealed main road, this well-marked track leads to spectacular rocky outcrops and brilliant island views.

Medlands Beach Experience Aotea surf along Medlands' sandy arc before adjourning for gin-sampling at Island Gin's summer-only tasting room.

Star Treks Join with born-and-bred islander Benny Bellerby on forest walks exploring the whaling and timber-felling history of the Whangaparapara Harbour.

Aotea Track Centuries-old stands of kauri trees and remote wetlands are the highlights of this popular 25km (15.5-mile) trail usually achieved across three days.

Tryphena Great Barrier's best harbour is popular for paddleboarding and kayaking, and dolphins are also regular visitors to its sheltered waters.

Codfish Island/ Whenua Hou

COUNTRY NEW ZEALAND • **COORDINATES** 46.7733° S, 167.6321° E • **AREA** 14 SQ KM (5.4 SQ MILES)

A small, uninhabited, forested speck off the southern tip of New Zealand's South Island, Codfish Island owes its conservation-world celebrity status to the rare, murky-green kākāpo parrot. Pushed to the brink of extinction by the late 20th century, the kākāpo's dwindling population seems to finally, slowly, be turning a corner. And this wild, wind-lashed island, which remains entirely off-limits to visitors, is one of its major homes. With little but wide-open sea stretching towards Antarctica, the dust-soft beaches, low dunes and seemingly impassable granite cliffs give way to shimmering wetlands, rustling shrubland and towering rainforests where centuries-old trees loom and bats flutter flap past after dark.

BRINGING BACK THE KĀKĀPO

The poster species of Codfish Island/Whenua Hou is the endemic, critically endangered kākāpo – a lovable, flightless, nocturnal green parrot that can live up to 90 years and is a talented tree climber. The kākāpo also holds strong historical and cultural importance for the Ngāi Tahu Māori, whose ancestors hunted it for meat and made cloaks from its feathers.

Forest clearance, infertility and the introduction of non-native predators (especially cats, dogs, rats and stoats) have devastated New Zealand's kākāpo population. By 1970, not a single kākāpo was known to exist, and a series of expeditions set out to find and recover the nationally treasured bird. In 1996, with only 51 kākāpo surviving despite intensive conservation efforts, New Zealand's Department of Conservation launched the Kākāpo Recovery project. Now, thanks to artificial incubation, activity trackers, hand-rearing of chicks and all kinds of other creative, experimental initiatives, there are 201 kākāpo waddling around four predator-free islands, including Codfish Island/Whenua Hou. Though it remains a long and challenging road, its hoped that the programme will eventually enable the reintroduction of this fabulous feathered species to mainland New Zealand.

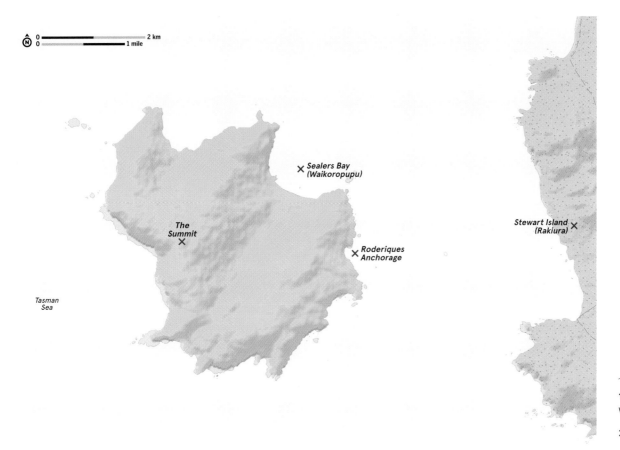

0 | 2 km
0 | 1 mile

Sealers Bay
(Waikoropupu) ✕

The
Summit ✕

✕ Roderiques
Anchorage

Tasman
Sea

Stewart Island
(Rakiura) ✕

1. Codfish Island/
Whenua Hou shore

2. Shrubland habitat

3. The flightless kākāpo

X MARKS THE SPOT

Sealers Bay/Waikoropupu
Creamy, dune-bordered
Sealers Bay, on the northeast
coast, is Codfish Island's
longest beach and main
landing point.

Roderiques Anchorage A
stretch of silvery sand curled
into the east coastline.

The Summit The island's
tallest point at 280m (919ft).

Stewart Island/Rakiura This
isolated next-door neighbour
is the place to spot several
other flightless birds,
including the southern brown
kiwi and the threatened
yellow-eyed penguin.

Kākāpo This large, flightless,
nocturnal parrot, rescued
from the brink of extinction,
survives only on predator-
free islands

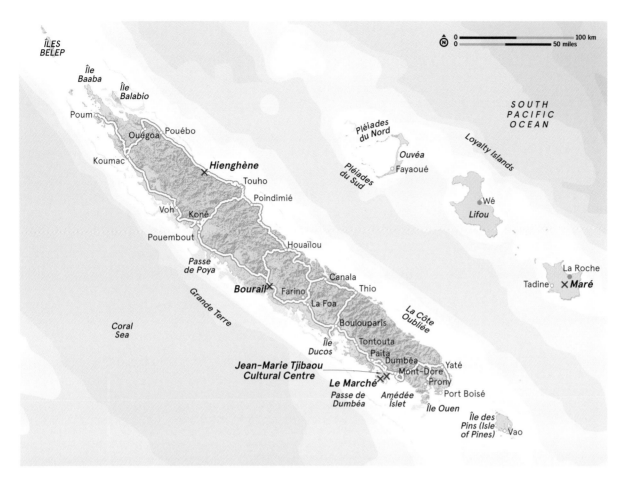

X MARKS THE SPOT

Hienghène Surrounded by black limestone coastal rock formations, this is the heartland of Kanak culture.

Jean-Marie Tjibaou Cultural Centre This Nouméa showcase of traditional Kanak history and culture is housed in a spectacular wooden building.

Le Marché Nouméa's central market blends French and Kanak culture. Combine croissants and cafe au lait with entertainment from a traditional Kanak string band.

Bourail New Caledonia's Caldoche community is strongest amid the ranches of Bourail and Grande Terre's sprawling west coast.

Maré Caves, rock pools and the carved-from-coral spectacle of the Natural Aquarium are highlights of New Caledonia's Loyalty Islands.

1. Kanumera Bay, L'Île-des-Pins

2. Pirogue, L'Île-des-Pins

3. Kanak totem, Mwa Ka

© CHRIStophe Robert HERVOUËT | 500px; © Onfokus | Getty Images; © Hemis | AWL Images

New Caledonia

COUNTRY FRENCH OVERSEAS TERRITORY
COORDINATES 20.9043° S, 165.6180° E • **AREA** 18,575 SQ KM (7172 SQ MILES)

Welcome to Melanesia with a French accent, as Gallic traditions and indigenous Kanak culture combine – and sometimes collide – on France's biggest Southern Hemisphere island territory. Downtown Nouméa is chic, casual and equal parts Europe and South Pacific, while the rest of Grande Terre, New Caledonia's main island, is divided by a central mountain range between the plains and ranches of the west coast, and the rocky coastline and lush river valleys of the east. Easily reached on day trips from Nouméa is the stunning L'Île-des-Pins (Isle of Pines), while traditional Kanak culture thrives on the smaller Loyalty Islands northeast of Grande Terre.

ONGOING CAMPAIGN FOR INDEPENDENCE

After French Catholics established a mission in 1843, France officially claimed New Caledonia in 1853. For the next century, the focus was first as a French penal colony, and then agricultural development driven by French settlers, the descendants of today's Caldoche population. Post WWII, New Caledonia's indigenous Kanaks were progressively given the right to vote, and the first Kanak political party was formed in 1953. Independence issues intensified in the 1960s and 1970s with the arrival of French migrants to work in the nickel-mining industry, and pro-independence Kanak political parties coalesced with the 1984 formation of the Front de Libération National Kanak et Socialiste (FLNKS), headed by

Jean-Marie Tjibaou. Following political violence, ending with the assassination of Tjibaou in 1989, the Nouméa Accord between France and New Caledonia was ratified in 1998. Setting out a 20-year transition period for independence from France, independence referenda were taken in 2018 and 2020. Independence was rejected twice with 56.7% and 53.3% respectively voting 'Non', and a third vote took place in 2021. Because of difficult voter access around Kanak mourning rituals during Covid-19, the FLNKS rejected the referendum, and 'Non' votes increased to 96.5%. A renewed referendum on New Caledonia's status in the French Republic is scheduled for June 2023.

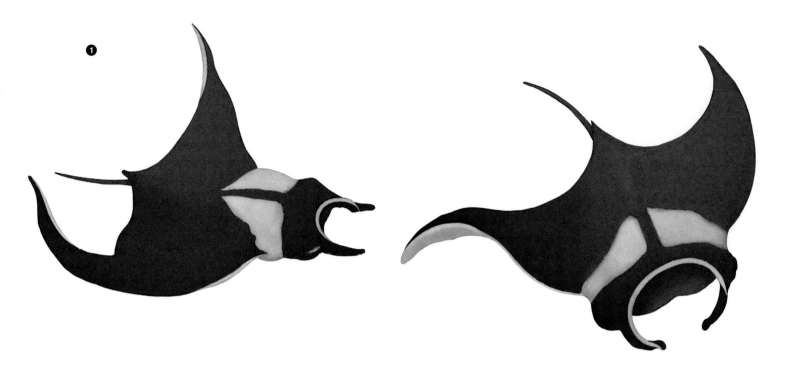

❶

Yasawa Islands

COUNTRY FIJI
COORDINATES 17.0000° S, 177.3833° E • **AREA** 135 SQ KM (52 SQ MILES)

White-sand beaches, swaying coconut palms and tranquil, turquoise waters – the Yasawa Islands are the image of a tropical island paradise. This archipelago of around 20 smallish islands forms an arc to the northwest of Viti Levu, the largest of the islands that make up Fiji. The islands were closed to tourism until 1987; there are resorts here now, alongside a thriving budget-luxe traveller scene. Here, following the flashpacker trail means hopping on the Yasawa Flyer, the high-speed catamaran that travels between the islands. Most of the population of roughly 6000 live on Nacula, Naviti and Yasawa, the three largest islands. All have no roads and no cars, so you'll be getting around on the footpaths.

SAWA-I-LAU

Tiny Sawa-i-Lau is unique among the Yasawa Islands. While all the other islands are volcanic, Sawa-i-Lau is made of limestone that reaches several hundred metres out of the sea. Its caves, formed by eons of lapping waves, are among the most spectacular natural attractions in the South Pacific. In Fijian mythology, the caves are known as the resting place of Ulutini, an ancient god with 10 heads, nine of which are shaped like snakes; the god's 10th head is human-like and beatific, with a shining stone set in the forehead. The caves are half-submerged in the turquoise waters that surround the island and the only way to enter them is to swim. One cave is called Qara ni Bukete (Pregnancy Cave), and reaching it requires swimming through an underwater tunnel. According to lore, anyone of any size or shape can manage it – except someone who is pregnant and hiding it. Another cave has a natural skylight that allows sunlight to filter in, flickering on the surface of the water and lighting up the striated limestone walls. Sawa-i-Lau is just south of Yasawa Island, the northernmost island in the chain.

X MARKS THE SPOT

Blue Lagoon This absolutely stunning natural lagoon on the coast of Nanuya Lailai was made famous by the film of the same name.

Vatuvula 'Big White Rock' is a volcanic plug – a tower of hardened magma – on Wayasewa Island offering vistas over the southern Yasawa Islands.

Long Beach On Nacula, the third largest of the Yasawa Islands, this is a superlative beach among many superlative beaches, with clear emerald waters.

Yasawa-i-Rara Traditional Fijian village on Yasawa Island and home to the Tui Yasawa, the High Chief of the Yasawa Islands.

Manta Ray Passage The waters between Naviti and Drawaqa islands draw squadrons of manta rays between May and October.

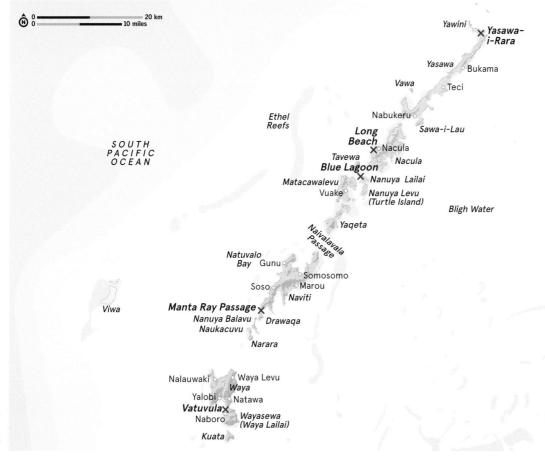

0   20 km
0   10 miles

N

Yawini   ✕ **Yasawa-i-Rara**

Yasawa   ○ Bukama

Vawa   ○ Teci

○ Nabukeru

Ethel
Reefs   *Sawa-i-Lau*

SOUTH
PACIFIC
OCEAN

Long
Beach   ✕ ○ Nacula

Tavewa   ○ Nacula

Blue Lagoon

Matacawalevu   ✕   *Nanuya Lailai*

Vuake ○   *Nanuya Levu*
                    (Turtle Island)

                    Bligh Water

                    Yaqeta

          Naivalavala
          Passage

Natuvalo
Bay Gunu

          ○ Somosomo

Soso ○   ○ Marou

          Naviti

Manta Ray Passage ✕

Nanuya Balavu   *Drawaqa*
Naukacuvu

Viwa

          Narara

Nalauwaki   ○ Waya Levu
           Waya
Yalobi ○   ○ Natawa
Vatuvula✕
Naboro ○   *Wayasewa*
           (Waya Lailai)

Kuata

~~~~~~~~~~

1. Manta rays

2. Green, serene
Yasawa Island

Vanua Levu

COUNTRY FIJI • **COORDINATES** 16.6268° S, 179.0179° E • **AREA** 5587 SQ KM (2157 SQ MILES)

Fiji's second-largest island is rangy and wild – even compared to its neighbour, Viti Levu, the country's largest island. Vanua Levu means 'Great Land' in Fijian; to the European traders who stripped the island of sandalwood in the 19th century, it was Sandalwood Island. Sharp peaks covered in dense green bisect the island: to the southeast is tropical rainforest and to the drier southwest, sugar-cane fields and coconut plantations. There is only one sealed road on the island, connecting the two largest settlements, Labasa and Savusavu. Vanua Levu has significant geothermal activity bubbling under the surface, which one day may power the island.

GREAT SEA REEF

Cakaulevu, also called the Great Sea Reef, is the world's third-largest continuous barrier reef, after the Great Barrier Reef and the Mesoamerican Reef. It stretches some 200km (124 miles) from Vanua Levu's northernmost point, Udu, all the way down the coast, crosses the Vatuira passage and then trails off past the Yasawa Islands. Seen from space, it is an aquamarine streak in the deep blue waters of the South Pacific. Underwater, there are groves of branch coral and ethereal sea fans – so far researchers have found over 300 coral varieties here. The reef is home to playful spinner dolphins, endangered green sea turtles, giant bumphead parrotfish and graceful manta rays. Cakaulevu is also vital to the lives and livelihoods of tens of thousands of Fijians. Traditional Fijian management of fishing grounds understood the need for sustainability, and periodically certain areas would be declared *tabu* (taboo; yes, that's where the word comes from). However, in recent decades the reef's delicate ecosystem has been threatened by poachers, as well as pollution and climate change. This has spurred local communities, along with the WWF and the Fijian government, to ramp up conservation efforts.

1. Savusavu marina and Nawi Island

2. Palm-shaded beach on Natuvu Bay

3. Underwater life

X MARKS THE SPOT

Waisali Rainforest Reserve This 120-hectare (296-acre) reserve is home to towering Pacific kauri trees, 30 species of orchids, rare red shining parrots and more.

Devodara Beach Strong contender for the title of Vanua Levu's best beach: a broad sweep of sand fronting shallow turquoise waters.

Yadua Tabu Small islet and protected sanctuary for the critically endangered Fiji crested iguana, which is bright green to match its tropical habitat.

Namena Marine Reserve Horseshoe-shaped barrier reef with a shocking variety of fish, thanks to early local conservation measures.

Dakuniba In the mountains above this otherwise ordinary village are large rocks marked with petroglyphs of mysterious origin.

SOUTH
PACIFIC
OCEAN

0 ————— 5 km
0 ————— 2.5 miles

Vai'utuaukau
Bay

Vava'u Island

Holonga

Leimatu'a

Ta'anea

Ha'alaufuli

Vaipua
Inlet

Feletoa

Mataika

Mangia

'Utui

Tu'anekivale

Tefesi

Taoa

Faleono

'Uatoloa

Vaimalo

Tulie

Longomapu

Lake
'Ano

Mt Talau
National Park ×

'Utulei

Clan
× McWilliam
Wreck

× Friendly
Islands
Kayak

Makave

Okoa

Koloa

Tu'anuku

Luafatu

'Utungake

'Olo'ua

Faioa

Hunga

Faihava Channel

Swallows'
Cave ×

Pangai

Talihau

Toula

Mafana

'Umuna

Luamoko

Ava Pulepulekai

'Otea

Mala

Pangaimotu

'Ofu

Kenutu

Kalau

Oto

A'a

Kapa

Falevai

'Ofu

Lolo

Fofoa

Nuapapu

Luaofa

Kapa

Tapana

Foelifuka

Foe'ata

Vaka'eitu

Sisia

X MARKS THE SPOT

Whale Haven Vava'u is an important breeding ground for humpback whales, and the leviathan mammals are regular visitors from June to October.

Mt Talau National Park Above the safe harbour of Port of Refuge, the 131m-high (430ft) summit of Mt Talau is tackled via a 40-minute track.

Friendly Islands Kayak Day-long explorations of Port of Refuge or multi-day adventures incorporating island camping and snorkelling are good ways to discover a stellar sea-kayaking destination.

Clan McWilliam The 1927 foundering of this steam-powered cargo ship in Neiafu Harbour now reveals shape-shifting shoals of fish at a depth of just 30m (98ft).

Swallows Cave Visited on snorkelling and boat tours, the natural attraction of Swallows Cave is carved into the rocky coastline of compact Kapa Island.

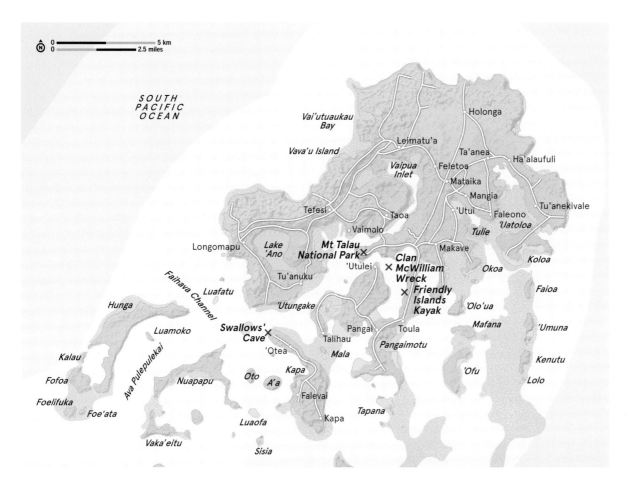

1. Market-fresh produce, Neiafu

2. Vava'u islet

3. Humpback whale

❸

Vava'u

COUNTRY TONGA

COORDINATES 18.6228° S, 173.9903° W • **AREA** 138 SQ KM (53 SQ MILES)

Vava'u is the most northerly of Tonga's three main island groups, around 300km (186 miles) from the national capital of Nuku'alofa. Around 50 smaller islets surround the main island, and the many sheltered harbours and anchorages make it one of the South Pacific's best yachting destinations. Kayaking is equally popular, especially on longer adventures exploring sea caves and Vava'u's smaller islands, while adventurous travellers can get their action fix by hiking in tropical forests or exploring caves. During the Tongan winter, the biggest and most important visitors to Vava'u have come all the way from the icy waters of Antarctica.

WHALE ENCOUNTERS

For millennia, humpback whales have been visiting Tonga's warm waters for mating and raising their calves during the South Pacific winter, before migrating south again to feed in Antarctica's nutrient-rich waters. The first operators in Vava'u to offer swimming with the whales began in 1993, and it soon developed into a vital part of the island's tourism industry. Whale-watching regulations and a cap on the number of licenses for tour operators were established, and Tonga was regarded as an international leader in the promotion of sustainable tourism. Unfortunately, across recent decades and contradicting the recommendations of conservation groups, there has been an increase in the number of licenses, and this peaked in 2019 with a total of 22 different operators. Across preceding years, the strong growth of inbound tourism also saw more people swimming with the whales than was recommended, and the use of boats not suitable for whale watching. Reputedly, fewer whales have been visiting Vava'u's more sheltered inner islands across recent seasons. In 2020, a reduction in the number of licenses in Vava'u was announced – from 22 to 20 – and it's hoped this decrease and the Covid-19-enforced slowdown of Tonga's tourism industry will restore greater sustainability to an industry that had been growing too too fast for its own good.

Upolu

COUNTRY SAMOA • COORDINATES 13.9134°S, 171.7349°W • AREA 1125 SQ KM (434 SQ MILES)

It's possible to drive all the way around the coastal road encircling Samoa's main island in under five hours. But it's worth allowing at least a week – ideally two – to properly explore this enchanting Pacific isle. Most visitors devote themselves to the dazzling strips of sand skirting Upolu's southern shoreline, with forays into azure offshore lagoons that shelter colourful coral groves and marine turtles. But Upolu also has its fair share of terra firma treasures: the tangled rainforest of the mountainous interior; rough coastal cliffs formed by the cooling of lava rivers; and fascinating craters and caves. The urban delights of Apia shouldn't be neglected either, from Samoan fusion restaurants to buzzing markets.

Hiring a car is the best way to see the island, giving you the freedom to pull over whenever you fancy to photograph plunging waterfalls, purchase seasonal tropical fruit from roadside stalls and swim at gorgeous beaches fringed by colourful *fales* (traditional open-air shacks).

TAKE ME TO CHURCH

Beneath the light-heartedness of Samoan culture, the strict and demanding Fa'a Samoa (Samoan Way) is rigorously upheld. The three main pillars of Fa'a Samoa are `aiga (your extended family group), the community you belong to, and the church. The third pillar has particular weight. Every village has at least one large church, ideally a larger one than in neighbouring villages. These operate as the village social centre, the place where almost everyone makes an appearance on Sunday, dressed up in their formal best. Sunday-morning church services are inevitably followed by *to'ona'i* (Sunday lunch), when families put on banquets fit for royalty.

Modestly dressed visitors are welcome to attend Sunday mass. With services often led by beautiful choir singing, it's an interesting way to spend a morning. Next to beach lazing, there aren't many other options, as most businesses on the island close on the holy day.

SOUTH PACIFIC OCEAN

Apolima

Manono

Fale'ula

Leulumoega

Vaitele
Vaigaga

APIA ✕ *Paddles*

Vailele

Apolima-uta

Solosolo

Saoluafata

Falefa

Manono-uta

✕ *Robert Louis Stevenson Museum*

Si'ufaga

Falelatai

Lake Lanoto'o

Falevao

Fagaloa Bay

Ta'elefaga

Giant clam sanctuary ✕ Safa'atoa

O Le Pupu-Pu'e National Park

Ti'avea

Lefaga

Samusu

Salamumu

Sa'anapu

Maninoa

Sa'agafou

Sale'a'aunua

Fanuatapu

Malaemalu

Vavau

Lepa

Namu'a
ALEIPATA ISLANDS

Nu'usafe'e

Lotofaga

✕ *To Sua Ocean Trench*

Lalomanu

Nu'utele

Nu'ulua

0 — 20 km
0 — 10 miles

X MARKS THE SPOT

To Sua Ocean Trench Climb down the ladder for a dip in the magnificent turquoise pool of this idyllic sinkhole in the island's southeast.

Robert Louis Stevenson Museum Tour the restored former residence of the late *Treasure Island* author.

Paddles It's a family affair at this convivial Samoan-Italian fusion restaurant, arguably the best on the island.

Giant Clam Sanctuary Pay a small fee and snorkel out into the lagoon fringing the west-coast village of Safa'atoa to marvel at enormous clams at this little-known attraction.

Fale Stay Sleeping in a traditional open-air shack on the beach is a quintessential Upolu experience.

1. *Fales* (traditional open-air shacks)

2. Inviting waters at To Sua Ocean Trench

3. Wild cordyline

Niue

COUNTRY SELF-GOVERNING IN FREE ASSOCIATION WITH NEW ZEALAND
COORDINATES 19.0544° S, 169.8672° W • AREA 261 SQ KM (101 SQ MILES)

To its resident population of around 1600 – and around 35,000 Niueans living in New Zealand and Australia – Niue is known as 'The Rock', and it's unlike any other South Pacific island nation. As a raised coral atoll forged by volcanic activity, there's only one small, sandy beach. Instead, Niue's coastline is studded with caves, natural swimming holes and reef pools. Some, like Avaiki Cave and the narrow canyon of Matapa Chasm were sacred bathing spots for Niuean nobility in past centuries; even today, swimming is still banned on a Sunday as Niueans focus on relaxation, traditional family life and attending church.

SWIMMING WITH HUMPBACK WHALES

Adrift in a South Pacific triangle framed by Tonga, Samoa and the Cook Islands, Niue is one of the smallest and most remote nations in the world. The nearest neighbouring country is at least 600km (373 miles) away, and Niue's only regular air links are with New Zealand, almost 2500km (1553 miles) to the south. But despite Niue's remoteness, giant humpback whales overcome this extreme isolation every year to breed and calve in the warm waters surrounding the island. Niue's migrating cetacean visitors usually arrive around July, and stay until September or October, before returning to feed in the much cooler waters of the Antarctic.

Interactions with Niue's whales are carefully regulated, and experiences are only possible with certified local operators. Inflatable Zodiacs travel along the island's rocky coastline of sea caves and natural arches, and when a whale is sighted in gin-clear waters just 50m (164ft) off the coast, the boats carefully slow to a stop. Donning a mask and snorkel and respectfully viewing them from above is an exceptional experience, and the whales are usually perfectly content to remain feeding in the presence of visitors. When they're ready, often after a compelling couple of minutes, they swim powerfully away with a languid flick of their tail flukes.

1. Sea snake

2. Niue's coral-stone coastline

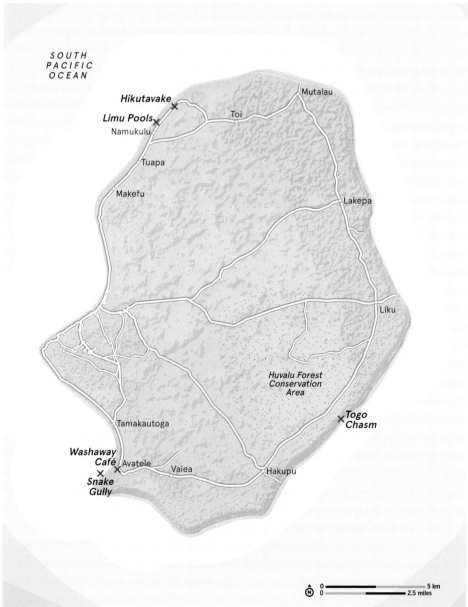

X MARKS THE SPOT

Limu Pools Warm seawater and cooler spring water combine in Limu's divine brace of coral-framed natural swimming pools.

Togo Chasm Traverse a careful trail through a landscape of indigo coral-stone pinnacles before climbing down a ladder to a palm-tree-studded oasis.

Snake Gully One of Niue's excellent diving spots, Snake Gully is populated by tangles of tricot raye sea snakes, while adjacent caverns reveal crayfish and moray eels.

Hikutavake Negotiate a cliffside trail to explore capacious reef pools that are home to sea turtles and scores of tropical fish.

Washaway Cafe Overlooking Avatele's compact sandy cove, the South Pacific's best little self-service bar is only open on a Sunday afternoon.

Cook Islands

COUNTRY SELF-GOVERNING IN FREE ASSOCIATION WITH NEW ZEALAND
COORDINATES 21.2367° S, 159.7777° W • **AREA** 237 SQ KM (91 SQ MILES)

With 15 tiny islands arrayed across more than 2 million sq km (8 milllion sq miles) of the aquamarine expanse of the Pacific Ocean, the Cook Islands are one of the most far-flung nations on the planet. The most populous island of Rarotonga is a blend of modernity and authentic Polynesia, with cafes and food trucks equally at home in Auckland or Sydney combining with the heavenly harmonies of Sunday morning church services. Easily reached by plane, Aitutaki and 'Atiu are equally compelling destinations, while the Cooks' Northern Group is a sparsely populated scattering of islands and atolls on the bucket list of yachties and other adventurers keen on exploring the South Pacific.

GETTING ACTIVE ON RAROTONGA

With plenty of palm-tree-fringed beaches, the Cooks' main island of Rarotonga ticks all the boxes for a relaxing South Pacific holiday, but it's also a destination packed with adventures for active travellers. Traversing an exciting path via Rarotonga's island-crowning 'Needle', the Cross Island Track is an iconic hike negotiating verdant valleys to end at the Papua Waterfall on the island's southern coast. Bicycling and walking experiences with Storytellers Eco Cycle & Walking Tours explore the island's scenic, cultural and historical highlights, and often end with a waterfall or beach swim. Popular ways to explore the warm and shallow waters of Muri Lagoon include kayaking and stand-up paddleboarding, while Muri-based Ariki Adventures also offer underwater 'sea scooter' experiences to spy sea turtles and a 100-year-old shipwreck. There's a popular snorkelling spot along the island's southern coast at Tikioki – also known as 'Fruits of Rarotonga' – while excellent diving locations include the northern coast wreck of the SS *Maitai*, and the canyons, caves and underwater tunnels of the island's southern side. Muri Lagoon is also an excellent place to safely learn kiteboarding and windsurfing.

1. Muri Beach

2. Lionfish patrols the Cook Islands' reefs

3. All aboard for some ukulele downtime

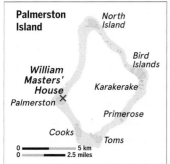

Palmerston Island

North Island

Bird Islands

William Masters' House ✕

Palmerston

Karakerake

Primerose

Cooks

Toms

0 — 5 km
0 — 2.5 miles

SOUTH PACIFIC OCEAN

Aitutaki

Arutanga Passage

Aitutaki Lagoon ✕

Akitua

'Angarei

Ee

Arutanga

Mangere

Nikaupara

Vaipae

Papau

Tautu

Coral Ridges

0 — 2 km
0 — 1 miles

Rarotonga

Avatiu Harbour

Black Rock

Punanga Nui Market ✕

Takitumu Conservation Area

Avana Harbour

Motutapu

Muri Lagoon

Sheraton Resort

Koromiri

Rutaki Passage

Papua Passage ✕

Avaavaroa Passage

Taakoka

↖ⓃN 0 — 5 km
0 — 2.5 miles

'Atiu

Taunganui Harbour

Tarapaku Landing

'Atiu ✕

Lake Te Roto

Sinkholes

0 — 2 km
0 — 1 miles

X MARKS THE SPOT

Punanga Nui Market The island comes to town at Rarotonga's Saturday morning market. Foodie treats include smoked-fish crepes and tropical fruit smoothies.

Sheraton Resort Abandoned since construction stopped in 1993, the quirky and forlorn shell of this Rarotonga hotel complex is a fascinating place to explore.

Aitutaki Lagoon Best negotiated on a kayak or paddleboard, Aitutaki's spectacular lagoon studded with *motu* (islets) is a South Pacific stunner.

'Atiu Combine exploration of subterranean caves, birdwatching and a *tumunu* (bush-beer) session on the Cooks' most idiosyncratic island.

Palmerston Courtesy of their lineage from William Masters, who arrived in 1863, modern residents of far-flung Palmerston Island still speak with a Gloucestershire accent.

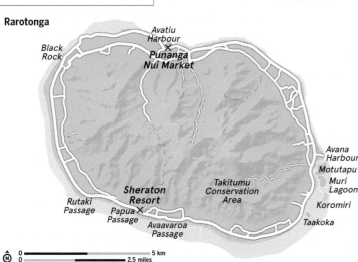

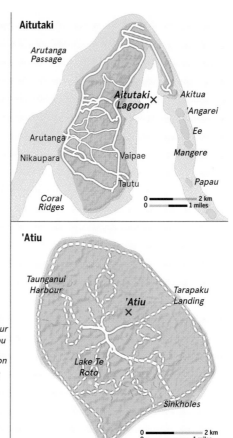

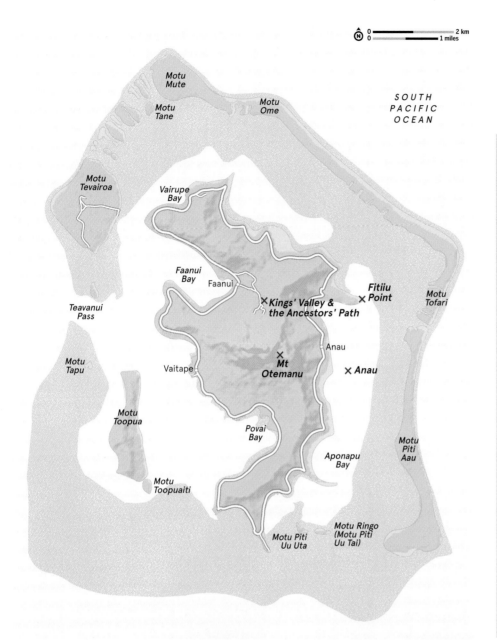

Motu Mute

Motu Tane

Motu Ome

SOUTH
PACIFIC
OCEAN

Motu Tevairoa

Vairupe Bay

Faanui Bay

Faanui

✕ *Kings' Valley & the Ancestors' Path*

Fitiiu Point ✕

Motu Tofari

Teavanui Pass

Anau

Motu Tapu

Vaitape

✕ *Mt Otemanu*

✕ *Anau*

Motu Toopua

Povai Bay

Motu Toopuaiti

Aponapu Bay

Motu Piti Aau

Motu Piti Uu Uta

Motu Ringo (Motu Piti Uu Tai)

X MARKS THE SPOT

Bora Bora Lagoon An essential highlight of any French Polynesian sojourn is exploring Bora Bora's lagoon. Experiences Include feeding rays, snorkelling and an island barbecue.

Mt Otemanu Soaring steeply and improbably to a height of 727m (2385ft), this verdant peak is the remnant of an ancient volcano.

Anau Anau's reputation as a world-renowned snorkelling and diving location is enhanced by manta rays, sea turtles and sharks.

Fitiiu Point Highlighting a slender promontory on the island's east coast, this elevated lookout features excellent lagoon views and well-preserved WWII coastal guns.

Valley of the Kings Bora Bora's most popular hike, best experienced with a local guide, includes the remains of ancient *marae* (Polynesian temples).

1. Lagoon snorkelling in Bora Bora

2. Overwater bungalows with a Mt Otemanu backdrop

Bora Bora

COUNTRY FRENCH POLYNESIA

COORDINATES 16.5004° S, 151.7415° W • **AREA** 30 SQ KM (11.5 SQ MILES)

Towered over by the jagged forested peak of Mt Otemanu, Bora Bora has been a byword for South Pacific spectacle and natural beauty for more than 250 years. Located in the Leeward Islands northwest of Tahiti, the romantic (and very pricey) overwater bungalows framing Bora Bora's lagoon are popular with honeymooners. Iconic actor Marlon Brando fell in love here, and for many travellers, Bora Bora may well be the most romantic destination they'll ever visit. There's also plenty of appeal for other travellers, with superb diving and snorkelling taking place in the warmest of South Pacific waters; opportunities for hiking including exploring the cultural heritage of Polynesian history.

BORA BORA & BRANDO

With its stellar natural beauty and luxury resorts, Bora Bora is considered a dream South Pacific destination. Western admiration for the atoll's stunning good looks started a few centuries ago, when British maritime explorer Captain James Cook dropped by in 1769 and declared Bora Bora the 'pearl of the Pacific'.

Fast-forward almost 200 years, and a 1962 film about a different British naval captain was filmed there, reinforcing the star-status of actor Marlon Brando and catapulting Bora Bora into the imagination of international travellers. During the filming of *Mutiny on the Bounty*, Brando grew close to his Bora Bora–born co-star Tarita Teri'ipaia, and the couple married and established a home on the Windward Islands atoll of Teti'aroa as an escape from the pressures of Hollywood.

The couple divorced after 10 years of marriage in 1972, but the simple guesthouse they built on the atoll has now expanded to become The Brando, one of the South Pacific's most exclusive private resorts. This luxury enclave has hosted actors Johnny Depp and Leonardo DiCaprio, while in 2017, soon after leaving the White House, Barack Obama decamped to The Brando's three-bedroom villa to start writing his autobiography.

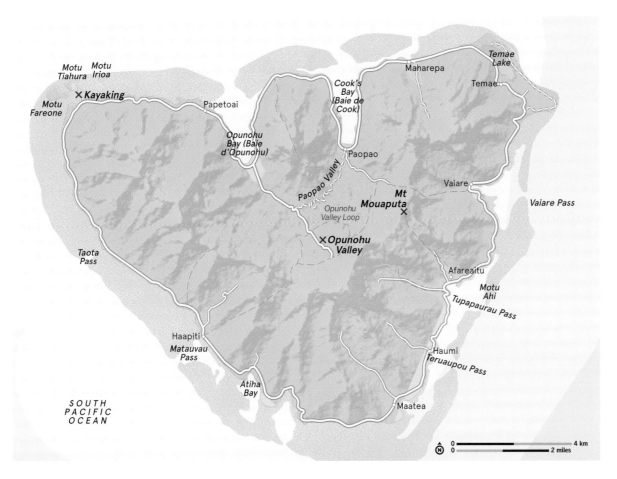

Motu
Tiahura
Motu
Irioa

✕ **Kayaking**

Motu
Fareone

Papetoai

*Opunohu
Bay (Baie
d'Opunohu)*

Cook's
Bay
(Baie de
Cook)

Maharepa

*Temae
Lake*

Temae

Paopao

Paopao Valley

Vaiare

Vaiare Pass

**Mt
Mouaputa**
✕

*Opunohu
Valley Loop*

✕**Opunohu
Valley**

*Taota
Pass*

Afareaitu

*Motu
Ahi*

Tupapaurau Pass

Haapiti

*Matauvau
Pass*

Haumi

Teruaupou Pass

*Atiha
Bay*

Maatea

*SOUTH
PACIFIC
OCEAN*

| 0 | | | 4 km |
| 0 | | | 2 miles |

Ⓝ

1. Cooks Bay,
overlooked by Mt
Mouaputa

2. Fare Natura museum

❶

Mo'orea

COUNTRY FRENCH POLYNESIA • **COORDINATES** 17.5388° S, 149.8295° W • **AREA** 134 SQ KM (52 SQ MILES)

Dreaming of holiday-brochure turquoise lagoons, white-sand beaches, dramatic peaks and lush landscapes? This gem of an island, just a half-hour high-speed ferry ride from its big sister, Tahiti, has got them all. Yet Mo'orea absorbs its many visitors so gracefully that the island feels surprisingly non-touristy, particularly in the south. Most visitors flop in a resort on the island's northern coast, fringed by a turquoise lagoon and backed by some of the island's most impressive mountain scenery. From snorkelling and diving to kitesurfing and kayaking, there's plenty of fun to be had on the water. But there's more action beyond. With public transport only servicing the ferry docks, it's worth renting a car to access inland waterfalls, lookouts and hiking trails. Allow a whole day (or more) to drive the 60km (37-mile) road hugging the coast all the way around the W-shaped island, as you'll want to make plenty of stops.

21ST-CENTURY ECO MUSEUM

Appealing to culture vultures, eco-warriors and architecture nerds alike, the futuristic Fare Natura museum, opened in 2021 at Opunohu Bay (a 30-minute drive from Mo'orea's ferry terminal in Vai'are), is another fantastic reason to visit Mo'orea. Conceptualised by the next-door Centre of Island Research and Environmental Observatory (CRIOBE), internationally renowned for its research into coral reefs, the museum is designed to educate visitors about French Polynesia's natural environment; its excellent permanent and temporary exhibitions are informed by both science and Polynesian culture. You can 'explore' fragile ecosystems via a virtual reality headset, while the eco-garden offers insights into the cultural and ecological roles of native plants and crops.

But this innovative museum isn't just for tourists. Designed by renowned French architect and oceanographer Jacques Rougerie, the eco-sensitive facility, which resembles a giant conch, also trains locals to become ecotourism professionals, and supports masters and doctorate students.

X MARKS THE SPOT

Street Food Experience Polynesian culture through your taste buds on a tour of the island's culinary gems with Tahiti Food Tours.

Opunohu Valley Explore ancient *marae* (traditional temples), breathtaking vistas and hidden walking paths in this green valley.

Kayaking Paddle from Hauru Point across the lagoon to Motu Tiahura for lunch at seaside restaurant Coco Beach.

Whales From July to November, Mo'orea is one of the few places in the world where you can swim with humpback whales.

Mt Mouaputa Take an unforgettable day hike to the summit of this spectacular peak (803m/2635ft).

❷

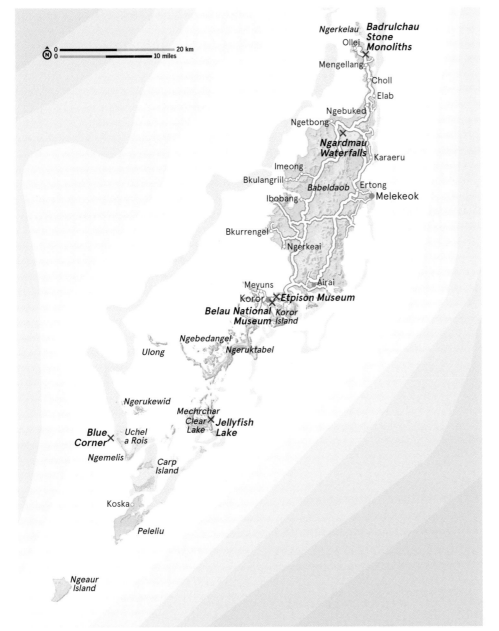

Map labels:

Ngerkelau
Badrulchau Stone Monoliths
Ollei
Mengellang
Choll
Elab
Ngebuked
Ngetbong
Ngardmau Waterfalls
Karaeru
Imeong
Bkulangriil
Babeldaob
Ertong
Melekeok
Ibobang
Bkurrengel
Ngerkeai
Meyuns
Airai
Koror
Etpison Museum
Belau National Museum
Koror Island
Ngebedangel
Ngeruktabel
Ulong
Ngerukewid
Mechrchar
Clear Lake
Jellyfish Lake
Blue Corner
Uchel a Rois
Ngemelis
Carp Island
Koska
Peleliu
Ngeaur Island

0 — 20 km
0 — 10 miles

X MARKS THE SPOT

Blue Corner Dive one of the world's most thrilling sites in the Unesco-listed Rock Islands Southern Lagoon.

Babeldaob Ponder Palau's mysterious past at the Badrulchau Stone Monoliths and take a refreshing dip at the spectacular Ngardmau Waterfall on the rural island of Babeldaob.

Jellyfish Lake Snorkel with millions of harmless transparent jellyfish in a Rock Islands marine lake.

Peleliu Spend a day spotting rusty WWII relics around this laid-back island.

Museums Gain insights into Palau's intriguing history and culture on the island of Koror at the Belau National Museum & Bai, and the Etpison Museum.

1. A sprinkling of Palau's 200 tropical islands

2. Palau lifeguard tower

3. Snorkelling with stingless golden jellies at Jellyfish Lake

Palau

COUNTRY PALAU
COORDINATES 7.5150°N, 134.5825°E • AREA 459 SQ KM (177 SQ MILES)

For such a tiny area of land, the Republic of Palau packs a big punch. It's hard not to be overwhelmed by its extraordinary array of natural wonders: this is an archipelago of about 200 spectacular limestone and volcanic islands, blanketed in verdant emerald forest and surrounded by a shimmering turquoise lagoon. Unsurprisingly, diving is the number-one activity in this corner of the western Pacific, with divers raving about Palau's exciting seascape, fascinating wrecks and stunningly diverse marine life – it's not dubbed 'the underwater Serengeti' for nothing.

But there's much more to do in Palau. Kayaking, snorkelling and off-road driving are all fabulous, with the added appeal of endless otherworldly settings. And for history buffs there are plenty of WWII relics scattered in the jungle, as well as a handful of well-organised museums in Koror City. Palau's commercial centre (really more of a town) is also home to some excellent seafood restaurants.

PALAU PLEDGE

In 2017, amid a massive increase in tourist arrivals, Palau became the first nation on Earth to change its immigration laws for the cause of environmental protection by introducing the Palau Pledge: a commitment to the children of Palau to preserve and protect their island home that must be signed by visitors upon entry. The pledge involves committing to behaviours that address the environmental, social, cultural and economic impacts of tourism, including treading lightly and exploring mindfully.

Ranked #6 in The Good Report's 'Most successful campaigns promoting good causes 2018' list, the Palau Pledge was widely considered to be a huge success from a marketing perspective, boosting the island's brand awareness and inspiring other destinations to follow its example. Researchers who have explored the effectiveness of pledges as a tool for destination management, however, have claimed that further research is required to establish the impact of national destination pledges on actual visitor behaviour.

1. Ofu Island church

2. Ta'u Island shore

Manu'a Islands

COUNTRY AMERICAN SAMOA (USA)
COORDINATES 14.2341° S, 169.4985° W • **AREA** 56 SQ KM (22 SQ MILES)

Ofu, Olosega and Ta'u, anchored about 100km (62 miles) to the east of American Samoa's main island of Tutuila, are among the most ravishing – and remote – of all the Pacific isles. The three share the same marvellous natural characteristics: enormous cliffs sheltering seabird colonies; expired volcanic cones; pristine lagoons stocked with a brilliant array of coral; and a soul-soothing sense of quiet. The twin islands of Ofu and Olosega, separated by a deep channel but linked by a bridge, are as close to paradise as it gets. Ofu's lone village crouches at its western end, leaving the rest of the island largely – and delightfully – uninhabited. Ofu Beach ranks as one of the most splendid stretches of sand in the world.

On the dramatic south coast of the remote, sparsely populated volcanic island of Ta'u, some of the highest sea cliffs in the world rise 963m (3158ft) to Mt Lata, the territory's highest point. The main settlement on Ta'u consists of the villages of Ta'u, Luma and Si'ufaga in the island's northwest. From Ta'u village there's a good walk south to secluded Fagamalo Cove. It was in Luma that Margaret Mead researched her classic anthropological work, *Coming of Age in Samoa*, in 1925. Despite the book's impression of a permissive society, Ta'u is the most conservative part of American Samoa.

SUBSEA SPECTACLE: THE VALLEY OF GIANTS

Ta'u, with its soaring sea cliffs, creation legends and preternatural sense of remoteness, is an extraordinarily exotic island. But its otherworldly feel isn't limited to land: Ta'u's surrounding waters are home to one of the largest, oldest and most mysterious coral colonies on the planet. Known as the Valley of Giants, this remarkable reef is populated by massive live boulder corals known as porites. The biggest is the gargantuan Big Momma, which looms 6.4m (21ft) high, has a circumference of 41m (135ft) and is believed to be at least 530 years old. How Big Momma and her colossal counterparts have managed to thrive despite centuries of climate change has baffled the few scientists that have been able to study this underwater wonder.

X MARKS THE SPOT

Ofu Beach Flanked by outrageously picturesque peaks that rise behind it like giant shark's teeth, the beach is 4km (2.4 miles) of shining, palm-fringed white sand.

Maga Point Favourite fishing spot on Olosega's southern tip; the 1.5km (1-mile) walk in offers great views of the point's steep cliffs, colourful reefs and distant Ta'u.

Mt Tumutumu The 5.5km-long (3.4-mile), often indistinct track to the summit of Mt Tumutumu (491m/1371ft) begins just north of Ofu village wharf and twists up to the mountaintop TV relay tower

To'aga Site At this site (just behind Ofu Beach) archaeologists uncovered an unprecedented array of artefacts dating from early prehistory to the modern day.

National Park of American Samoa Some of the Samoas' best underwater action: huge schools of coloured fish dart through jaw-droppingly clear waters, occasionally pursued by reef sharks.

Index

First Edition
Published in October 2022
by Lonely Planet Global Limited
CRN 554153
www.lonelyplanet.com
ISBN 978 1 83869 503 3
© Lonely Planet 2022
Printed in Malaysia
10 9 8 7 6 5 4 3 2 1

General Manager, Print & Publishing Piers Pickard
Associate Publisher Robin Barton
Commissioning Editor Darren O'Connell
Design & Image Research Lauren Egan
Cover & Illustrations Whooli Chen
Editors Gabrielle Stefanos, Polly Thomas
Photo Editor Ceri James
Index Polly Thomas
Print Production Nigel Longuet

Written by: Brett Atkinson, Anthony Ham, Mark Johanson, Rebecca Milner, Isabella Noble,
Etain O'Carroll, Sarah Reid, Regis St Louis, Nicola Williams

Background map data:
© Lonely Planet © OpenStreetMap contributors
NASA/METI/AIST/Japan Spacesystems, and U.S./Japan ASTER Science Team (2019). ASTER
Global Digital Elevation Model V003 [Data set]. Distributed by NASA EOSDIS Land Processes
DAAC, https://doi.org/10.5067/ASTER/ASTGTM.003.
NASA JPL (2013). NASA Shuttle Radar Topography Mission Global 1 arc second [Data set]. NASA
EOSDIS Land Processes DAAC. https://doi.org/10.5067/MEaSUREs/SRTM/SRTMGL1.003
British Oceanographic Data Centre (BODC) (2015) The GEBCO_2014 Grid [Data set]. https://www.
bodc.ac.uk/data/documents/nodb/301801/

LONELY PLANET GLOBAL LIMITED
Digital Depot, Roe Lane (off Thomas St), Digital Hub, Dublin 8, D08 TCV4, Ireland

STAY IN TOUCH
lonelyplanet.com/contact